D1106952

101018

American Alpine Club Library

APPROACH TO THE HILLS

AMERICAN ALPINE CLUB LIBRARY
710 10th ST., SUITE 15
GOLDEN CO 80401
(303) 384 0112

BLANC GREFFIER

APPROACH
TO THE HILLS

BY

C. F. MEADE

AMERICAN ALPINE CLUB LIBRARY
710 10th ST., SUITE 15
GOLDEN CO 80401
(303) 384 0112

LONDON
JOHN MURRAY, ALBEMARLE STREET, W.

GV
200
.M4
1940 b

First Edition . . 1940

Printed in Great Britain by
Wyman & Sons, Ltd., London, Fakenham and Reading.

8285

PREFACE

EIGHT of the twenty-three essays in this book have appeared previously: the material for "The New Adventurers" in the *Quarterly Review* and the *Nineteenth Century and After*, "A Tragedy on Nanga Parbat" and "An Ascent of the Watzmann" in the *Quarterly Review*, "The Attempts on the Eigerwand" and "An Episode on the Dru" in the *Cornhill Magazine*, "Losing the way on a Dolomite" in *Blackwood's Magazine*, "A Neglected Pastime" in the *Contemporary Review*, and "Everest and the Future" in the *Fortnightly Review*. I thank the Editors of these journals for their permission to use the articles in question.

Part II of the book deals with the Himalaya and describes experiences as an explorer on Kamet, the great peak on the Tibetan frontier, ultimately ascended by an expedition under the leadership of Mr. F. S. Smythe.*

I wish to thank Colonel E. L. Strutt, recently Editor of the *Alpine Journal*, for generously supplying me with information, and Mr. L. H. Myers for much assistance and advice.

Pen-y-lan,   C. F. MEADE.
   Meifod,
      Montgomeryshire.

* See F. S. Smythe's *Kamet Conquered*, Gollancz.

CONTENTS

PART I (Alpine)

PART II (Himalayan)

Contents

LIST OF ILLUSTRATIONS

List of Illustrations

MAPS

PART I
Alpine

THE INACCESSIBLE MEADOW

ANTOINE DE VILLE, Seigneur of Domp Julian de Beaupré, was an artillery officer and engineer in command of four hundred and fifty bowmen and men-at-arms at the court of King Charles the Eighth of France. One fine summer day in the year 1492 this intrepid courtier was setting out on a mission that any ordinary man might well have regarded as desperate, for the King had directed him to ascend the celebrated and redoubtable Mont Aiguille, a rock-peak in Dauphiny, 6,880 feet above sea-level, and referred to by Rabelais as "the inaccessible", for no man had ever succeeded in climbing it. The mountain's formidable reputation seems to have been well deserved, and the King must have suggested the expedition to de Ville in rather the same spirit as that in which Mark Twain deputed his agent, Harris, to ascend the Matterhorn.

The enterprise was certainly enough to discourage the boldest adventurer, and the fame of the Mont Aiguille was the more significant because in those days even the most striking mountains in the Alps could obtain very little recognition from a public that was strangely indifferent. Indeed, it is a curious fact that in all classical antiquity only two Alpine summits are mentioned by writers, and, even after the Middle Ages had come to an end, the Alps still succeeded in maintaining a certain degree of incognito. In fact, the exhaustive researches of that great Alpine authority and mountaineer, Coolidge, could not discover more than forty mentions of Alpine peaks before the beginning of the seventeenth century. Thus, when the first map of Switzerland appeared in 1495, the conspicuous Monte Viso and an obscure peak called the Crête du Vallonet, both of which had been known since classical times, had only two serious rivals in the limited amount of limelight that was available for mountains in those days. One of these two rivals was the Mont Aiguille. It had first been noticed, apparently, as early as 1211, when an Englishman residing in Provence, in a work dedicated to the Emperor Otho the Fourth, refers to its inaccessibility and the remarkable plateau on the top.

It is not surprising that the Mont Aiguille incurred some attention, and modern authorities have agreed with the opinion that mediæval writers held of this mountain's unique peculiarities. The experienced guideless mountaineer, Kirkpatrick, ascending it in 1913, declared it to be the most extraordinary peak that he had ever seen, and Coolidge calls it the most curious and interesting of all the numerous ascents that he had made. He also points out that if Petrarch was the first Alpinist to be inspired by love of mountains, and Rotario, the conqueror of the Rochemelon in 1358, was the first mountaineer, it was Antoine de Ville who, by storming the heights of the Mont Aiguille in 1492, became the prototype of all modern rock-climbers.

So we may claim that the first modern rock-climb took place as long ago as the year in which Columbus discovered America.

The hero who performed the climb was certainly no ordinary man, and was well fitted for the exacting task that his royal master had set him. He is supposed to have been one of the earlier teachers of military engineering who influenced the great Vauban, that famous master of the art of fortress construction, and, like Vauban, he was doubtless proficient in storming fortresses, as well as in building them. Moreover, his courage and determination were phenomenal. It may be said of him, too, that he was a specialist in regard to Mont Aiguille in much the same sense as the modern "mechanical" school of mountain-climbers are specialists. These men, who started their activities in the Eastern Alps soon after the Great War, take a pride in working their way up overhanging precipices by hammering in a series of rings, hooking themselves on to them by means of clasps attached to their waists, and festooning the cliffs with balustrades of rope. De Ville's usual technique in reducing the fortresses of the King's enemies was probably equally elaborate, and, like his modern imitators, who are quite accustomed to do their work while receiving missiles discharged by the mountain they are attacking, he was probably quite unperturbed by the harassing attentions of the garrisons that he besieged.

In organizing his mountaineering expedition the Seigneur showed considerable foresight, for among ten men that he took with him he included the King's ladder-man, a carpenter and a couple of royal chaplains. We have Rabelais's authority, too, for stating that he was equipped with "engins mirifiques", the mediæval military engineer's equivalent for the modern "mechanical" climber's ringed pegs, spring-hooks, stirrups, hammers and ropes.

Modern visitors to the Mont Aiguille have stated that it is as steep all round as a house, and they have compared its difficulties with those met with on the abrupt Dolomite rock-mountains of Tyrol, where, it is said, the ascent would have a great reputation, but more for its dizziness and sensational qualities than for its difficulty. The rocks, however, are admitted to be smooth and bad to climb. The way is described as lying through several deeply cut fissures or hollows of the most extraordinary nature, and at one moment the climber finds himself in the bowels of the mountain, in a great cavern, where scarcely any light penetrates. The smoothness of the rock is such that there is very little to hold on to, and to lose one's balance might result in a fall of several hundred feet.

No doubt the King's ladder-man proved useful, for, after struggling with terrible difficulties, de Ville's whole party reached the top, where they most unexpectedly encountered a very old ram, a portent that must have been puzzling to account for, considering the inaccessibility of the locality. In fact, as Rabelais's narrative admits, the astonished climbers could only guess who could have brought it there. The top of the mountain, they were delighted to find, consisted of a luxuriant meadow, smothered in wild flowers that possessed a special fragrance, and among which lilies were conspicuous as well as many unknown varieties of plants. It was, they said, "the most glorious place you ever saw", and from it Mont Blanc could be seen at a distance of ninety miles, but they were not aware of this fact, for in those days the great mountain was still unknown to fame.

Soon after they had arrived some tame rabbits were released by one of the priests, and mass was said. Three crosses were also erected, and a house was built. Fortunately, as there had been no casualties, there had been no occasion for the priests to perform their last offices, but they could still serve de Ville's purpose in christening the mountain by the name of "Eguille Fort", although unfortunately the effect did not last, and the old name continued to be used.

Meanwhile, with an uncanny prescience that doubts might be cast on the veracity of his story, and with more gumption in this respect than modern climbers have sometimes shown, de Ville took the wise precaution of despatching a letter to the

President of the Dauphiny Parliament at Grenoble, inviting him to send a delegation to visit the successful party while it was still on the summit, so that the achievement might be adequately verified. He significantly added to his invitation the suggestion that they should only come, "provided a sufficient number of brave men are available, for this is the most formidable and dreadful experience that either I or my men have ever had". He continue to explain that he had only got up by the grace of God, and admits employing implements with ingenious devices, in this latter respect anticipating the mountaineering methods of a generation born more than four centuries later.

On receiving this letter the President hurriedly sent a lawyer on the following day to investigate the truth of so astonishing a report. The lawyer found ladders placed at the foot of the precipice, and observed de Ville and his men on the summit-plateau. The climbers eagerly shouted to the visitors to come up and join them, but the lawyer was shy; perhaps he was intimidated by the remarks in the letter; at any rate, he preferred not to run so evident a risk of perishing, and decided that "it would be unwise to tempt providence, for the mere sight of such a mountain was terrifying". Although most of his followers stood by him and remained below, a few were more courageous, and among those who visited the top was one whose descendant subsequently made researches into the history of the mountain, and published them in 1880 in the annual volume of the *Société des Touristes du Dauphiné*.

The lawyer's men eventually accomplished their mission by signing formal certificates testifying to the genuineness of de Ville's ascent. Altogether, the whole party remained six days on the top, and noted the presence of a herd of chamois, one of which they killed for food. As in the case of the ram, the origin of these animals is wrapped in mystery, for as de

Ville admitted, there was no possibility for them to get up or down.

Nearly three hundred and fifty years were to elapse before this audacious ascent was repeated. In 1834 Jean Liotard, an inhabitant of the district, aged twenty-six, made an attempt, and his progress was watched by a party who accompanied him to the foot of the western precipice with ropes, ladders and mason's hammers. Finding it impossible on this side, they went round to the north, and climbed a quarter of the total height without artificial aids. Then, removing his nailed boots, Liotard clambered obliquely across the north face of the precipice. After disappearing from view, he reappeared on the summit-plateau and explored it in every direction, making his stentorian voice resound in the distance, and attracting the attention of neighbouring communes by hurling enormous boulders down into the valley.

He found the grass on the plateau six inches high, and the remains of a hut were visible. Just as de Ville had done in 1492, Liotard commented on the many varieties of flowers, and the peculiar sweetness of their smell. There were birds to be seen, but no quadrupeds; the chamois and de Ville's rabbits had left no descendants. As Liotard reached the highest part of the plateau, he crossed himself and reflected that without God's help he certainly would never get down again; finally, however, he succeeded in returning by the same route. His companions were much impressed by his performance, and spoke of the Aiguille as "one of the seven wonders of Dauphiny".

The mountain's great reputation for inaccessibility persisted for another forty-three years till Monsieur Rochat made the first tourist's ascent in 1877. On the summit he found the announcement of an otherwise unrecorded ascent in 1849 by three inhabitants of a neighbouring village. During the latter half of the nineteenth century, however, mountaineering had come into fashion, and standards of difficulty were higher. The more or less intelligent passenger, harnessed to the rope between a couple of the most efficient guides available, was beginning to perambulate the Alps in all his glory. Nothing that his guides could climb would stop him, and the reputation of the Aiguille was bound to suffer at his hands. In 1878 the French Alpine Club had chains fixed to the more difficult passages on the cliffs. The final climb up very steep rocks could now be pronounced "not altogether easy, in spite of the numerous cables", and the descent of the precipice that the pioneers had so justly dreaded "took only an hour and five minutes".

Various Englishmen, among many others, made the ascent, and the view of the mountain from the top of its higher neighbour, the Grand Veymont, was said to be most extraordinary. One writer mentions the instinctive reluctance felt in treading under foot the rich grass of the meadow, although it was a crop that no one owned and no one would ever mow. The area of the summit-plateau was estimated at about five hundred yards long and a hundred yards wide. The lilies, it seems, are still numerous, and one climber counted twenty varieties of other wild flowers.

Now that this mountain has been tamed with chains, the modern mountaineer may not appreciate the formidable impression that its precipices must have made on the pioneers before artificial aids had been fixed to the rock. To the accomplished rock-climber the Mont Aiguille may no longer offer difficulty, yet this remarkable mountain, with its smooth vertical walls, and the magical meadow of wild flowers on its summit, will still remain one of the seven wonders of Dauphiny. Moreover, its fame will endure as the scene of one of the earliest and greatest feats of mountaineering.

A GREAT GUIDE

I was lucky in my first guide, for I fell almost at once into the hands of that famous Savoyard, Blanc, nicknamed "le Greffier," one of the pioneers of the Alps.

I knew him at first only by reputation—everybody had heard of him in Maurienne and Tarentaise early in the century. Indeed he was known and loved throughout the Western and Central Alps, both in France and in Switzerland. Each of his distinguished sons in turn had undergone a drastic education at his hands, for he had taken them with him wherever he had climbed, and, as he began to age, made them lead for him whenever the difficulty became extreme. It was a hard schooling, and his third son, Pierre, has told me how once, and once only, on one of the more sensational climbs at Chamonix, after failing to swarm up an exposed crag on the extreme crest of a dizzy ridge, he complained angrily to his father that the place was unclimbable, and how his father, still more angrily, drove him at it again, and gave him no respite till he had succeeded in grappling his way up.

Apparently the old man thought it demoralizing for a youngster to reach the status of guide too soon, and he always adopted a deprecating attitude whenever the great qualities of his sons Auguste and Pierre were mentioned. Auguste—who was afterwards killed on Mont Dolent*—he would occasionally praise meagrely, but only in his absence, and the by no means

* A.J. . . .

inferior merits of the impudently argumentative Pierre he was never willing to admit. "Vous avez été trop bon pour mes vagabonds de fils," he would say, and Pierre's retort that it was unusual for an employer to climb for years with the same guide, if the latter was a vagabond, was received in silence.

He was old-fashioned in his ways. The sum of twenty francs a day, with ten for the porter, was all that he would allow his employers to pay, and on these terms he would undertake the most difficult climbs in the Alps; whether he had ever seen them before or not made no difference.

When I first engaged Blanc Greffier I had done practically no climbing, and besides knowing next to nothing about mountains I was ignorant of the character of the formidable old man whom I had to deal with. Had I known Blanc and his mountains better, I should never have dreamt of proposing so ambitious a programme of ascents that it could only be successfully accomplished, with the help of an iron determination, and three weeks of more or less continuous fine weather. I could not guess that fate would provide the fine weather, and that Blanc had a good deal more than his share of the necessary iron determination. In fact, as things turned out, the indomitable *amour-propre* of the old guide caused him to accept my proposals as if they had been a challenge, so that he carried out every item to the bitter end, completely disregarding the protests of his exhausted companions. Thus for three weeks we continued indefatigably, always climbing three days running, each day a peak, with an intervening day for getting to huts, or even occasionally for resting. Blanc's third son Pierre accompanied us as porter.

Strictly conscientious in every respect, Blanc, with a most masterful temperament, simply forced us to keep going. His methods were peculiar. Whenever difficulties occurred he was accustomed to take more or less command of all the parties on the mountain, provided they happened to be within earshot, and he lavishly distributed praise or blame wherever he judged it would be salutary. To a capable but rather awkward guide who was in charge of another party, and climbing down one of the less difficult pitches of a Chamonix peak without displaying that degree of fearless agility that Blanc thought desirable, orders were sharply given to turn his back to the cliff that he was descending. "Face au vide, je vous dis, face au vide, mon Dieu; combien de fois voulez-vous que je le repete?"

He very nearly succeeded in preventing me in moments of exhaustion from freely slaking a frantic thirst at every spring that we met. The only drink that he approved of on a mountain was the sour red wine that I had not yet learnt to love, and which he carried in a skin smelling strongly of the goat which had originally supplied it. "Il faut boire pour prendre de la force," he would observe. Nevertheless he was most abstemious, although on a proper occasion he would think nothing of finishing a whole bottle of brandy with an old crony before going off to sing in the choir at the village church.

Blanc had strict ideas on what was fitting. On the climb he took as his right the position of an autocrat, but, when the climb was over, and the party was nearing its destination, the firmness of the autocrat gave place to a sort of ritual. The amateurs might well have been ciphers during the heat of the day, but now, if Blanc could contrive it, they were to come into their own, and achieve the prominence that he considered due to them in the stately pageant of the arrival. Accordingly, as the imposing façade of some grand hotel came into view, conversation ceased, Blanc hastily drew back, concealed himself behind his employers, pushed the reluctant Pierre still further to the rear, and thus the little procession that he

13

had organized could advance with the formality that he deemed proper.

Eventually the elaborate programme that I had so rashly planned was all duly accomplished within the given three weeks. It was evident that the old man was firmly determined that if only he could get me to the end of the performance alive, not a single detail should be left out. Towards the end of the tour, I remember, we were spending the night in a cowherd's chalet. My comfortable bed was a sheet stuffed with hay, and after a surfeit of climbing I was sleeping the sleep of exhaustion, when at midnight Blanc appeared with his lantern, and sternly commanded me to get up, drink some black coffee, and prepare for an immediate ascent of the Charbonel, the highest mountain in that part of the country. Ten minutes later he was again calling me for, although I had not dared to get back into the bed, I was sitting upright on the edge of it, fast asleep once more.

It was a relief when we arrived at his home at Bonneval, and our taskmaster told us that we should not be wanted for a few days, as he had business to attend to. He was at that time mayor of the village.

Several times during our stay at Bonneval, and on many subsequent occasions, Blanc acted as my host. It was characteristic of him that when I wanted to buy provisions to take with us in the mountains, I found that in his own estimation almost everything he supplied us with was either not good enough to have any value, or else too good to justify him in putting a price on it, so that in neither case could payment be accepted. In the priceless category were the bottles of delicious, altitude-matured wine, made from the muscat grapes of Asti, and coming—with a certain amount of mystery—from a friend, the Prior of a monastery across the frontier.

Our porter, Pierre, was as young as I was, and found his father's fondness for perpetual motion rather too much, even for his own abundant energy; indeed, Pierre was undisguisedly thankful to be released on the last day of our prodigious tour, when we left him at the parental home and crossed the mountains to sleep at Val d'Isère. On this occasion Blanc as usual was determined at all costs to complete my wretched programme, and was adamant in insisting that the last four peaks which I had rashly inscribed in the list should all be climbed before we could think of descending to our destination. That night at Val d'Isère I slept the clock round, and, on coming down for luncheon next day to enquire for le Greffier, I was told that the indefatigable old man had borrowed a rifle in order to set out that morning at three o'clock in pursuit of chamois.

La chasse was not the only outlet for Blanc's insatiable energy: there was also *la contrebande*. In those days there were no Fascists patrolling the frontier to prevent Italians from crossing into France, and it was still possible to do a little smuggling. This was rarely profitable, but it was not the hope of profit, it was rather the element of adventure which had for Blanc an irresistible attraction. He used to travel far afield into Italy, sometimes right into the south, bringing back hundreds of sheep, travelling with them by slow stages from railhead to the high Alpine valleys along the French frontier. From Alpine resorts such as Ceresole Reale, proceeding by infinitely slow marches, with only his sons to help him, he would drive his flock across the frontier by some glacier-pass that was considered impassable except for climbers, and camp in the open among the sheep, high up near the snow-line. Since it was quite out of the question to allow Italian animals to be seen in any of the French frontier villages, where they were absolutely prohibited, days had to be spent in conducting the flock over a whole series of glacier-passes till the party had penetrated sufficiently far into the interior of France to make it safe for them to appear, and descend in a region where frontiers, Customs officers and smugglers were alike unthought of.

Sometimes these expeditions would involve a week of this high-level touring, and on one occasion, at least, a decoy informer was employed to send an anonymous warning to the Customs to say that a flock of sheep could be caught crossing a certain pass on a certain night. The inferior animals were then drafted out from the rest, and sent round by the route indicated, till they met the Customs officers, and while the latter were preoccupied with what seemed in the darkness a most satisfactory capture, the conductor of the flock of crocks had no difficulty in making his escape. At the same time, in the absence of the Customs men, the choicer animals were safely driven across a less obvious pass.

Perhaps Blanc's most famous, if not his most arduous, exploit was his raid from Courmayeur to Chamonix, when he successfully brought a flock of many hundred sheep over the Col du Géant, a pass 11,000 feet above sea-level. Mountaineering parties who crossed just afterwards were astonished to find the upper reaches of the glacier above the rather formidable ice-fall covered for miles with sheep-dung. Pierre assured me that he and his brother spent the whole of one day and a moonlight night continuously lifting sheep up a vertical pitch of rock high up on the steep Italian side of the pass. It is not surprising that the sons disliked the experience, and, every time that their persuasive father induced them to accompany him on one of his smuggling trips, vowed that it would be the last.

Another *grande passion* of this remarkable old man was the pursuit of the ibex. At that time these animals were strictly preserved in Piedmont for the King of Italy, and the Blanc family had only to cross one of the neighbouring frontier-passes of nine or ten thousand feet to find themselves in the heart of the royal hunting country. The ibex, though not so clever as the chamois in dealing with snow and ice, is even more agile on rock, and probably, for Blanc, the excitement of out-manœuvring the King's keepers gave the pursuit of the ibex an attraction that was lacking in the comparatively tame legality of chamois-stalking. Sometimes the whole family would spend the night in a royal shooting-box, one son on sentry-duty outside, on the watch for keepers, while the rest of the party inside were busy cutting up and cooking the meat from the animals they had shot that day. On another occasion they were surprised and put to flight by a patrol of keepers, and once they were chased the whole way up one side of a mountain, down the other side into the valley beyond it, and then, still on the run, they ascended the slopes of yet another range, so that, as night came on, they looked down on the lights of their pursuers flitting from house to house, as the search passed through the village, thousands of feet below. The fugitives lay out in the open all night, and next day a long circuitous march by devious passes took them back across the frontier into France.

Towards the end of his life, when he was over seventy, Blanc caused a good deal of anxiety to his family of sons and daughters. Like other guides, he was in the habit of dispensing with a porter when he accompanied a trusted client who was also an old friend. But unfortunately he often extended this practice, and undertook long, severe climbing-tours as the only professional in charge of a party of indifferent climbers. After such expeditions he would return home in such a state of fatigue that often he could hardly remember where he had been. It was to save him from these dangers that the French Alpine Club artfully induced him to take on the uncongenial rôle of hotel-keeper, and consent to be the caretaker of the excellent club-hut at les Evettes, a few hours above his home. The officials of the club charitably hoped that this new occupation would keep him out of mischief, but as the summer drew on, the call of the mountains became irresistible. The victim of the kindly plot was quite unaware of the solicitude that had prompted it, and at last one day, impatiently exclaiming "Gardez votre vieille boîte, moi, je fiche le camp," he went off to join an old employer in the mountains of Switzerland.

It was on his return from one of these trips, while he was recuperating at Bonneval, that I last saw him. I had not climbed with him for many years, and one day Pierre remarked that he thought his father would be pleased if we invited him to take us up the Albaron, mentioning one of the principal neighbouring peaks, a summit of about 12,000 feet. Le Greffier agreed to the suggestion, and our day together was a great success. On the top of the mountain there was a fog, and it was quite like old times, for Pierre, who had always been independent in mountaineering matters from the very earliest years of his Alpine apprenticeship, expressed his own opinion as usual on the question of the best way down. Accordingly the usual fierce quarrel took place between father and son, and the old man, as was his custom, went on his way, regardless of all argument, and quite unperturbed, even by the vehemence of his own language. Indeed, according to Pierre, these angry scenes always passed from his father's consciousness like water off a duck's back, leaving the younger generation, on the other hand, dazed and shattered by the violence of the storm.

Blanc Greffier's death occurred during the last war, and came with merciful quickness. In earlier life the toughness of his physique had enabled him to take liberties with his health, and when he lived till beyond the age of seventy-five, he never properly realized that he could no longer play these tricks with impunity. He would never have allowed a drink of cold water to any tourist in his charge who was over-heated by exertion. Yet one autumn afternoon, when he returned exhausted from hunting, he drank cold water, and lay down to sleep on some stones. When he awoke he was ill. He sent for one of his sons. "Je suis perdu," he remarked, "il n'y a rien à faire; le médecin ne pourra rien." He made his will, and in three days he died of pneumonia.

He was a passionate lover of the mountains, and it was characteristic of him that his last words were "Tout ce que je regrete en abandonnant cette terre sont les montagnes et les chamois". Pierre's epitaph on his brother Auguste applies equally well to le Greffier himself: "Il etait fier et juste."

OTHER GREAT GUIDES

ANOTHER great guide whom I used to meet in the Alps was Aloys Pollinger, father of famous sons. Blanc Greffier and he, whenever they met, were inseparable and devoted friends, although neither of them understood a single word of the other's language. Pollinger's method of training his sons as leaders was similar to Blanc Greffier's. On the Grépon, for instance, he not only always sent his boys up first, but, instead of accompanying his party to the actual summit, would take the opportunity to have a nap on a ledge some distance below. It was said that never in his life had he set foot on the peak itself, till one day two of his sons determined to give him the experience. Seizing his rope, regardless of his indignant outcries, they hauled him resisting furiously right up to the summit.

One of Pollinger's most faithful employers was an Englishman. Year after year they travelled and climbed together. It was a strange relationship, for in spite of the mutual affection that united them, they were constantly differing and bickering. Once the hostilities reached such a pitch that one of the two disputants, taking advantage of his position as last man on the rope during a descent, vented his feelings by kicking down stones on his less fortunate companion. On another occasion the day began with an angry wordy warfare even as they set out from the hotel—probably at two o'clock in the morning. Victory in the first round was undoubtedly Pollinger's, for, after three hours of toiling uphill, when the unhappy employer, feeling unusually fatigued, halted to untie his rucksack at the breakfast-place, he was mortified to discover that there was a very large stone in it, surreptitiously placed there by Pollinger.

Martin Schocher, of Pontresina, was another of these magnificent bearded veterans whom I rightly venerated when I climbed with him in my youth. I can see him now in memory, strolling casually along the skyline of the dizzy knife-edged Crast'aguzza with the ponderous yet firm and easy balance of a climbing bear. Mountains meant more than a living to him, and he inspired his daughters with his own passion for climbing, taking them up the great peaks near his home. In these days of ski-ing, winter expeditions are relatively easy, yet we spend less time on skis than the Schochers and Blancs did on those unwieldy, laborious and exhausting implements, the *raquettes*. These were their only means of locomotion on their constant hunting-trips, day after day, winter after winter. The men of that generation were certainly made of stern stuff.

In recent years there has been one guide who, if a plebiscite could have been held among experienced climbers, might have been voted unanimously to be *primus inter pares*, just as an earlier generation might have acclaimed Christian Klucker as the greatest guide of his day. I refer to Franz Lochmatter, the fifth of a band of brilliant brothers. On a mountain, this tall, lean, almost awkwardly built guide became transformed, and as one of his old employers once expressed it, Franz's climbing seemed to be completely effortless, however great the difficulty. As his followers watched him from below, everything seemed absurdly easy, but when it was their turn to advance they were soon undeceived. Once at the end of a successful season, when I praised and congratulated my

Photo: A. H. Meade

PIERRE BLANC, 1926

guide Pierre Blanc rather more warmly than usual, he smiled in deprecation of my enthusiasm, and replied: "You mustn't overestimate my powers; I can think of several guides in the Alps who are quite as good as I am, and I dare say Franz may be rather better." This was spoken by a man who was never prevented by insincerity or false modesty from forming a true estimate of his own outstanding merits as a mountaineer.

But testimony to Franz's great qualities is plentiful. Of his leadership on that desperate expedition, the ascent of the south face of the Täschhorn, Mr. Winthrop Young wrote:

"Franz Lochmatter's mountaineering feat was the greatest I have ever witnessed, and after a number of years I can still say the greatest I can imagine. It is right that it should be recorded; for I do not suppose that in its mastery of natural difficulty, in its resistance to the effects of cold and fatigue and to the infection of depression and fear, it has often been equalled on any field of adventure or conflict."

Franz's death, caused by a slip in an easy place—easy, that is to say, for a climber of his powers—when descending the eastern *arête* of the Weisshorn, was an irreparable loss to mountaineering and to everyone who was privileged to be his friend.

In the Dolomites during the first decade of the century the two most famous guides were Sepp Innerkofler and Antonio Dimai. These two men were magnanimous rivals, and as different in respect of temperament as any Teuton and Latin can be. The following story well illustrates their attitude towards one another.

Innerkofler was staying with the late Sir Edward Davidson at the Vajolet hut for the purpose of making the second ascent of the Delagoturm. This mountain is one of a group of three giant rock-fingers projecting into the sky, and had long remained virgin. It had just been reported that a brilliant young solitary climber, whose name was afterwards given to the peak, had recently succeeded in making the first ascent, but only after the most desperate struggle, and the formidable shape of this astonishing obelisk gave it a semblance of utter inaccessibility. It was therefore with some curiosity that Innerkofler and Davidson observed two tiny figures approaching in the distance, evidently two other climbers gradually ascending the valley towards the hut. The two turned out to be Dimai with a German doctor who was his employer, and the conclusion was inevitable that they must be coming to attempt the same mountain that Innerkofler and Davidson had in mind.

When the newcomers had arrived and had admitted their intentions, Innerkofler drew Davidson aside and said that as both parties would now be making a combined assault next day, there were certain stipulations that he had to make. He then explained that he must insist on being allowed to lead the combined parties himself; and in case he found the climb so difficult as to compel him to retreat, Dimai must undertake not to make any attempt until Innerkofler and Davidson had left the neighbourhood. At first Davidson was dismayed at what seemed such an uncompromisingly personal attitude towards a rival, and expostulated, but to no purpose.

"No," replied Innerkofler, "I am not jealous of Dimai, I think a lot of him, and believe he is as good a climber as I am."

"Then surely," said Davidson, "you might agree to Dimai's taking his turn at leading the party?"

"No," was the answer, "if that mountain is difficult enough to be dangerous, even for me, it will be equally dangerous for

Dimai, and if he insists on taking his turn—you know what is likely to happen when the leader falls off."

"But," pursued Davidson, "even if you do decide to turn back, why should you object to Dimai and the doctor having a try by themselves on the same day?"

"Because," said Innerkofler, "I know what Dimai is like, and if he's allowed to have a try when he sees me turn back, he will either get up or fall off, and I don't want a fatal accident to happen while I am still on the mountain, and sharing the responsibility."

As this proposal seemed fundamentally reasonable, it was agreed to by all. Next day, however, the difficulties nowhere proved to be too great for the powers of such climbers as Dimai and Innerkofler, so that the stipulations of the latter did not require to be carried out.

Probably neither Innerkofler nor Dimai were ever acquainted with the kind of fear that many climbers experience fairly often in the mountains. Yet I believe that at some stage or other in the course of mountaineering fear affects everybody. If this is not apparent, it is because the control of fear tends to become automatic and instinctive. Fear affects people variously; some are nervous before an exciting climb, and some seem free from nervousness until the difficulties begin. The fact is that since the emotion of fear has a biological purpose, a climber totally lacking in it would have a poor chance of survival. It is at any rate remarkable that such a man as Dimai, who was quite devoid of insincerity or vanity, once admitted to me, when we were starting on a difficult expedition together, that he had slept badly that night from thinking of a climber, who, some days previously, had fallen off the peak that we were about to ascend and been killed. In my own case such reflections never interfered with sleep, but whenever Dimai and I reached the field of action there could be little doubt which of us was completely unhampered by any form of nervousness. It would seem better to discount one's fears, as Dimai had done, at the cost of an occasional indifferent night suffered long before arrival on the scene of operations.

Innerkofler and Dimai were both men of the highest character. When Innerkofler was still almost a boy, and was climbing one of his own difficult Dolomite peaks, a friend of the man who was employing him was a member of a party close by, and slipped, with the result that he fell to the bottom of the vast precipice that they were climbing, and was dashed to pieces. Innerkofler's employer, remarking that after such a fall as they had just witnessed there could be no doubt about the death of his friend, suggested that they might as well go on to the top and finish their climb. Innerkofler not only indignantly refused the cold-blooded suggestion, but as soon as they had returned to the hut, told the man that he would have nothing more to do with him, and they parted company forthwith.

During the war Innerkofler was killed by machine-gun fire in a gallant single-handed attack that he made on an enemy position on one of the terrific precipices of his own mountains.

I once climbed with Dimai for a season in the Dolomites, together with Pierre Blanc. On rocks he was the fastest and neatest climber I have ever seen, and—on the few occasions when we encountered any—he appeared to be equally proficient on snow. He was very well known throughout the Dolomites, and the fact was obvious wherever we went. Blanc remarked of him that whenever Dimai entered a room "tout le monde vibre, et moi-même maintenant je commence a vibrer aussi". The regard that Pierre had for him was warmly reciprocated. A year or two later I was alone with

Blanc climbing a peak in Tyrol,* when we inadvertently strayed from the ordinary route and found ourselves exposed on a sheer precipice like flies crawling up the wall of a house; in fact we owed it entirely to Blanc's courage and agility that we were able to reach the top of our mountain alive. Dima also happened to be climbing in the neighbourhood that day and had witnessed our struggles from a distance. Afterwards I asked him: "Did you think we were done for?" "No," was the laconic reply, "I knew Pierre."

* See page 33.

LOSING THE WAY ON A DOLOMITE

THE sensational development of Alpine climbing in recent years has to a great extent depended on the lavish use of what mountaineers in former days would have considered unfair mechanical devices.

The following true story of what happened to Blanc and myself in the Alps of Northern Italy deserves to be recorded, because the events occurred out of their time—thirty years ago—long before it became fashionable to carry engineering tools. The difficulties we had to encounter were as formidable as those that the rock specialist of to-day is willing to face, even when armed with a complete mechanical outfit.

In 1909 Pierre Blanc, already well known as a guide throughout the Alps, was spending part of the summer with me in the Rifugio della Tosa, the club-hut which is the chief centre for climbers in the Brenta group. These mountains belong to the geological formation known as Dolomite, and are situated west of the River Adige; they are described by Freshfield as a mysterious range, utterly unlike anything in the Central Alps, and remote from the more frequented Dolomite district east of the Adige valley, but, in the opinion of many connoisseurs, superior to the Eastern Dolomites both in beauty of shape and richness of colouring. Moreover, the difficult rock-work to be found in the Brenta group will satisfy the most exacting climbers.

The long rough walk over the pass known as the Bocca di

Brenta leads from Pinzolo past the Tosa refuge to the picturesque Lake of Molveno through a narrow gap in the recesses of the range, and is perhaps the most beautiful Alpine expedition in Europe. The ascent is through a forest of beech and pine into a high valley of peaceful streams, pine-woods, and rich meadows, leading into a mountain cul-de-sac. When all farther progress seems to be barred by an impassable cirque of cliffs, a path, masked by bushes, is found winding its way up the precipice, and emerging on a platform of Alpine meadow above the tree-line. Here, to quote again from Freshfield's book, "before the traveller's eyes rise towers, horns, cupolas, columns, and spires, crowded together in endless variety". In the midst of the whole array of fantastic peaks appears the gap that constitutes the pass of the Bocca di Brenta. The Tosa hut where we were staying at the time of the story is on the Molveno side of the watershed, and only a few minutes downhill from it.

One of the attractions that had brought us to this hut was the celebrated Guglia di Brenta, a peak of over nine thousand feet, reputed to be as difficult to climb as any of its famous rivals east of the Adige. It was among the last summits of its size to be ascended, and had held out successfully till 1899. Its appearance is sensational, for it towers into the sky, some say, like the finger of a god; others less romantically compare it to a factory chimney.

At the time of this visit it was known to very few guides, for most of the earlier ascents had been made by brilliant amateurs. The only local guide who was acquainted with it was reported to be unwilling to renew the experience, and his services were in any case engaged elsewhere. It seemed, therefore, that we should have to find the route by ourselves, and this might be a complicated matter, because, in the Dolomites, soft climbing-boots are always worn where

Photo : Leo Bahrend (Merano)

GUGLIA DI BRENTA

the rock is difficult, so that there are no tell-tale scratches made by the nailed boots of predecessors to guide the climber.

It was on a fine August morning, a few days after we had arrived in the hut, that we set out for the Guglia. The hut-keeper's wife bade us good-bye rather emphatically, saying she would pray for us; she wished us well, but evidently believed that a foreign guide could not be expected to find the proper way to the top. Her misgivings, which seemed at the time so unreasonable, were destined to be justified. However, once we had started, we lost no time in getting to close quarters with the mountain, walking quickly up a low ridge that disappears into its eastern base.

The view of the Guglia, especially as we had seen it a few days earlier from the top of its loftier neighbour, the Cima Brenta Alta, revealed how little it resembles any ordinary mountain. It is more like an immensely tall church tower, without a spire, built on a scale that is utterly overwhelming in its effect on the spectator.

The moment had now arrived when the serious climbing was to begin, and at the foot of the precipitous eastern wall of the mountain was accomplished the familiar Dolomite ritual of removing nailed boots and putting on *scarpetti* or *kletter-schuhe*—that is to say, rope-soled climbing boots. After we had taken off our jackets, and emptied all waistcoat pockets, I took charge of the rucksack containing a few scraps of bread, meat and cheese, as well as a quart-sized thermos bottle of tea made with lemon, sugar and wine. Blanc was to carry nothing, for on such climbs as this the leader must be absolutely unencumbered. Tying ourselves together with a hundred and twenty feet of rope, we climbed into a chasm that slants upwards from right to left across the base of the east wall. The route is curiously complicated, and before reaching the summit half encircles the mountain. At the head of the chasm, scrambling over a boulder that was jammed in it and traversing a few yards in a horizontal direction, we emerged on the south face. Here we reached the foot of the first instalment of the slabs which constitute one of the two chief obstacles of the ascent. These slabs consist of about sixty feet of perpendicular rock, seamed at intervals of a few yards with horizontal and vertical cracks, offering scarcely adequate holds for fingers and toes. It was consequently essential that the leader should be that "expert climber with steady head" so often referred to in the pages of Baedeker's guide-books. Indeed, one place was so awkward that Blanc found my shoulders useful to take off from.

When at length we had reached the top of the slabs we found ourselves on a notch or shoulder in the practically vertical eastern ridge, and then passed along rock and shale ledges, a foot or two wide, that closely skirted the brink of the enormous northern precipice. Next a series of chimneys had to be ascended—steep, as is all the climbing on this mountain, but not exceptionally difficult. These gave access to a broad, easy horizontal shelf or terrace. This magnificent promenade, several feet wide in parts, extended for about three hundred yards as far as the south-east ridge, which is perpendicular like all the ridges of the Guglia. Here, where the terrace came to an end, another vertical chimney began, about a hundred and eighty feet high, rather tiring, but not excessively difficult, although it had to be climbed by forcing a way up it, and exerting the pressure of knees, back, and elbows against its opposite walls. At the top of this chimney is the southern terrace running east, and easy to follow; it is the second great terrace, and is only a hundred and fifty feet or so below the summit of the Guglia. This attractive-looking path is a terrible trap; for the correct way lies in the opposite direction, up the final instalment of slabs which lead immediately to the summit.

Probably by this time we had both of us become careless, perhaps elated at finding the actual difficulties less terrifying than the descriptions volunteered by imaginative natives. At any rate we fell into the trap, and followed the broad easy terrace towards the east, instead of quitting it as we should have done in order to ascend the slabs. The terrace was from two to three feet wide, and we strolled rapidly along it. Presently I overtook Blanc who had been brought up short, in some dismay at the sensational ending of this seductive highway, which now faded gently into the smooth, blank, perpendicular wall of the huge southern precipice. In fact the terrace vanished utterly in a manner that was uncompromising and most disconcerting.

While I was overtaking Blanc, I heard distant shouts coming up from below. It seemed that there was a party at the foot of the mountain trying to communicate with us. Had we only known what was being shouted, we might have been saved from the terrible predicament in which we were soon to find themselves. Unfortunately it was impossible to distinguish what was being said.

Blanc and I might indeed have recoiled from the sinister smoothness of that forbidding precipice, had we not happened to see, several yards obliquely above us in the face of the wall that fell sheer for more than a thousand feet, a small iron ring fixed to a spike in the rock, and it seemed to beckon us on. At first sight of this place the same reflection must have occurred to both of us simultaneously: surely it could not be as bad as it looked. Obviously the ring must be an indication of the route, for we assumed it must have helped numerous climbers to overcome this very formidable-looking *mauvais pas*. Only later did it appear that this assumption was unwarranted.

33

Blanc, when in action, was a man of few words, and had already hitched a spare coil of the rope to a projecting rock, probably more from habit than from any confidence in the usefulness of this precaution in such a place. He then invited me to kneel down as near the vanishing point of the terrace as possible, so that by standing on my shoulders he could reach out sideways to the right, higher up the cliff, in hopes of getting a grip that would enable him to pull himself up. His new position would then be one of complete exposure on the bare face of the precipice, and from it he must attempt to reach the iron ring by continuing to crawl in an oblique direction higher and higher up the cliff. The crouching position that I now took up on the very brink, where the shelf ended, provided me with a sickeningly uninterrupted view down the thousand feet to the foot of the mountain. Every pebble that either of us dislodged fell clear, and hummed as it vanished into the depths.

Unfortunately I proved an unsatisfactory footstool. The rock above was overhanging, forcing Blanc backwards and outwards in an alarming fashion, so that he kept imploring me to lean farther out over the formidable gulf that seemed to be waiting for its prey. I must also contrive somehow to raise myself to a standing position, to enable the leader to find handholds that appeared to be desperately out of reach. All the time, while I struggled, the sound of distant shouting echoed in my head, like an incessant refrain in a nightmare, or the singing of a sick man's pulse. Eventually, after what seemed an endless struggle, I managed to raise myself to my feet, staggering under my companion's weight, and leaning as far over the edge of the abyss as I dared. Blanc, having mounted from my shoulders to my head, succeeded, after much kicking and wriggling, in launching himself on to the wall, with the result that in some miraculous way he

34

contrived to hoist himself over the overhang. There was no sound but the scuffling of his boot-soles seeking non-existent holds, till, after a prolonged *tour-de-force*, he reached the iron ring where he could pause and cling in order to recover his breath. He called down to say that there was a second ring in sight, and that it would be necessary for him to reach it before he could be approximately secure. As for me, having no one to give me a leg-up, I should have to depend considerably on the help of the rope if I was to be able to follow; and Blanc, if he was to give any assistance at all, would be compelled to find a better position for himself still higher. But, before attempting to advance any farther, Blanc was anxious, for security's sake, to pass his rope through the ring, a laborious process; for in order to accomplish it he was obliged to untie the rope from his waist, and subsequently put it on again. He then passed quite out of sight, obliquely above my head on the right, struggling up the precipice like a fly on a wall, and in silence, so that I could only imagine what was happening. All that could be assumed from the slowness of the process, and the forbidding appearance of the cliff, was that the struggle to which we were now committed was something that exceeded all our past experience of the more formidable Dolomite expeditions. It could only be supposed that we had gone astray, with the consequence that we had now no choice but to continue forcing our way up the mountain till we reached the top or fell off.

Very slowly, with prolonged pauses that caused me the deepest anxiety, the rope uniting us slid upwards, a few inches at a time, gradually following the invisible leader above. Again there was a long and anxious delay as the leader reached the second ring; for here he was obliged for safety's sake to repeat the difficult manœuvre of threading the rope as he had done lower down.

At last he must have made himself relatively secure; for, after repeated shouting, he succeeded in making it clear that I could now advance in my turn, for the rope was securely hitched. Unfortunately, however, it had stuck somewhere, either in the lower ring or on the rocks. Moreover, Blanc was too badly placed to be able to give any help by hauling, or even by drawing in the slack, so that I had to help myself, especially at starting, by pulling myself up hand over hand on the rope. To a self-respecting mountaineer, who would in ordinary circumstances scorn to help himself by grasping the rope, this task might seem easy, not to say ignominious, but it must be remembered that the situation here was peculiar. The last man had no human ladder from which to take off, and the line of ascent, besides being perpendicular, was also oblique, a fact which greatly added to the difficulty. At the starting-place, too, there was the overhang, where hand and footholds were practically non-existent.

But I had already had time enough for thought, and now was the moment for action. As I grasped the rope, and clutched at any small asperities that I could find in the rock, I was obsessed by anxiety lest the rope, which had stuck in its transverse position, might, owing to the violence of my efforts to surmount the overhang, suddenly detach itself from the rock-face and swing me off sideways across the precipice to dangle to and fro like a pendulum over the revolting abyss into which I had so long been gazing. I felt pretty sure that such a situation would admit of no recovery. Another danger was that since the rope had jammed above me, the slack of it drooped in a great coil below me as I ascended, and it was evident that if my grip were to fail I should shoot down the full length of the slack. Since no man in Blanc's position could be expected to resist the jerk of such a violent fall, both of us would then inevitably fly off into space.

In such circumstances the niceties of mountaineering are easily forgotten, and pride is not likely to deter the last man from firmly grasping the rope, thankful that if he cannot be pulled he can at any rate try some pulling on his own account.

With a desperate effort I somehow succeeded in getting over the overhang. Providentially, too, the rope continued to adhere to the rocks, with the result that in course of time, exhausted as a fish out of water, I reached the first ring, there to cling, gasping for breath. Then followed the difficult and uncomfortable job of standing bolt upright, pressed against the cliff, with only one good foothold, untying the rope at my waist, re-tying it, and maintaining a precarious balance while doing so.

Once more it was Blanc's turn to advance. Fortunately he had reached a point where the direction, although still vertical, no longer slanted so unpleasantly across the face. Nevertheless the climbing was just as difficult. Then, as soon as Blanc could establish himself securely, I recommenced the struggle, again having to unrope and re-rope as I passed the second ring. It afterwards struck me as curious that throughout this long battle with the mountain my exclusive preoccupation had been a vivid conviction that to die in bed must be the most agreeable way of ending one's life. Moreover, the desire for such a peaceful consummation increased in intensity as every moment it seemed less likely to be realized.

How long this nightmare lasted it is difficult to say, but I well remember my astonishment and relief when the rock suddenly became easy, and I found myself stepping on to the spacious square top of the Guglia. I threw myself down beside Blanc, and we lay recovering our breath, swearing that never again would we be such fools.

After a thorough rest Blanc went to peer over the edge of the vertical western precipice, and with very little trouble discovered the orthodox route. It might be difficult, but it was certain not to be as bad as the way by which we had come, and we confirmed our suspicion that in following the south terrace we had made a mistake that might have been fatal. Presently we realized that the party which had been shouting to us was coming up the mountain. It was led by two well-known guides of Cortina, Antonio Dimai, whom Blanc usually referred to as "the king of the Dolomites," and Agostino Verzi. These two explained how local guides whom they had met at the foot of the Guglia had declared that we had deviated on to a false route and were bound to fall off; hence the attempt to communicate with us by shouting, which we had failed to understand. Dimai described the strange appearance that we presented seen from below, "human specks crawling up through the air," quite detached against the sky.

Certainly this was the most difficult rock-climb in Blanc's experience, a performance that was thoroughly up to the standards of the modern climbing of to-day, and which we had inadvertently accomplished some twenty years before its time.

But Alpine history moves apace, and to-day this route, or rather variation of a route, is classified, and may be repeated by modern rock-specialists, but it will not provide the emotions experienced by the two involuntary pioneers. With the tools and engineering methods of climbers belonging to the "mechanical school", all mountains become everywhere equally accessible, but unfortunately it is insufficiently realized that they also become equally uninteresting to climb. It is, alas, only too likely that the Guglia will suffer an increasing degree of mechanization in the future.

The existence of the misleading rings requires an explanation. Certainly the man who could climb into such a position

and fix two rings there can have been no ordinary mountaineer. We subsequently discovered that he was an Austrian
professor of gymnastics who, with a friend, had been on the
mountain only a few days earlier. They had made the
attempt from the vanishing-point of the south terrace, perhaps
in ignorance of the proper route. The leader had successfully
climbed the overhang, and had hammered the two rings into
the precipice, one after the other, while his companion was still
at the taking-off place, with the joint rope of the party securely
belayed to a rock. Above the second ring the leader's strength
probably failed, for he lost his hold on the cliff and slipped
backwards. It is not surprising that the sudden jerk of his
fall snapped the rope, with the result that the unfortunate
man fell a thousand feet through the air and was dashed to
pieces on the rocks at the foot of the mountain.

AN EPISODE ON THE DRU

On the gigantic cliffs of the Little Dru, that superb aiguille dominating the lower reaches of the great glacier at Chamonix known as the Mer-de-glace, French, Swiss and Italian mountaineers a few years ago fought a heroic battle against the forces of nature, and this epic struggle that lasted four days and three nights deserves to be recorded.

The two Drus, when seen from the Montenvers, produce the impression of a monolith soaring miraculously into the sky to a single sharp point, but this apparent pyramid is in reality divided at a height of about 12,000 feet into two peaks known as the Great Dru and the Little Dru, 12,315 and 12,247 feet respectively. An English climber who in 1883 made the second ascent of the Little Dru, wrote of it as follows:

"The race of mountaineers may greatly improve as time goes on, and laugh our puny efforts to scorn; yet I believe the ascent of the upper portion of the western Aiguille du Dru will always rank high among the most difficult rock-climbs in the Alps."

Certainly time has not falsified this prophecy. Nevertheless, if the conditions of snow, rock and weather are favourable, the ascent nowadays does not generally take more than six hours from the club-hut, and on the 12th of August in 1928 the conditions happened to be such that the four young guideless Frenchmen who had come up to the hut that day had every prospect of getting up and down the mountain in good time. If Jean Choisy, Jean Charignon and Georges Clot were relatively rather inexperienced for such an exacting expedition, Pierre Daurenson, who joined them from Lyon at the last moment, was a guideless climber who was accustomed to lead on first-class peaks. By the irony of fate it was he that was destined to be the cause of the tragedy that eventually overtook them.

The next day, Monday, the weather was doubtful, so that the young men only reconnoitred the route, and remained in the hut most of the day. On Tuesday their alarum woke them at half-past one in the morning, but as the weather was still doubtful they waited till it grew finer, and then set out at seven o'clock, a late hour for starting such an important undertaking. At first all went well, and they climbed fast on two ropes, Choisy leading Charignon, and Daurenson leading Clot. For the first two or three hours the difficulties are not excessive, and the whole party reached the shoulder of the mountain without incident. From here the route follows alternately either side of the south-west ridge, over "terrace after terrace of forbidding rock" as an earlier climber has described it. There is a succession of what are called 'chimneys', interrupted by vertical walls of rock, 'chimney' being the name given to cracks or narrow gullies which have to be climbed by inserting hand and foot, or sometimes the whole body. As time went on, the climbers zigzagged to and fro over precariously narrow ledges in order to get from one chimney to another. Signor Guido Rey has described his own reactions in scaling this tremendous precipice:

"I began," he says, "to feel a tingling in my shoulders. The hardest part of the work fell to the upper muscles; in such climbs as these it is not the legs that push the body up,

but the arms that pull it, and the knees act as props to keep
the body away from the rock, while the feet become useless
appendages, and swing in space."

So complete an abandonment of the normal procedure in
climbing usually implies that the mountain which calls for
such awkward manœuvres is getting the better of its
assailant.

After some three hours of this sort of gymnastics the four
young men had almost reached the top of the mountain, and
just as the second pair had surmounted what is known as
the '*petit mur vertical*', all the serious difficulties of the climb
being disposed of, Daurenson, who was working his way up
a crack, found that he was awkwardly placed, and attempted
to alter the position of his hands. Suddenly he became
exhausted, and, crying out "I'm letting go" ('*Je lâche*'),
slipped backwards. Clot, who was behind him, managed
to check the impetus of the fall with the rope, so that
Daurenson landed on a small platform after falling only
four or five yards, but in doing so he received severe injuries
to his back.

The situation was now very serious, for although
Daurenson remained conscious he had lost the use of his
limbs, and the party were in an utterly exposed position,
close to the summit of the Dru, with their injured companion
suffering such pain that evidently the three men that were
available would not be able to move him very far. The
accident had happened at midday, and by four o'clock they
had only been able to lower him about a hundred and twenty
feet. It was obvious that something drastic must be done,
and it was decided that Choisy and Charignon should hasten
down at their utmost speed in hopes of fetching a search-
party from Montenvers or Chamonix to bring down

Daurenson the very next day if possible. Clot, meanwhile, volunteered to stay with Daurenson to look after him.

Even in midsummer a night in the open at 12,000 feet may be a terrible or even fatal ordeal. Rey wrote of his own similar but less dreadful experience:

"By night a mountain's mighty limbs are as still as if frozen to death, and its gigantic face stiffens into an immutable expression of mystery. . . . I instinctively clasped my arms to my breast that I might feel the warmth of my own body, and protect it from freezing in that embrace of stone."

Fortunately the night was calm and relatively warm for such heights as this. The two who were to fetch help sped downwards at such a pace that by stumbling on through the night they reached the Montenvers at one o'clock on Wednesday morning, and a few hours later had given the alarm in Chamonix.

Meanwhile on the same day one of the leading guides in Chamonix, Camille Tournier, who had heard the news of the accident on his way to the club-hut, was organizing the despatch of guides and climbers, with the result that a rescue-party of ten men reached the hut late on Wednesday night.

The weather was now threatening. Earlier in the day, however, three men from Geneva, the brothers Albert and Charles Fiaroli, and their friend Joseph Paillard, with an Italian party, Giuseppi Gandi and Nigra, evidently all of them first-rate guideless climbers, had left the hut, and, regardless of weather, were gallantly racing up the mountain, carrying food and clothing. They succeeded in reaching Clot and the injured man by three o'clock that afternoon. There were now ominous signs of an imminent storm, so the five men with the assistance of Clot made desperate attempts to

44

get Daurenson down the mountain, but in vain. All they could do was to lower him to a less exposed position on a tiny shelf in the cliff, and to build what stones they could into an inadequate shelter behind which the two men might pass a second night in the open. Clot had absolutely refused to leave his friend, and the two rescue-parties, before reluctantly turning to descend, handed over all their food and even their underclothes, an act of unselfish heroism which, alas, was to have fatal consequences.

The night that followed was terrible, both for the two men crouching on their shelf, and for the five good Samaritans descending foodless and underclad. Beginning at a quarter to seven that evening, and lasting throughout the night, one of the worst storms that had been known for many years raged continuously, deluging the cliffs of the Dru with snow and hail. The wind was so violent that trees were uprooted even down at Chamonix.

The next day, Thursday, at seven in the morning, Tournier's party of guides, who had spent the night at the hut, found four inches of snow on the ground, and, looking up the Charpoua Glacier, caught sight of the Swiss rescue-party returning, in the act of descending on to the glacier, after their all-night descent of the rocks of the Little Dru. It was terribly evident that they were in a state of complete collapse from exposure and exhaustion. After them came the Italians, who, perhaps more wisely, had bivouacked higher up, where there seemed to be a little more shelter. As the guides who went to bring in the three Swiss were carrying Joseph Paillard down to the hut, he died in their arms. Only the two Italians were able to descend unaided. It was fortunate that an English doctor named Shelford, undeterred by the fact that he was not a mountaineer, had climbed up to the hut in the hope of being useful, for his treatment with camphor injections revived the Fiaroli brothers, and probably saved their lives.

Meanwhile, during Thursday morning, up at the ghastly bivouac, Daurenson appeared to be dying, and Clot, as he subsequently admitted, had begun to despair. Suddenly a break came in the clouds, and, before it closed again, he saw, infinitely far below, and yet distinctly enough to be convincing, dots like men approaching across the Charpoua Glacier. What he saw was his indefatigable friend, Choisy, returning up the mountain with another climber, Stoffer, who had volunteered to help. These two men had come up to the hut with Charignon, and then, although it was already noon, and although the snow everywhere covering the rocks had decided the guides congregated in the hut to postpone all attempts at rescue till next day, this gallant pair, Choisy and Stoffer, started together undismayed. In only six hours' climbing, in spite of the appalling conditions, they reached Clot at his bivouac, and found that the unfortunate Daurenson had died at one o'clock that afternoon. They had reached the bivouac too late for the three men to do more than abandon the narrow rock-shelf where the body of Daurenson was lying, and then establish themselves a little lower down the precipice in a slightly more sheltered situation for passing another night in the open. This was the devoted Clot's third night on the mountain.

Dawn broke clear on Friday. There were by now no less than eighteen persons assembled in the hut, and a general assault upon the Dru had been planned for this day. At this juncture, however, there burst upon the scene with the violence of a hurricane the romantic figure of Armand Charlet, the leading spirit of the *élite* of the Chamonix guides. Up at the bivouac early on Friday morning, Stoffer, peering anxiously down from the eyrie where he and his two companions had passed a miserable night, perceived to his astonishment a solitary human figure bounding up the rocks of the Dru, and approaching at a prodigious speed. This was Armand Charlet, who, having been absent on an expedition, had arrived at the hut late on the preceding evening, and was now hastening to the rescue alone, without waiting for the main body of the guides who were following him as fast as they could. In the astonishingly short time of two hours and forty minutes he had reached the three men at the bivouac, and was afterwards joined by the other guides, all of them exhausted by their efforts to overtake him.

Charlet, however, was determined that his party should not only rescue the living, but should fetch down the body of Daurenson. It was probably now his haste that proved his undoing. In hurriedly traversing a narrow ledge with ice on it, he slipped and fell through the air, fortunately on to a small patch of snow, about ten yards below. With brilliant presence of mind the guide, Georges Cachat, was able to hold him with the rope, and save him from destruction, incidentally saving the lives of all the other men on the same rope. Charlet was seriously injured in the head. His wounds had to be bound up, and presently he recovered consciousness. He was then roped between two guides, while another pair took charge of Cachat, whose hand had been damaged by the pressure of the rope when he had so successfully checked Charlet's fall. The whole party of guides, under the capable leadership of Tournier, then began the descent. At the shoulder, an intrepid lady doctor, Madame Manoury, who had come up there in order to help, gave first aid to Charlet, and found that he was suffering from a fractured skull.

As the descent proceeded, Charlet realized that his strength was not likely to last, and he repeatedly urged the men to greater speed. The heroic Clot and his two brave rescuers, who were descending steadily, were caught up and passed. Continually Charlet pleaded for speed and still more speed. The pace, indeed, became so great that some climbers on a neighbouring peak, in ignorance of all that had been happening, were startled and amazed at the spectacle of a crowd of men apparently diving in headlong flight down the forbidding crags of the Little Dru.

Charlet's presentiment was justified, for, on reaching the glacier, he collapsed, and again became unconscious, so that for the remainder of the terrible journey down the steep mountain-side, and across the Mer-de-glace to the Montenvers, he had to be carried by his devoted colleagues.

Clot, who had lived through three nights of exposure, reached the hut safely with his two courageous companions soon after midday, and arrived at the Montenvers before seven o'clock that night. The next day a party of guides who went up to bring down Daurenson's body considered the conditions to be so unfavourable that they made their way to the bivouac-place by passing over the summit of the Great Dru, so as to deal with the difficulties of the Little Dru more easily, by encountering them only during the descent.

Finally, it is remarkable that during the course of this disaster on the Little Dru no less than fifty-one persons took part in the operations that were necessitated by the accident to one climber. The gallantry and unselfishness of so many of the participants in the rescue work is specially striking. Paillard had sacrificed his life in a manner that is beyond all praise. Fortunately Clot and Choisy, as well as the gallant Italian and Swiss parties, were soon none the worse for their magnificent efforts. That dashing guide, Charlet, not only made a complete recovery from his injuries, but subsequently made an equally perfect recovery from further severe injuries which he sustained in another accident later.

It is sad to learn that the heroic Choisy and Clot were involved, in the following year, in a fatality during a very difficult climb on the Meije, the famous rock-peak in Dauphiny. They were attempting to reach the highest summit from the north by ascending a precipitous ice-gully, when Clot slipped, and pulled his leader into a fall. Both men were hurled down the gully till Choisy, by being flung into a crevasse, automatically prevented his companion from falling farther. Choisy was killed on the spot, and Clot was seriously hurt. It was characteristic of Clot's intrepidity that in spite of his injuries he insisted on accompanying the search-party that brought down the body of his friend.

ATTEMPTS ON THE EIGERWAND

THE sensational exploits of a new school of Alpine climber have scandalized the mountaineering world, and with good cause. Nevertheless, there may be some excuse for the extravagances of the innovators. The fact is that the young desperadoes belonging to what is known as the "mechanical" school of climbing have begun to take alarm. These virtuosos who delight in forcing their way up a mountain by hammering pegs into overhanging rocks or vertical ice-falls—"conquering" the mountain they would call it—have realized that since the classical era of exploration has come to an end, there will now be no more laurels left for them to win.

However, this state of affairs that they describe as "the exhaustion of the Alps" is not yet quite complete, for at least one great climb survived untried until recently.

At Grindelwald, in 1935, the appalling northern precipice of the Eiger that overshadows the valley, and forms the sensational feature of the view from the village, still remained unclimbed, and its forbidding appearance had deterred everyone from meddling with it. It is true that a daring party in 1932 had skirted the brink of the huge cliff by following a difficult route that led along its eastern margin over very steep snow and ice to the summit; nevertheless the direct and dangerous route up the very centre of the colossal wall had never been attempted.

It is not surprising that such a climb should never have been seriously thought of before 1935, for this amazing north wall of the Eiger, the Eigerwand as it is called, is one of the biggest cliffs in the Alps. Throughout its five thousand feet of rock its steepness is such that, in spite of the altitude, permanent snow cannot rest anywhere. From top to bottom, too, the whole of the vast rock-face is shattered by constant bombardments of ice-fragments and boulders. Besides these there are smaller missiles in the shape of flying stones, and most of these projectiles, big and little, travel at a speed that renders them invisible, as they whistle and scream past the cowering climber clinging precariously to the precipice.

It seems as if the present phase in the evolution of mountaineering has evoked a new type of climber adapted to an environment that has become more and more exacting in consequence of the so-called exhaustion of the Alps. This new type of climber, proud of his skill in the use of hammers, pegs, rope-rings, balustrades, stirrups, slings and pulleys, finds a new source of joy in a mystical worship of danger as an end in itself, so that he considers even the most foolish feat praiseworthy, as long as courage, skill and endurance are displayed in performing it. In the sinister shadow of the Eigerwand the votaries of this strange cult have sought their valhalla. It may be profitable to learn from the story of their adventures the consequences of the doctrine that they profess. At any rate the self-sacrificing heroism of the guides who staked their lives repeatedly in desperate attempts at rescue deserves to be remembered.

In August of 1935 two young men from Munich reached Grindelwald. They spent some time reconnoitring the lower cliffs of the Eigerwand, and one of them devoted a whole day to ascending the Eiger by the ordinary way in order to leave a depot of provisions on the summit. Meanwhile at the foot of the mighty wall the two men prepared a

Photo: R. Schudel

THE NORTH FACE OF THE EIGER (EIGERWAND)

- - - - - Route attempted in 1935.
——— ,,   ,,   ,, 1936.
† Indicates scene of 1936 accident with line of fall.
o Bivouacs.

tent and sleeping-bags as their base-camp where they could remain with their stores of rope and tools. They then waited in hopes of an improvement in the weather, which, in fact, was so bad that they were several times sorely tempted to abandon their enterprise and go home.

At last, on Wednesday the 21st, the weather improved, and they began their attack upon the precipice. By the evening they could be well observed from the Eigerwand station of the Jungfraujoch Railway, through the window cut in the solid flank of the Eiger where the passengers pause on their way up inside the mountain in order to enjoy the panorama of northern Switzerland, and gaze down at the chalets of Grindelwald nestling in the green depths far below.

Everything seems to have gone well, for the climbers were now on a level with the station, and succeeded in accomplishing about one-third of their immense journey up the cliff.

On Thursday, however, the rate was not maintained. Moreover, as a critic has expressed it, the first half of the wall is only about a quarter as difficult as the whole; and still there were two-thirds of the formidable task to be achieved, for during the whole of this day, hampered as they were by the steepness of the ice, the climbers could only by their utmost efforts accomplish a paltry increase of some three hundred feet.

Already the prospects were disquieting enough, and again on Friday they had only ascended another three hundred feet. Obviously there was no longer any chance of victory, and the difficulties they were contending with were evident, for observers with telescopes could see the climbers hauling up their rucksacks after them by means of the rope. Later that evening a terrible storm suddenly concealed them from view.

On Saturday the whole mountain was ominously swathed in cloud, so that the men were still invisible. There was much fresh snow higher up the mountain, and avalanches, big as well as small, were pouring down the rocks.

On Sunday the anxiety of the watchers was reaching a climax, yet in such weather rescue operations were out of the question. The doomed men were again momentarily visible. They had made little progress, and were making their fifth bivouac, at about two-thirds of the way up the wall. Doubtless they spent the night in the customary manner of these devotees, crouching against the cliff without sleeping-bags or blankets, and with the climbing-rope that united them fastened for the sake of security by means of a steel clasp to a ringed metal peg driven into any available crevice in the rock. The clasp, it may be mentioned, is an important feature of the mechanical mountaineer's equipment, and is a contrivance resembling the clasp on some brobdingnagian watch-chain.

Meanwhile it had begun to rain all over the Oberland, and although snow was falling only at great heights, the danger from waterfalls, stonefalls and the increasing exhaustion of the climbers was growing constantly. At Grindelwald a rescue-party had been formed, but the weather remained prohibitive. An aeroplane had been warned to stand by, and on Tuesday, the first clear day, a pilot from Thun in a military plane flew for a full hour to and fro across the Eigerwand, scanning the cliffs. There were masses of fresh snow everywhere, and no living being was in sight. Several days later, when fine weather had definitely returned, another pilot, accompanied by an Alpine guide, actually flew to within twenty yards of the precipice, and caught sight of one of the two men standing upright, frozen to death, up to his knees in the snow, as if gazing down into the valley. The other man, they thought, must have been already buried in a drift. Probably both men had died where they had last been seen, on the fifth day of their attempt.

In 1936 another summer had come round, the tragedy of the
Eiger was fresh in men's minds, but a party was gathered once
more at the foot of the same forbidding precipice with the
same desperate ambition that had led the two youths to
destruction in the previous year. Eight young men had been
dreaming the same dream of the Eigerwand, and were muster-
ing their resources for the assault. They had collected
quantities of rope and the usual paraphernalia employed by
climbers of their way of thinking. Yet already death had
taken its toll among the aspirants, for two of them who had
been doing a practice climb on the Guggi route up the north
face of the Jungfrau had fallen, and one of them had been killed.
Of the others now waiting to make an attempt, Kurz, the
youngest, had qualified as a guide in the Eastern Alps. With
his friend, Hinterstoisser, who was to accompany him, he had
already accomplished formidable ascents such as the storming
of the vertical north wall of the Grosse Zinne. Two other
young men of the party, Rainer and Angerer, were from
Innsbruck. All these four showed equal determination.
"The Eigerwand is ours or we shall leave our bones on it,"
they declared.

Yet the weather was even worse than in 1935; it rained
constantly, and the Eiger was hidden in cloud. Only brief
glimpses through the cloud-curtain revealed the wall frowning
down at them and loaded with masses of fresh snow.
Avalanches thundered, and the crackling reverberations caused
by stonefall were almost continuous. Doubt began to spread
among the party, and no wonder. They must have known
that before committing themselves to a five days' struggle on
such a precipice a preliminary spell of settled weather was
essential, in order to stabilize the conditions, and that only a
prolonged spell of equable weather is likely to give more than
a day's warning before it breaks up. With several days'

warning it might be possible to retreat in time to escape before conditions prohibitive to life have supervened. In seasons that are variable the onset of dangerous conditions can occur with terrible abruptness. No wonder, then, that four of the less infatuated members of the group abandoned the adventure. However, the Bavarians, Kurz and Hinterstoisser, remained, and so did the Austrians, Rainer and Angerer. These four now decided to join forces.

In the meantime there were many visitors to the tents at the foot of the Eigerwand, and many sought to reason with the party, but the camp resounded with youthful laughter, and the four protested that they had no wish to die, although they admitted that luck was necessary for the undertaking. Down at Grindelwald they had even been told that the local authorities would take no responsibility for rescue operations, but they were confident that none would be required. All that was necessary was one more preliminary reconnaissance, and, with this object in view, the four set out together. They soon reached a suitable bivouac-place under a huge over-hanging cliff known as the Rothe Fluh. They had once passed the night there during a previous exploratory climb. Unfortunately, when they had got thus far, instead of staying where they were for the night, in order to reconnoitre further next day, they decided to return to their base, and at this juncture the Eigerwand gave its first warning. Hinterstoisser was beginning to descend, and was about fifty feet above Kurz's head. He trusted his weight to a peg that Angerer and Rainer had hammered into the rock some days previously. The peg suddenly gave way, and Hinterstoisser was hurled down for a hundred and twenty feet through the air past his horrified companion. The latter could do nothing to check the fall, for it happened with the rapidity of lightning, so that there was not even time to make a futile attempt to belay the rope. By a miracle the falling man not only hunched himself into a ball, but dropped into a patch of deep soft snow, where he saved himself from a further fall by acrobatic dexterity. Strange to say, the only damage was a wounded knee, and, although when they got back to camp the rain had begun again, the four men never wavered in their determination to pursue their adventure to its end.

On Friday the 17th of July the weather looked better, and all were satisfied that up to 10,000 feet the precipice had been sufficiently reconnoitred. Rucksacks were packed, and there was much amusement when Kurz made a comic story for the pressmen out of Hinterstoisser's hundred-and-twenty-foot fall. Hinterstoisser meanwhile was packing some photographs away in a sack that was to be left behind. "If anything happens to us," he remarked to the reporters, "you will know where to find our photographs."

It was regrettable that more food could not be carried. Sixty hand-forged pegs with rings attached were a heavy burden. Twenty of them, about a foot long, were for use on ice-walls, and forty of a shorter kind were intended for hammering into crevices in the rock-face in places where otherwise hand-holds would be lacking. Besides this weight of metal they had to carry hammers, a few steel clasps, two hundred and forty feet of spare rope, some string and the spirit cooker. Consequently, without overloading their rucksacks, the only provisions they could take were two pounds of bacon, five pounds of black bread, six tins of sardines, tea, sugar and solidified spirit. It was not nearly enough, but greater loads could not be managed.

Finally, at two o'clock in the morning of Saturday the 18th of July, the four set out from the Kleine Scheidegg. The news spread through Switzerland, and the ethics of the enterprise began to be discussed once more. A telegram from the commanding officer of the Bergsjaeger regiment forbidding Hinterstoisser and Kurz from taking part in the expedition came too late, for the young men had already started and were out of reach. By half-past nine that morning the whole party had gathered at the reconnoiterers' sleeping-place under the Rothe Fluh. Everything seemed favourable, and progress had been rapid, but from now on difficulties began, and observers at the Kleine Scheidegg and Grindelwald thronged the telescopes. It could be seen that from the sleeping-place a difficult traverse had to be made over some very smooth cliffs. Hinterstoisser succeeded in crossing at a point where Rainer and Angerer had already failed. A narrow belt of snow and a difficult descending traverse then enabled the party to join the route of 1935 at the lower of two small snow-fields. To the distant watchers at the telescopes progress seemed agonizingly slow, yet the men wasted no time, for they were expert at their work, hammering and chiselling the rock whenever one of the precious pegs could be spared, and there was a chance of forcing it into a suitable crevice. The rocks indeed were so steep and difficult that it was a long time before the party reached the second bivouac used by the two Bavarians in 1935, and situated between the lower and the upper snow-fields.

By five-thirty in the afternoon the last man had reached the foot of the cliff below the upper snow-field, night was approaching, and a site for a bivouac had to be found. The formidable overhang of the Rothe Fluh was now behind them, and they settled down to pass the night, partly sheltered by another overhanging cliff. They were now on a level with the third and last bivouac of the Munich pair where the latter were supposed to have perished. Here the four men remained all night without sleeping-bag or blanket, while the stones that thundered down the mountain continuously were deflected by the overhang above the sleepers' heads.

On the following day, Sunday, dawn broke threateningly with thunder-clouds, and only occasionally were patches of blue sky visible. At Zurich it was already raining, and although a north wind was driving the clouds upwards, the party in their bivouac, condemned to inaction by the cloud-bank surrounding them, could hardly have realized that there were signs of a momentary improvement in the weather. By six-forty-five that morning, however, they had started, and Hinterstoisser was leading, cutting steps up the steep *névé* of the upper snow-field, in order to rejoin the route taken by the party of the previous year. An hour later they were suddenly hidden by a curtain of cloud, and nothing more was to be seen of the Eiger that day.

It was not until eight o'clock on Monday morning that they were again observed to be on the move. Their second bivouac must have been at a height of about 11,800 feet, a little above the highest point reached in 1935, but soon they began to retreat and were back at the second bivouac once more. One climber was seen to be so long immobile that it was concluded he was injured, and it was believed that Angerer had been wounded by a stone, as he appeared to be wearing a bandage on his head. As late as five o'clock that evening they were still to be seen descending the upper snow-field, above the overhanging precipice called the Rothe Fluh. Two of the party seemed to be helping a third, presumably Angerert but the prevalence of clouds made it difficult to see what was happening. The situation had now become extremely serious, for the food supply had only been calculated to last over the third night, and the third night was now beginning, while the climbers were still far up on the mountain. The supply of pegs, too, was being used up, the weather was not improving, and avalanches of stones and snow continued to fall.

Tuesday's weather, unfortunately, was much worse, with pouring rain and quantities of fresh snow everywhere covering the rocks. The roar of avalanches became almost continuous. Cries could be heard. At nine in the morning three of the party were seen descending. Could the fourth have dropped out? However, two hours later all four were seen still descending the upper snow-field. Below them was a vertical and overhanging cliff that they had avoided on the way up. In order to avoid it again they must ascend the smooth and difficult rock-traverse down which Hinterstoisser had led them on their way up the mountain, three days before. It was at this point that they met with a fatal reverse. The passage had taken them only two hours on the outward journey, but now, facing the traverse in its ascending direction, foodless and frozen as they were, short of iron pegs, too, and with a rope frozen so stiff that it was unmanageable, they failed repeatedly to force their way up the smooth ice-glazed slabs. At length they must have realized that retreat was now cut off, and that the one remaining hope was to face the appalling precipice below them and make a desperate attempt at a direct descent of it. After two hours had been wasted in fruitless struggles to ascend the traverse, the conclusion became inevitable, although the ghastly prospect of attempting to lower themselves by ropes into the abyss below them may well have seemed hopeless. Clouds, too, were seething round them, and the artillery of the Eigerwand was incessantly in action.

Meanwhile, from a point only six hundred feet below the four men, through an opening cut to serve as a rubbish-shoot for the tunnel of the Jungfraujoch Railway a workman, peering out from inside the mountain, had been for several hours anxiously watching the manœuvres of the climbers, and was now exchanging shouts with them. At first they still hoped, and they shouted down courageously that all was well. Later, when the whole party became involved in lowering themselves down the three hundred feet of precipice, cries for help could be heard, and the anxious spectator hurried down to give the alarm at the Eigergletscher station. The assailants of the Eigerwand had all been warned before starting that they could expect no guides to risk their lives in futile attempts at rescue, but it so happened that at that moment three of the best guides in Switzerland were working for a cinema company at the Eigergletscher station, and the railway company at once supplied a train to take them to the workman's observation post at the hole in the tunnel. The three guides then climbed out through the hole, and in only three quarters of an hour, at an astonishing speed, traversed the face of the deadly Eigerwand in a horizontal direction, and reached the foot of the precipice that the four men had been trying to descend. As they toiled across the face, pebbles, invisible like bullets, hummed past them, and a flying boulder burst like a shell, close to the leader. From the first it had been evident that it would be impossible to effect a rescue that night, and now it appeared that Kurz alone of all the climbers was alive. He was suspended in a sling from the overhanging cliff, and was exposed to stone-falls as well as torrents of snow and water. "Can you hold out till morning?" he was asked, and "No, no, no!" came the heart-rending reply. But it was already night, and the guides had no choice but to retreat and disregard his cries. The return journey in storm and darkness must have been an unforgettable nightmare.

During the night another guide of the same calibre joined the original three, and by daybreak of Wednesday all four,

Adolf Rubi, Christian Rubi, Hans Schlunegger and Arnold Glatthard, climbed through the rubbish-shoot once more and again raced across the terrible wall. Kurz was still calling for help, and was even capable of telling something of his dreadful experiences. "Are none of your friends alive?" he was asked. "No, I am alone, they all died yesterday; one is frozen above me, one has fallen, and one lies hanging on the rope below."

It seems that the four men had fixed a rope to the cliff, and had begun to rope themselves down into space over the overhang. As there had not been enough rope for them all, Hinterstoisser had been obliged to untie himself. In doing so he fell, perhaps having been knocked over by falling stones, and was dashed to destruction at the bottom of the precipice. Angerer is said to have been strangled in the coils of falling rope, and Rainer was flung against one of the iron pegs with such violence that he died. Pegs and rope-rings had all been expended, and Kurz was helpless, third on the rope that linked him to his dead comrades, and crippled by having an arm and hand useless owing to frostbite. The guides, too, were in a desperate position, secured by their rope to a peg driven into an ice-slope of sixty degrees, and under fire from the relentless mountain. Glatthard, indeed, had narrowly escaped destruction. Moreover, they were still at a distance of a hundred and fifty feet below Kurz, and the interval that separated them consisted of smooth, vertical and overhanging rock, veneered with ice.

Since it was impossible to climb up to Kurz he was asked: "Try and cut the dead man loose from you." In order to do this he had to climb down forty feet—handicapped as he was by his crippled arm—and then with his ice-axe laboriously saw through the rope close to the loop round his friend's body. Afterwards he had to climb up again to where he was before

in order to fix the severed rope to the peg to which he had
been suspended. By a miracle of resolution and endurance,
after hours of toil, he succeeded in carrying out these exhausting
manoeuvres. At first the corpse could not be detached, for
it was frozen to the cliff; then, when it suddenly plunged into
space, it narrowly missed sweeping the guides with it, as it
hurtled past them in its three thousand feet fall. Then, after
Kurz, working with one hand and often with his teeth, had
climbed back to his former position, he had to lower the
severed rope to the guides, who attached to it some pegs and
rope-rings. These were then drawn up to Kurz, who
hammered in a peg, and passed the rope through the ring in
the head of the peg. The guides were so placed that it was
impossible for them to help Kurz by lowering him in pulley
fashion, and the whole series of Kurz's heroic efforts seemed
endless. Four hours were consumed in the terrible work
before the unfortunate man could begin the descent. As he
did so, it was noticed that he carefully removed any loose
stones which might otherwise have been dislodged and have
fallen on to the guides below him. As he slowly descended,
an avalanche swept over the whole party, concealing Kurz
from view for some moments.

And now, at the end of this heroically prolonged struggle,
Kurz's consciousness was beginning to fail. Yet he was
almost down. "Another step and you'll be saved," cried
the guides, and then with a supreme effort, one guide climbing
on the shoulders of another, while a third held him in position,
it became just possible to touch the ice-coated climbing-irons
of Kurz with the tip of an ice-axe, but he was still just out of
reach. At this moment occurred the final disaster: the knot
that joined the ropes together caught fast in the ring fifty
feet above the victim's head, and would allow him to descend
no further. This was the end. Suddenly, throwing his

axe to the guides, he let go his hold, and, swinging slowly out into space, he died. The devoted efforts of the heroic rescuers had been in vain, and death had come to Kurz at a moment when the reward of his unparalleled endurance and courage seemed to be close at hand. The guides, overcome by the spectacle of such unavailing fortitude, returned by the way they had come.

Note.—The north wall of the Eiger was eventually ascended by an Austro-German party in July, 1938. In spite of bad weather they succeeded in reaching the summit alive, and encountered the rescue party during the descent by the ordinary route.

THE BATTLES ON THE GRANDES JORASSES

In the domain of mountaineering one of the chief battlefields of Europe during the last ten years has been the northern precipices of the Grandes Jorasses, the magnificent rock-wall rising to nearly 14,000 feet above sea-level at the head of the Mer-de-glace, the glacier that flows down towards Chamonix from behind Mont Blanc.

A series of relentless battles has been fought on this awe-inspiring stage, for, although on the southern side the Grandes Jorasses are not very difficult, on the grim northern face climbers have made frequent unsuccessful attempts to reach the summit-ridge, and fatalities have occurred, not to mention hair-breadth escapes innumerable.

Only one Englishman has taken part in these attempts, Mr. Winthrop Young, who, by an exploration as long ago as 1907, first drew attention to the possibility that these formidable cliffs might be climbed. It was not until after the very dangerous ascents on the hitherto unclimbed faces of the Matterhorn had been triumphantly accomplished in the years 1931 and 1932 that the mountaineering hot-heads of Europe began seriously to turn their attention to the north wall of the Grandes Jorasses, for this terrible barrier was now almost the last great rock-wall in the Alps to remain unscaled.

Certainly the north face of the Grandes Jorasses constituted a challenge that only the most foolhardy could accept. The precipice is more than 3,000 feet high, and culminates in four summits exceeding 13,000 feet above sea-level. This imposing row of peaks is really more comparable to an upright slender screen than to a wall, and its crest, when seen from aeroplanes, or by climbers balanced on it precariously like tight-rope walkers, resembles a saw, not merely on account of the numerous jagged teeth that adorn it, but because of the extreme narrowness and dreadful sharpness of the edge that cuts the sky. The fact, too, that this grim precipice faces north ensures its being terribly exposed to cold, and always as richly clothed with snow and ice as the extreme steepness of the angle will allow. Moreover, the moment the early morning sun begins to thaw the crags, they burst into a murderous activity, and a hail of projectiles in the form of boulders, pebbles and ice-fragments roars and whistles down the cliffs, to overwhelm any climber who ventures to approach. This artillery and musketry of the mountain are more or less continually in action according to the variation in temperature, and a climber who is caught in one of the bursts of fire in a gully is fairly certain to be killed.

Of the many attempts to climb the face, two in particular were noteworthy, if only because they were the most typical of what is good and bad in the extreme methods of the new school of mountain-climbing. The two attempts were made by pairs of Munich climbers who were friends and rivals, each party being keenly ambitious to be the first to conquer the difficulties of the notorious wall. Of the four young men concerned, Brehm and Rittler were first in the field, and in August of 1931 were already sleeping at their base-camp on the glacier. Of them we shall hear more later. In the meantime their friends, Heckmair and Kroner, who were out of employment, and practically without means, had ridden the three hundred miles or so between Munich and

Photo: Edouard Frendo

NORTH FACE OF GRANDES JORASSES

*The great central couloir is seen in deep shadow. The route up the
buttress ascends to the right of it*

Chamonix on a couple of old bicycles, carrying with them a bivouac-tent as their headquarters in order to save as far as possible the expense of sleeping at club-huts. On arrival they set themselves to accomplish all the most arduous expeditions within reach, in a district that provides the most difficult climbing in the world. It was characteristic of their methods that throughout their constant strenuous activities they showed an almost total disregard for bad weather. Later, when some English mountaineers invited them to share a meal in one of the high huts on Mont Blanc, they admitted that, although their equipment was good enough, their lack of means often prevented them from getting enough to eat. At that moment, in fact, they were evidently famished.

Eventually, when the weather became so bad that even the fanatical enthusiasm of these gallant youths could no longer cope with it, some form of relaxation seemed desirable, so they abandoned their camp equipment at Chamonix in order to ride off on their bicycles to the Riviera, sleeping at night on the roadside in the open. Within a week, however, they were back again at Chamonix.

Their next proceeding was to pitch their tent underneath the north face of the Grandes Jorasses, at the foot of the ice-slope 800 feet high, where the real climbing begins. They had already made one attempt on the face that summer, and had reached a considerable height. While they had been under fire from falling stones on that occasion, one missile hurled by the mountain had smashed the head of an ice-axe that one of the climbers was carrying slung to his waist, and another stone had severed the rope that united the two men.

And now they were ready to start once more, but before doing so they turned aside in some trepidation to investigate the empty camp of Brehm and Rittler, their fellow competitors. It was known that these two had set out five days previously, and, in spite of a severe storm, it was thought that they might have reached the summit and have descended on the other side into Italy. Perhaps they were even now on their way back to Chamonix in triumph. Accordnigly Kroner and Heckmair anxiously examined the vacated tent, and discovered an abandoned diary in which they read with a thrill of excitement the following words written by one of their absent friends:

"Here we are at the base of the north wall. It appears quite harmless (sic). [Heckmair and Kroner themselves had believed this once.] If it wasn't snowing we should try the climb immediately. Hourly we are expecting Heckmair and Kroner, our strongest competitors."

Evidently there was not a moment to be lost. Consequently, Heckmair and Kroner set off at once on a resolute attempt to reach the summit by storming the great central couloir that divides the face in two. They succeeded in cutting steps up the first and biggest of the three glittering ice-plaques that adorn the precipice, but failed to get any higher than they had done six weeks earlier. During a terrible retreat amid falling stones and avalanches they barely escaped with their lives, and on getting down to the foot of the cliffs, were dismayed to come upon the bodies of their two friends, still roped together, and lying lifeless on the glacier. It is believed that the two unfortunate men had climbed about twelve hundred feet up the wall, and, owing to the fact that their gloves were in their pockets, it is supposed that they had begun to descend before the onset of the storm, and slipped while doing so.

This was the last appearance of Heckmair and Kroner on the scene, for they now abandoned the stage to other antagonists.

Among these latter perhaps the best known was Armand Charlet, one of the *élite* of the Chamonix guides. With various colleagues he had made repeated attempts on the north wall, and had twice been driven back by falling stones. In 1934 he returned to the attack with an amateur. Members of previous parties who had happened to find themselves on the north face with Armand Charlet have described the experience. It appears that he would set out from the hut in the small hours at such an incredible pace that more ordinary mortals were thankful to abandon the attempt to keep up with him, and consoled themselves with the reflection that it was on the man in front at any rate that the strenuous labour of step-cutting would devolve, and that they might just as well leave this exhausting job to one who was so pre-eminently efficient in performing it. However, they were soon dis-illusioned, for Charlet was not quite so distinterested as it appeared. Thus when the leisurely rear-guard had crossed the great crevasse at the foot of the slope where the severe climbing begins, they found to their disgust that the steps were not being cut in the convenient zigzags that they had anticipated, but rose vertically up the slope in the manner of a ladder. The consequence was that the blocks and splinters of ice hacked out so rapidly by Charlet's skilful axe came bounding down in an almost continuous stream, and hummed about the ears of everyone who tried to follow. There was nothing for it but to stand aside and wait till Charlet's party had increased their distance, so that they were no longer immediately overhead. This was decidedly inconvenient, and for climbers to be strung out above each other at great distances on the very loose rocks that were to be found higher up the mountain, was not only inconvenient but highly dangerous. In fact, for the second party retreat was inevitable, since it had become painfully evident that the ascent was not going according to plan—unless indeed the plan was Charlet's.

To return, however, to Charlet's expedition in 1934: it must be explained that three great buttresses support the north wall, and between the easterly pair lies the prodigiously steep gully known as the great central couloir. After crossing the big crevasse at the foot of the mountain, Charlet's party reached the great central couloir, and followed it until they could effect a lodgement on the central buttress, on their right. There was now the same fatally seductive foreshortening that had lured Brehm and Rittler to destruction, and Charlet noticed that owing to this distortion, the peak named Michel Croz, which was the ultimate objective on the lofty frontier ridge overhead, appeared to be fantastically near at hand. At first there was an air of hope and the climbing on the buttress went quickly, but soon an overhang was encountered, and then, to free the leader for greater exertions, his companion took over both rucksacks for a while, with the consequence that he had to be given considerable help with the rope, and this diminished the rate of progress. Step-cutting in steepest ice also began to alternate with the rock-climbing. Some of the perpendicular rock-pitches were surmounted with the help of iron pegs hammered into convenient crevices. Above the climbers the vertical perspective now seemed to increase, instead of diminishing, and the blunt crest of the buttress on which they were climbing for hour after hour soared endlessly overhead up the face in massive outward-leaning steps. As the party rose, the mighty Aiguille Verte, across the Mer-de-glace, seemed to rise with the climbers and dominate the landscape to the north.

At last the men had cut steps up the second of the three ice-slopes, or plaques, and had reached a platform that was big enough to sit on, so they rested for half an hour. The

immense height and width of the wall was now overwhelm-
ingly impressive, yet hope was rising again, for it seemed that
time was in their favour, as it was only ten o'clock. Time
indeed was still most necessary to them, for they were now
about to begin work on that most critical portion of the
precipice, where the buttress that they had hitherto been
following, lost itself in the rugged barrier of sheer rock that
supported the actual summit-ridge. Abandoned by the
buttress, the party were at a loss what to do next. Climbing
down a few steps from the vanishing-point of the buttress,
Charlet attempted by making a détour to work his way
painfully up on to the appallingly exposed rock-wall above
his head, but he found that though the rock-wall was seamed
with several shallow gullies, each one of them terminated in an
insurmountable overhang. Yet the wall between the gullies
was still more intimidating. So Charlet tried two of the
gullies and then got stuck in a third, and this one was not only
shallow, but nearly vertical. When he tried to traverse out
of it with the help of his axe, cramp seized his arm, and his
companion suffered intense anxiety, as there was no means
of making the rope fast, in case of the leader slipping.
Finally, by hammering in an iron peg, Charlet contrived to
transfer himself into a fourth chimney, and swarmed up it a
little way, until he had to leave it again by following a descending ledge. But the ledge came to an end, and he was obliged
to return once more. It was half-past twelve, there seemed
to be no way of overcoming the rock-barrier, and they had
taken two hours to climb only seventy-five feet. So, with
reluctance they abandoned all hope of the summit, and began
the terrible descent. Yet there was cause for congratulation,
for they had climbed higher than anyone else. The rock-
barrier that they had failed to climb would have given them
access to the uppermost of the three ice-slopes on the face,

and it was this slope that abutted on the foot of the final four hundred feet of cliff that formed the actual summit-ridge.

As Charlet and his companions descended, the air seemed alive with falling stones, all of them invisible owing to the speed of their flight, but by keeping on the crest of the buttress, the two men remained safe from all missiles, except ricochets. Projecting rocks were used for fixing the spare rope wherever possible, for they were running short of the essential iron pegs. When, later, they were obliged to enter the dangerous couloir again, stones and avalanches were no longer so active, for the sun had quitted this side of the mountain. The *bergschrund*, or great crevasse at the foot of the cliffs was a fitting climax to the descent, and they passed it with their hearts in their mouths with one tremendous leap. It was twenty minutes past seven in the evening. Difficulty alone had been the cause of their defeat. The dominant impression had been the profound emotions caused by the spectacle of the grandeur and immensity of the face seen at such close quarters.

The next four battles on the Grandes Jorasses took place almost simultaneously, about a month later. One was a remarkable effort by two Germans from Munich, Haringer and Peters, another was a further raid by Charlet, a third was an attack by two Italians, Gervasutti and Chabod, and the last of the four ventures was a performance by three Austrians.

Haringer and Peters were perhaps the most determined of the assailants, and had gone into serious training in 1933. During the winter they had been practising rock-climbing and bivouacking in the snow in the *klettergarten* of the Isar valley. Their attempt was launched on the 28th of July in 1934, when they left the hut, crossed the *bergschrund* successfully, and after climbing for two hours up the first precipitous ice-slope, made a horizontal traverse which enabled them to get foothold on the central buttress, now the recognized highway to the upper regions. They were just in time to find space for an exiguous bivouac before darkness overtook them. During the night they even succeeded in dozing a little, and just as day was breaking, Peters was wakened dramatically by a wet rope brushing against his face. It signified the arrival of that formidable antagonist, Armand Charlet, who, accompanied by a professional colleague, was in the act of carrying out one of his lightning attacks. So the Germans now bestirred themselves with preparations for an advance, but in the semi-darkness before the complete arrival of day-light, and without pause, the two French aces hurried past them, leaving them far behind, and rapidly vanishing up the precipice overhead. Meanwhile the Germans made slow progress, and Charlet's party still at racing speed, completely outdistancing their rivals, had reached a point somewhere below the second of the three ice-slopes. But now the weather seemed to be definitely breaking, so that Charlet and his friend determined to retreat, and, descending with the utmost swiftness, passed by the Germans again, vanishing from the scene as rapidly as they had come.

But other rivals were advancing to the attack; the two Italians, Gervasutti and Chabod, who subsequently distinguished themselves on the mountain in the following year, had been hotly pursuing the Germans, and now overtook them at a height of about 12,000 feet, still almost 2,000 feet below the highest peak. Here they halted, not liking the look of the weather, but the Germans continued to ascend.

The fact was that the weather was not only threatening, but was every moment getting worse, and the north face is never a safe climb for more than one party at a time, on account of the risk of dislodging stones. There is no doubt that it would have been imprudent to go on. The Germans were at work overhead, there was another party loitering on the cliffs in an undecided manner, and finally, when salvoes of stones dislodged by the still advancing Germans began to whistle past, the Italians decided to go down. Accordingly, a general retreat began, long, dangerous and exhausting. Eventually they crossed the *bergschrund* at the foot of the mountain at nine o'clock that night. During most of this time, to the astonishment of everyone, the German party was still ascending, and was far up the mountain out of sight.

Two days then elapsed, during which blizzards raged on the precipice, nothing could be seen of the Germans, and naturally the greatest possible anxiety was felt for their safety. On the third day it seemed impossible that they could have survived, but at five o'clock that afternoon, Peters descending alone, staggered down on to the glacier at the foot of the cliffs, and was succoured by friends who had come to look for him. This was the terrible story that he told: When the others had turned back, and Peters had decided with Haringer to push on in spite of the weather, it was already their second day on the mountain. Disregarding the conditions, they continued to climb exceedingly difficult rocks, and to cut steps in ice till they were compelled by darkness to halt for their second bivouac on the precipice, sitting astride a narrow boss of rock. They had already reached the second of the three ice-slopes, and next morning with astounding pertinacity they succeeded in reaching the third. They had now beaten Charlet's best effort, but the badness of the weather was now reaching a climax, snow fell heavily, and enormous masses of it poured incessantly in avalanches down the cliffs. So the inevitable retreat began. To help in the descent they used two spare ropes, each a hundred and fifty feet long. These could be hitched doubled to any available rock-projections, and pulled down afterwards, as soon as the climbers had slid down them. Unfortunately, owing to the smoothness of the precipice, it was difficult to find trustworthy projections.

All day they continued the terrible labour of lowering themselves down the enormous cliffs. Night again overtook them, and it was necessary to organize another bivouac. It was their third night on the mountain. In the increasing darkness Haringer unroped for a moment, and withdrew for a few paces to try to kick standing-room in the snow-slope of seventy degrees on which they might pass the night. In his attempt to do this he must have come upon ice, for with a single shout of "Ice!" he slipped and vanished to his death in the darkness of the abyss.

Peters spent that night alone in the raging blizzard, and during the whole of the next day continued his exhausting task of lowering himself down the cliffs, till he was again obliged to stop by nightfall, and bivouac for his fourth night upon the mountain. Next day he still had sufficient strength to complete the descent. The body of his friend was found eighteen hundred feet below the place where the slip had occurred.

There had now been twenty-five unsuccessful attempts, and the tragic adventures of Peters and Haringer closed the season of 1934. Peters claimed to have reached a point that had never been reached before, only five hundred feet below the summit, but, chiefly because the pace of his party had been observed to be so slow, doubts were expressed on the soundness of his claim. However, undismayed by his companion's death, and by the five days of appalling hardship that he had suffered, Peters, as he took his departure, uttered only one comment. "I shall return," he said, and in June the following year, true to his word, this astonishing man was back at the Leschaux hut with another companion, and busy studying the conditions of the precipice.

But there were others, too, in 1935, waiting and watching. The Italians, Gervasutti and Chabod had never given up hope of being first on the top. Gervasutti had already had two experiences, and Chabod had attempted the climb in 1932. A Swiss lady, Mademoiselle Boulaz and her guide, Lambert, had also made a previous attempt and were absorbedly dreaming of this ill-omened face. In addition to these, an Austrian, Steinhauer was in the offing, and on a previous occasion, had made an exploration with a Bavarian named Maier. Of all the possible competitors, however, the most formidable was that dashing French guide, Armand Charlet, the doyen of them all and the best mountaineer. Would he return to the attack? No one could tell.

The month of June in 1935 had been very hot; the heavy snowfall that had taken place earlier in the year had melted, and the rocks on the north side of all the great peaks were dry almost right up to the summits. Surely this was the season of seasons! As Gervasutti and Chabod approached the Leschaux hut, they were astonished to see that the north face of the Grandes Jorasses was in such perfection of condition as they had never seen before. With this wonderful weather they might well expect all the principal performers to be assembled on parade. Accordingly they were not surprised on reaching the hut to be greeted gloomily by one of their rivals, Steinhauer, with the laconic remark, "Peters is up there." They soon discovered that Peters was with Steinhauer's former companion, Maier, also an addict of the north wall.

All that was known of the two men was that they had started, and Steinhauer had no idea on what date they had begun the climb. He was now beside himself with anxiety at having as yet failed to secure a companion with whom he could join in the general assault.

In the meantime the two Swiss, Mademoiselle Boulaz and the guide Lambert arrived, whereupon, suddenly, while they were all discussing the situation, four figures were visible approaching from the scene of action across the glacier. They turned out to be a party who were returning in discomfiture, owing to their leader having dislocated his shoulder. They brought no news, but the assembled parties now reached the melancholy conclusion that by this time the two Germans must either have died or reached the top.

While these gloomy speculations were going on in the hut, the two Germans were wasting no time on the mountain. As he had done with Haringer, so also with Maier, Peters had undertaken severe winter climbing as training for the great ordeal. When they had first arrived at their base-camp on the Leschaux Glacier, on the 26th of June, the unusually warm weather had made the mountain unapproachable, for the whole of the north face was undergoing bombardments of stones. On the 29th, however, the heat had abated, and by four o'clock that afternoon, their opportunity had arrived, and the two men were hard at work cutting steps in the bare ice of the first ice-slope. A well-marked gully giving access to the central buttress was now too dangerous a route, owing to its being under fire from falling stones, and in the smaller gully that they chose in preference, a stream of water poured over them, soaking them to the skin. At half-past six that evening they had climbed on to the backbone of the buttress, and were preparing to pass the night in the bivouac-place of the year before. The low temperature that accompanied the clear sky was a favourable sign, and as the evening wore on they were relieved to notice that the streams of water ceased cascading down the cliffs.

A clear cold night such as this was wanted for checking the bombardment from above. All boulders and ice-blocks must be firmly frozen into the mountain before there could be any reasonable security.

It must not be supposed that a bivouac on the north wall of the Grandes Jorasses is accompanied by any of the comforts usually associated with a mountaineer's bivouac before a big climb. There are no snug tents or cosy sleeping-bags, and the climbers, when overtaken by darkness, are sometimes obliged to stand upright all night, lashed to pegs driven into suitable cracks in the rock; they are thankful if they can change place every hour or so, in order to relieve the intolerable constraint of their position. The cold increases as the night goes on, and the hours pass interminably; every now and then the roar of a stone avalanche in one of the gullies punctuates the intensity of the silence; and occasionally one of the climbers dozes where he stands, till the jerk of the rope, when he falls forward, wakes him once more.

Afterwards the Germans spoke well of the security of their resting-place, but its amenities can have been only relatively desirable, for, during the night a falling stone hit the cooking-stove and smashed it to atoms, so that when they started climbing again at six in the morning, it was without the support of a hot breakfast. Once they were under way, however, the great couloir on their left that descends between the two main buttresses of the face, seemed to be dry and quiet, and they climbed fast over dry rocks, keeping always on the great central buttress till they reached the second of the three ice-slopes. Here they put on climbing-irons and divided all the iron pegs that they carried into equal shares. They now adopted a special technique, for there was not time for the laborious cutting of steps. They relied a good deal on two special prongs projecting horizontally from the toe-pieces of their climbing-irons, and the leader dispensed with cutting until each time that he came to the end of his rope, when he hacked out a step for one foot, hammered in one of the longer ringed pegs, in order to secure himself, and then the second man followed, till he reached the leader's level, partly pulling himself up by the rope in order to ensure more rapid progress.

Suddenly, while they were thus engaged upon the second ice-slope—without any warning—a rock-avalanche swept down on them through the air. Maier was struck and hurled from his footholds, but Peters fortunately only had his hat knocked off, and was able to support Maier with the rope and prevent him from falling any further. Maier had received a large open wound, but insisted on continuing the climb.

An hour later they had left the second ice-slope behind them, and were at the foot of that formidable vertical rock-barrier which had defeated Charlet, and which separates the second from the third ice-slope. On their left they could now gaze down the great central couloir plunging in a succession of black and ghastly cliffs, till it emerged on the Leschaux Glacier, thousands of feet below. The early arrival of the sun on the mountain had already started avalanches as well as stone-falls, and the whole face seemed alive and hostile.

A direct assault on the smooth, water-worn, slabs of the barrier was out of the question, and a wide détour was necessary. The difficulty of the climbing increased, and although the steepness presently diminished a little, the protection that the vertical angle of the cliff had at first afforded to the climbers was now absent and left them more exposed to avalanches and stone-falls. They now ascended continuously difficult cliffs, past the place where Peters had bivouacked the previous year with Haringer, and from time to time, where handholds or footholds were conspicuously lacking, the leader would hammer in one of his dwindling store of iron pegs.

At two o'clock in the afternoon they reached the third and uppermost of the three ice-slopes, and came upon a hollow in the ice, with a great flat boulder overhanging it, the only site really suitable for a bivouac on the whole of this inhospitable precipice. Here they had an hour's rest. Peters knew the spot well. It was where he had turned back with Haringer in 1934, when no one had believed him. No other mortals had ever been here before. Perhaps this time the world would believe. Could it now be possible that he and Maier had already stormed the key-position of the whole climb? He did not yet know that the north face was keeping its best for the last.

After their rest they climbed the third ice-slope in only forty-five minutes. Above the ice-slope a great hidden chimney led to a pinnacle on a buttress, and thence fine climbing over good granite enabled them to move simultaneously till fresh difficulties once more compelled them to climb one at a time. At last they arrived beneath the final rampart, and found that the last three hundred feet of the mountain rose uninterruptedly in a vertical sweep of the most forbidding rock to the snowy culmination of the Pointe Michel Croz. Here again direct assault was out of the question. A détour to the left could just be managed, although the difficulty of the climbing was almost prohibitive. This precarious traverse brought the men into a position of fearful exposure, suspended vertically above the great central couloir, which descended almost sheer, so it seemed, between the two great buttresses of the face, that is to say the central buttress which had earlier been their route, and the formidable-looking eastern buttress on their left.

The climbing now verged on the impossible. There were smooth brittle slabs with overhangs, and abrupt crests of rock offering only minute crevices as supports for fingers and toes. In order to free himself for more violent exertions, the leader contrived to remove his rucksack and hang it on a peg, so that the second man could take charge of it when he had got up to it. Hammer-blows resounded as pegs were driven into the rock. The work was supremely exhausting, a feat of strenuous gymnastics, and these last three or four hundred feet formed the climax of the whole expedition. At length, however, the difficulties were overcome, and at eight o'clock in the evening of the second day the leader clambered triumphantly on to the summit of the Pointe Michel Croz. Here on one of the highest peaks of the Grandes Jorasses, 13,484 feet above the sea, the exhausted climbers were obliged to bivouac, but what did the precariousness of such a situation matter to the men who had conquered in the final battle for the north wall?

THE NEW ADVENTURERS

THE new methods of climbing, such as I have described in the last two chapters, can be explained, if not excused, for it must be remembered that it is the gradual and inevitable changing of conditions that has just as gradually and inevitably produced the modern methods. The new technique, outrageous as it appears to the majority of mountaineers, is in fact only an adaptation to altered circumstances.

In the happy days in the middle of the last century, when the vogue of mountaineering may be said to have started, there seemed to be an unlimited number of unclimbed peaks. This period may be designated as the first phase of Alpine climbing, and it was not until the end of the last century that the seeker after virgin peaks had to look further afield than the Alps. Towards the end of the last century, however, the decreasing number of unclimbed summits had compelled the more adventurous to find distraction in discovering new routes to the familiar mountain-tops. Nor was this unreasonable, for the pioneers who had climbed the Swiss and Italian sides of the Matterhorn or traversed Monte Rosa from Italy into Switzerland, or had explored the classic routes on Mont Blanc, had long ago realized that each new way of approach to even the most familiar peak constituted a completely different and novel expedition. For instance, only an expert would guess that the Matterhorn, whose vast bulk dominates the Italian pastures at Breuil, is the same mountain that towers so gracefully and impressively above the Swiss village of Zermatt. In fact, when approached from opposite sides, it is as different to climb as it is to look at, and this applies to all great peaks.

So for a time the profusion of variety to be found on every great mountain satisfied even the most adventurous: it was the Indian summer of mountaineering; the evil day on which it had been expected that the Alps would be "exhausted" seemed to be indefinitely postponed, and new routes sufficed instead of new peaks. This period may be called the second phase of Alpine climbing, and it continued approximately until the end of the European War. Throughout this second phase there was a growing tolerance on the part of the Alpine world towards guideless climbing, a practice which the majority of the pioneers had looked upon as a dangerous form of naughtiness. Since the earliest days, it is true, there had been successful guideless ascents, but they were only sporadic instances, and Canon Girdlestone's prolonged guideless activities in the 'sixties, did little to change opinion, for his ingenuous narrative revealed too many hair-breadth escapes to encourage others to follow his example.

However, a campaign in 1876, accomplished by Messrs. Charles and Lawrence Pilkington in company with Mr. Gardiner was a very different affair. Within the limits of a comparatively short holiday these three carried out with unvarying success a series of guideless expeditions of all degrees of difficulty. The effect of this performance was decisive, and guideless climbing from that day gradually became respectable. Later on, too, the advent of a class of amateurs who could spend more time and thought on mountaineering than even the best guides could spare made it evident that men with the necessary leisure and aptitude were at least as trustworthy for any expedition as guides were.

Subsequently, with the general impoverishment that followed the European War there were few climbers left with money enough to pay guides for long engagements, and after the war, guideless expeditions became so common that they no longer excited comment.

But even so, during the second phase of Alpine climbing, apart from this relenting attitude to the question of guideless expeditions, the view of the majority of mountaineers remained orthodox, and strict attention was still paid to the fundamental principles as preached and practised by the pioneers. The latter had always drawn the sharpest distinction between difficulty and danger. While admitting that mountaineers might enjoy difficulty with clear consciences and not be deterred by danger, they maintained that true mountain craft consisted not merely in conquering difficulties, but also, as far as possible, in circumventing dangers. Thus they held that no degree of difficulty could excuse an experienced mountaineer if he fell off his mountain. But they also declared that it was inexcusable for anyone to venture deliberately into the sort of place where the mountain was likely to do the falling and might fall upon the mountaineer. According to this theory risk from falling stones and avalanches could nearly always be avoided. To run such risks voluntarily was, in the orthodox view, prejudicial to the good name of mountaineering.

After the war these ideas, which had worn so well, came to be discredited and repudiated by the new school which now arose among the numerous young guideless climbers. The third phase of Alpine climbing may now be said to have begun, and the greatest revolution that the ethics of mountaineering have yet undergone began to take place. It was partly caused perhaps by a war-worn attitude of mind, but chiefly by what has been often described as the "exhaustion" of the Alps. Now, it has been maintained very plausibly that the Alps can never be exhausted, and this is true, no doubt, in the case of those who love them best. On the other hand, in the case of a man whose motive in climbing may be a passion for exploration, he will surely find that for him the Alps have been exhausted long before each gully, ridge, face or quarry has been charted with dotted lines and classified in the last and most exhaustive climber's guide-book of some future age.

The Alps have been referred to by a great writer and mountaineer as the playground of Europe. Such an analogy is disagreeably suggestive of gymnastic apparatus and asphalt schoolyards. Certainly, if the Alps have become a mere playground to us to-day, there is some excuse for the young generation's rejecting the hallowed traditional methods of mountaineering, and the present state of affairs can be accounted for. When the best pitches of the playground are overcrowded, when play is becoming stale and the peaks, with all their routes have been traversed again and again, what novelty or uncertainty is there left? The only solution is to alter the rules of the game, and the young generation will not hesitate to do so. They will make the new principles clear by their deeds; dangers must be courted, chances must be taken, uncertainty can be improvised. Are not the very few great mountaineering problems that are left in the Alps all of them dangerous to solve as well as difficult? The word "impossible" is to have no meaning to the new mountaineer; he is to conquer tempests as well as precipices of ice and rock; it is not for him to wait upon the weather. For him mountaineering is to be the same thing as war, and as the enemy gives no quarter, all means are fair. Thousands of feet of rope, scores of hooks, clasps, pegs, wedges, stirrups, slings, hammers, pulleys, chisels, or anything else in the world that can be dragged or carried up a mountain, may be used: no manner of mechanical means need be rejected; this is the new spirit.

It is curious that no English names are to be found in the records of this peculiar school of mountaineering. It seems that its general principles do not appeal to Englishmen; at any rate the English do not appear to put them into practice as far as climbing mountains is concerned. Yet the new attitude to mountains, whatever Englishmen may think of it, is responsible for some astonishing exploits, edifying and the reverse.

Perhaps the most notorious of these was the celebrated *tour de force* of the brothers Schmid on the previously unclimbed north face of the Matterhorn. One of the young men had already taken part in a new ascent of the Ortlerspitze, in Tyrol, and the route chosen on that occasion had been described as "an enormous ice-couloir situated between threatening rocky banks and under the constant menace of the gigantic overhanging sérac-bastion of the upper Ortler Glacier." The critic went on to say that only a person desirous of uselessly exposing his life would dream of ascending this funnel, swept as it is by continuous stones and ice avalanches. But the brothers' ascent of the Matterhorn was a longer and more serious business, for the north face of this mountain is peculiar in that it is probably only possible to attack it with any chance of getting up alive when the conditions may be said to be at their worst—that is to say, when the rocks happen to be plastered with ice and snow. Without the coherence which an armour of ice and snow supplies, the whole face is a precipice in process of disintegration, discharging incessant volleys and avalanches of stones. Owing, therefore, to the conditions under which the brothers were obliged to make the attempt, holds for hands and feet had to be scraped with an axe in the ice and snow. Slowly they worked their way up the long steep slope, grooved by stone-falls. Occasionally the leader was able to hammer in a peg in order to secure the rope uniting him with his companions, but there was no security from the stones falling from hundreds of feet above. In places the thinness of the ice that coated the rocks allowed only the smallest notches to be scratched for hands and feet. Only one halting-place could be found before the onset of darkness obliged them to bivouac, crouching roped to the cliff. The constant toil had enabled them only to eat one bar of chocolate since dawn, and the rope was frozen as stiff as a hawser. Next morning at seven o'clock they staggered on again from their roosting-perches and reached the top of the Matterhorn at two in the afternoon. Throughout the latter part of the climb they had been in great danger from the storminess of the weather, and in descending from the top to Zermatt they wasted considerable time, because, as they had never been on the mountain before, they were unfamiliar with the way.

Of a similar ascent on the south face of the Matterhorn, also only recently effected, one of the successful party writes:

"With the rising sun stones began to fall methodically, and we were involved in their unpleasant company during ten hours. We were obliged to proceed by rushes, steering towards big boulders or other obstacles that might afford shelter. But the stones were kind to us and fell only at regular intervals, thus permitting us to pass between successive showers."

Yet another side of the Matterhorn to be recently climbed for the first time is the east face. It is easier than the other two faces, except in the upper part, where the victorious party were occupied during eleven hours in climbing only a thousand feet. On this side, too, the mountain is notorious for its avalanches of stones, and so great is the danger from this cause that on several occasions it has proved impossible to recover the bodies of victims that have fallen to the base of the precipice.

One more performance on the Matterhorn may be quoted as typical of the new spirit. On this occasion the new methods themselves were not in question, but the disastrous familiarity with which a tragic party of climbers treated a great peak that was totally unknown to them is only too typical of the new point of view.

It was the summer of 1934, and the weather that season was remarkable for the sort of chronic instability that all habitual climbers become acquainted with sooner or later in their Alpine careers. In view of the daily afternoon storms it is not surprising that the Matterhorn was only in mediocre condition. In the little club-hut, perched at a height of nearly thirteen thousand feet on the vast southern precipices of the Italian face, were four guideless climbers from Bergamo. They were new to the Matterhorn, though they had done some good climbs on smaller peaks. There were also in the hut two Italian guides accompanying two military officers. The guided party proposed to start for the peak at four the next morning, and offered their company to the men of Bergamo, but the latter refused it with the scornful comment that to start four hours later would be quite early enough for a mountain like the Matterhorn.

The guided party accordingly set out by themselves, traversed the summit in good time, descended into Switzerland, and, by crossing a pass in the afternoon, were back in Italy before dark that evening. They had found snowy conditions with occasional ice on the cables, and a bitter wind had been blowing all day. On the same morning at four o'clock three Turinese guideless climbers had also started on the same route up the Matterhorn, but from a lower Italian hut called the Rionde. They overtook the four guideless men from Bergamo shortly after the latter had left the club-hut, and in their company began the first day of what was to prove a long and tragic journey.

For a short time after the parties met all went well; then one of the three Turinese became exhausted or perhaps mountain-sick, and it was eventually agreed that he should be left alone where he was, on the terribly exposed precipice, till his companions could pick him up again on their return. It was already close on midday, and the Turinese party, now reduced to two, pushed on ahead of the four Bergamo men and reached the rope-ladder by themselves. This ladder, a well-known feature of the climb, hangs about two hundred feet below the summit, in a position that is extremely exposed and sensational, for it dangles loosely over the steepest part of the gigantic Italian precipice. The climber is obliged at a certain point to change his position from the inner side of the ladder to the outer. At a moment in the afternoon when the Bergamo party, following at a slower pace, were scaling the vertical cliffs on the way up to the ladder, they suddenly heard a crash overhead, and, looking up, saw two human beings hurtle past them through the air, so closely as almost to collide and sweep the helpless party headlong from the mountain.

The experience, one would have thought, must have been appalling; yet the strange fact remains that the four men were so little moved that after commenting on the event, the cause of which was unknown to them and remains unknown to us, they wrote off the loss of their two fellow-climbers and decided to continue their own ascent as before. It was a strange decision from more than one point of view, for the weather had now become worse, so that it was with consider-able difficulty and alarmingly late in the afternoon that they finally succeeded in reaching the summit. Night was coming on fast, and they now found themselves in a state of indecision. Should they take the easier route and descend by the Hoernli ridge into Switzerland, abandoning to his fate the unfortunate man who was awaiting their return, or should they go back to him by the way they had come? Eventually the conclusion was forced upon them when they realized that they dared not face the Italian precipices again, and, darkness having come on completely, they were obliged to stay where they were, crouching together all through the night on the very crest of the peak itself.

Thus not till dawn of the second day did they venture to attempt the descent of the Hoernli ridge into Switzerland. As for the man abandoned on the precipice without the knowledge that his two friends had already been killed and that the other four climbers had enough to do to look after themselves, he had waited all day in miserable uncertainty and spent the night in the open. During the afternoon of the second day, frost-bitten and utterly exhausted, he succeeded in climbing down to the Italian club-hut, where first aid was given to him by a number of parties who, owing to the bad weather, had decided not to start for the summit that morning.

Meanwhile, as the second day of the tragedy wore on, the unfortunate men from Bergamo were toiling frantically down the Swiss ridge towards the inn on the Hoernli which they could see at an immense distance below them. After they had fought their way for some fifteen hundred feet one of them dropped dead from exposure and exhaustion. The dead man's brother, with the aid of his two companions, tied the corpse to the rocks and staggered on once more. Slowly and painfully the day passed; one storm after another swept over them, and at nightfall they had failed in their attempt to reach the Solway hut which is the emergency refuge midway between the summit and the Hoernli. Thus they were still at a great height on the ridge, and were faced with the prospect of spending another night in the open.

But by this time the alarm had been spread, and Italian guides were moving to the rescue with admirable promptitude and a heroic disregard of the terrible weather. Already on the morning after the ill-fated Bergamo men had reached the summit, two guides had crossed the frontier and were examining the Swiss ridge of the Matterhorn through a telescope, in the hope of detecting some trace of the missing parties descending towards the Hoernli inn. As the clouds cleared, signs were obvious enough, but to their dismay the reconnoiterers saw that the tracks stopped short at some considerable distance above the emergency refuge, which stood at a height of about thirteen thousand feet. With this disconcerting news they returned into Italy, and, after a consultation at the Rionde hut, set out at six that evening to cross the frontier once more. Their intention now was to make for the Hoernli inn and from there, disregarding darkness and storm, to climb the Swiss ridge in order, if possible, to bring rescue to the descending men.

Earlier on the same day, too, five other guides with similar intentions were making preparations to climb right up the Italian ridge to the summit of the Matterhorn. This was a venture that might well have deterred the boldest, for all that morning the bad weather had continued and the great mountain, whenever it was visible through gaps in the racing clouds, showed white from head to foot; everywhere deep snow lay in drifts, and long streamers of it were blowing off in the gale. Nevertheless the men continued to get ready, and at eight o'clock that morning, during a temporary lull in the storm, set out on their desperate errand. They succeeded in reaching the little club-hut, and thence three of them actually managed to force their way to the summit, arriving there at the dangerously late hour of five in the evening. The conditions were terrible, ice was on all the fixed ropes, and in places they sank up to their hips in the snow. On the top they discovered a clue, the vacated bivouac-place of the four missing climbers.

By this time the weather was improving, and as night came on the heroic three guides began the descent into Switzerland. Fifteen hundred feet down they came upon the frozen corpse of the tourist who had first succumbed to exhaustion, and when they arrived at the emergency-hut they found another climber, delirious and in a state of collapse. Here, therefore, they left one of their number to stay with the exhausted man until he could be got to safety. Two of the guides then continued the descent. At nine that evening, still descending and scarcely six hundred feet below the emergency-hut, they found two more of the unfortunate party, sprawling in the snow, helplessly awaiting a second night in the open and the certainty of death. To the astonishment of the rescuers the climbers were wearing thin summer clothes, having left their only warm garments, as well as most of their food, at the club-hut from which they had started. Fortunately, the other two guides who, by eleven o'clock that night, had crossed the frontier from Italy and reached the Hoernli, did not pause, but ascended immediately in the darkness, joining forces with rescuers and rescued. They were therefore able to take over the terrible duty of helping down the surviving climbers, while the two guides who had come the whole way over the summit descended in advance in order to make tracks through the masses of soft snow.

Gradually the night passed, and, soon after half-past four in the morning of the third day of this tragic Odyssey, another climber collapsed and died. His companion, however, was successfully brought down in safety to the inn on the Hoernli, and was actually fit to return to Italy over the Breuiljoch that very afternoon. Later, the man found in a state of delirium in the emergency-hut was conducted down by the guide who had been detailed to look after him, and was able subsequently to go home by train. Thus out of seven men who had started so confidently for the summit, four had perished during those three fatal days. But the work of the heroic and devoted Italian guides was not yet finished, for they still had to accomplish the strenuous task of conveying down the two bodies left out on the mountain. The tragedy, too, was to have an aftermath, for two of the men who had perished were brothers, and their father, shortly after attending the funeral, went out of his mind and died.

Another typical catastrophe that happened in the summer of 1934 differed from the last chapter of accidents, for it was more directly due to the actual technique of the modern extremists than to their attitude of mind. The victim was young Herr Toni Schmid, the most famous exponent of the ultra-modern methods. It was he who, with his brother, had achieved the terrible ascent of the north face of the Matterhorn referred to in this chapter. His final climb and its dreadful ending is described in the review published by the French Alpine Club. The young man and his companion were engaged in the ascent of the desperately steep and difficult ice-wall on the north side of the Wiesbachhorn, in the eastern Alps. Schmid was more than ninety feet above his companion, and was hard at work knocking a ringed iron peg into the ice by means of a hammer that he had just taken from his belt. He was standing upright in a narrow ice-step while the man below cautiously paid out the rope to him whenever it was needed, and hitched a coil of it round the head of his ice-axe, which was precariously anchored against the unyielding ice. Schmid was so awkwardly placed that he was obliged to work in a hurry, and the blows of his hammer resounded rapidly on the iron peg. Unfortunately the ice was particularly hard and brittle, with a tendency to split instead of gripping the pegs. However, this particular peg seemed to be at last secure, as half of it had been successfully driven in. Accordingly, Schmid fastened the spring-hook in his belt to the ring in the head of the peg, and began to apply his weight to it as a test. Suddenly the peg came away, breaking off a chunk of ice as big as a dinner-plate, and the peg itself fell from his grasp. As it was the only peg left, it was essential to save it, so Schmid made a desperate effort to catch it, lost his balance, and slipped, his climbing-irons grinding vainly against the glassy ice. Then noiselessly, with increasing momentum, he slid helplessly down upon his companion, who was snatching in despair at the descending slack of the rope in the frantic effort to draw it in, but to no purpose, for the glissade instantly became a fall, and like lightning the shock was upon him. The companion, who miraculously survived the disaster, has described the fatal moment.

"My axe," he wrote, "is wrenched from the ice—the violence is too great, and now at last fear paralyses me, the rope hums through my fingers, burning them, as the overwhelming force of the fall tears me from the mountain . . . falling in prodigious bounds . . . shocks from the rope as it spins round, a terrifying leap, then things whirling in my head, the fall increases its terrible speed . . . crazy thoughts . . . an impression of flying, another wild leap, and without transition black darkness. How gentle is death. . . . Recovery astonishes me, and only vague recollections assail me of the hours that follow. One tragic thought suddenly burns itself into my battered brain: my friend is dead. With a

last effort I drag myself towards him. I look into his eyes . . .
in vain. Again unconsciousness overwhelms me."

A further illustration of the attitude of the modern school is
the remark made by one of the infatuated assailants of the
Eigerwand when bad weather seemed likely to prevent his
party from starting. "It almost looks," he said, "as if Providence wants to preserve us from death." A compatriot of
the young Bavarians seems to have been similarly inspired
when he declared, just before he perished in the desperate
attempt to force a new route up the northern face of the
Morgenhorn, "For us Germans there is nothing more to
lose." Indeed such men as these seem to be consumed by a
passion for self-destruction in a cause so obscure as to defy
definition. Yet we must remember that at the opposite pole
to these fanatical enthusiasts are the still more intemperate
advocates of the sacred principle of "safety first", these
unattractive arm-chair critics, getting on in years, and ready
for almost any sacrifice for the sake of a quiet life, yet frequently exasperated to the point of frenzy at the obnoxious
spectacle presented to them by the exuberant recklessness of
youth. It is between such irrational extremes that we must
look for the golden mean.

Nevertheless, it is hardly surprising that many young men
seek notoriety in performing these strange exploits when we
see what extravagant hero-worship is lavished on those who
become star performers in the new style of climbing. A recent
expedition in the Dolomites is a case in point. In the summer
of 1935 an Italian party succeeded in engineering their way
up the north wall of the Westliche Zinne. The climb was
described in the Italian Press as one of the few remaining major
problems in the Dolomites, and credit was claimed for the
climbers because they incurred grave extra risk from bad

weather in order to anticipate some Germans who were competing with them for the honour of achieving the first ascent. The climb was also classified, in the curious lingo of the new mountaineers, as belonging to the "upper sixth standard" ("*scala di sesto grado superiore*"), and the fact that it contained a horizontal traverse across an overhanging cliff made it—according to the victorious party—worse than any direct ascent. Moreover, so difficult was this face of the mountain that there had previously been twenty-seven unsuccessful attempts on it.

The expedition was in this respect typical of up-to-date Dolomite climbing. In five hours the Italians worked their way up the precipice till they reached a great overhang, and here it took them seven hours to climb twenty-five yards. They then bivouacked in a light tent-sack while a storm of wind, snow, and rain raged over them. Next day the remainder of an ascending traverse of sixty yards took them ten hours to climb. They were stimulated at this point by the reflection that it was now too late for retreat. The rocks were treacherously rotten and were, moreover, veneered with ice so that they provided inadequate holds for fingers and toes. When another storm came on, the party bivouacked a second time, and next morning, after two hours of struggle, they succeeded in overcoming a difficult passage that had defeated them on the previous evening. Then, in two hours more, forty yards of height were gained, and the climbers sheltered from a snowstorm under a rock, while the water which they drank froze as they collected it. After a relatively easy interval and a rest, they encountered more frozen rocks of the "fifth and sixth standards", and at last succeeded in reaching the top of the mountain after fifty hours of toil.

Yet the most significant facts in the story have still to be told, for when the party descended after their achievements and encountered their German rivals at the foot of the peak, the Germans, who had given up the climbers for lost, presented them with a magnificent floral tribute. In fact, even the vanquished regarded the Italian performance as a national victory, and the Press declared that it was a fine example of the valour and audacity of the young men of the era of Mussolini. But the rejoicings over the victory were destined to be still further protracted, and when the victors reached their native town they were "surprised and confused" (as well they might be) to be greeted by a procession of their fellow-townsmen, and to receive congratulatory addresses from the provincial authorities. Finally the two victims of this ovation were presented with medals for valour, and received a telegram of felicitation from the cousin of the king.

Such manifestations as these are, as the Italian newspapers admitted, novelties in the history of mountaineering, yet in the newspapers' view such popular reactions are desirable, on the assumption, apparently, that the performance of these two young climbers was as meritorious as the winning of a bicycle race or a victory at a boxing match, and should, therefore, be similarly rewarded. On the other hand, there are critics who may agree with some of the young men who perform these desperate deeds that it is the battle that counts rather than the victory, a maxim that is more desirable as an incentive than any system of rewards. It is likely that celebrations of the kind just described will encourage a type of climber who is more disposed to covet the meretricious fruits of victory than to value the struggle for its own sake.

But besides this respect for material rewards, this recklessness of life, and this predilection for mechanization, there is another striking peculiarity that is characteristic of these mountaineering extremists. It is the spirit of bitter nationalism that inspires them. Foreign competitors on the same mountain—and the extremists are nothing if not competitive—are even spoken of as "the enemy", and the Bavarians, who were the first to succeed in storming the north wall of the Grandes Jorasses, actually went so far as to avoid the nearest club-hut, and camped secretly in the neighbourhood so as to be out of sight of possible competitors. So successful was this ruse that on the day when these Bavarians won their victory an Italian party attacked the mountain without having the slightest idea that rivals had so cunningly forstalled them.

Various nations encouraged this spirit of nationalism, and a certain government even condoled officially with the relations of one of the casualties on the Grandes Jorasses, asserting that the victim "had died on the field of honour" for his country. A foreign Alpine organization has also been known to make travelling allowances to impoverished young climbers on condition that "respectable" climbs are made by "direct routes". Nor when we consider that no foreigner has ever taken part in British expeditions to Mount Everest can we reasonably claim that our own country is entirely free from this sort of chauvinism. Apart from nationalism, too, the spirit of mere competition is so fierce that the death of a friend on a climb seems to count as little in comparison with the glory that the successful survivor may win by achieving an important ascent.

Yet another eccentricity of mountaineering is undoubtedly attributable to the new school. It is the attempt to classify the great peaks of the Central and Western Alps according to their difficulty, just as the new mountaineers have already compiled categories of the smaller mountains that are to be found in the Eastern Alps. It is strange that those who wish to classify the Alps in this way forget that since many of the new ascents can only be accomplished with the aid of mechanization, all classification is futile, for it must vary according to the amount of mechanization that each climbing-party employs. The proud conqueror of a "sixth grade" ascent will have to specify the exact number of pegs he has used before the proper amount of kudos due to him can be estimated. Moreover, among the higher peaks this grading is always useless, for it must vary constantly according to the conditions of snow and rock that the climber happens to encounter.

It is probably the modern spirit of competition that inspires this eagerness to classify climbs, and the real motive for doing so may well be a desire to classify climbers rather than climbs and to give to mountaineering the status of a regulated competitive sport. In fact, it is this confounding of mountaineering with sport that is at the bottom of so much misunderstanding. It is the failure to realize that mountaineering is a pursuit in which the sporting instinct may enter at times, but that the deepest motives behind it are a longing for adventure, a love of nature, and a sentiment that can only be called mystical. The traditional mountaineer matches himself against the forces of nature, and does not seek to vie with other men in the sort of competition that requires regulations and rewards. Nor does he consider that a "victory" over a mountain justifies the sacrifice of men's lives.

The new spirit, however, is active everywhere, in the Himalaya as well as in Europe. The campaign on Kangchenjunga, for instance, is frankly regarded by many of the protagonists as a prolonged battle with human lives as the stake. The exaltation of such a state of mind will seem strange to most Englishmen. An English member of the international expedition that attempted Kangchenjunga, although he was a hardened mountaineer, wrote as follows:

"After nineteen days it was a relief to get back to the base camp. I have never spent a more nerve-racking time in my life, for during the majority of those nineteen days we never felt safe from the huge avalanches that fell down Kangchenjunga . . . I can only say that anyone who approaches this side of Kangchenjunga must take his own life and the life of his porters in his hand."

These remarks were scarcely surprising, for the expedition was encamped all the time on glacier plateaux that were liable to be swept by ice avalanches a mile wide. Some idea of the difficulties may be gathered from the fact that one of the climbers while step-cutting on an ice-slope, although at least four yards below the knife-edged crest of the ridge in which the slope culminated, suddenly saw to his horror that a blow from his axe had broken right through the mountain, and that blue sky was showing through the hole that the axe had made. As the editor of the *Alpine Journal* wrote in regard to the second Bavarian expedition in 1931:

"No one can have realized hitherto how terrible and tremendous is an attack on Kangchenjunga pushed right home. . . . Two solid months anchored to a knife-edged and bepinnacled ridge; never a single step to be taken lightly, never a moment of relaxation of tension, and with the ever-present menace of the Kangchenjunga tempest."

Indeed, these attacks on Kangchenjunga were quite a new departure in Himalayan mountaineering, for before these attempts very few Himalayan climbers would have ventured to embark on climbs that would have been considered difficult and dangerous even according to the most exacting Alpine standards, quite apart from the question of altitude. Bauer, however, perhaps the greatest mountaineer of his generation, in writing of the superb achievements of the German Himalayan expeditions which he has led, expounds an ideal which compels respect. "In those joyless days," he says,

"We needed some means of proving that he who was dauntless and undeterred, he who was prepared to make the greatest sacrifices, and he alone, could aspire to the highest attainment. Defiantly resisting the spirit of that time, we had to show again and again what these virtues could achieve in spite of the heaviest odds."

Moreover, even in the case of the most extravagant of the Alpine exploits that I have recorded, the assumption that such performances are all inspired by vanity or a craving for notoriety is absurdly inadequate. It seems much more likely that the strange heroes who perform these feats are sometimes dismayed by the glaring publicity in which they find themselves involved, and one explanation of their actions may be that these are the result of a new attitude to the conduct of life. It is possible that the mainspring actuating the behaviour of the generation subsequent to the war is a contempt for life so deeply buried in the unconscious mind that no pessimism or despair betrays itself on the surface, save when it leads to the perpetration of deeds such as these. At any rate, whatever the cause, it may be worth while to study the method of this madness, for it is possible that those who have a more conventional outlook on life than the new adventurers might find that there is something to be learnt from them.

AN ASCENT OF THE WATZMANN

A few years ago there occurred on the Watzmann, a peak of nearly nine thousand feet in the Bavarian Alps, a mountaineering drama that surpassed any other Alpine extravaganza that has ever been performed—not even excepting the notorious attempts to climb the Eigerwand in 1935 and 1936. The originators of the drama were two youths, uncle and nephew, each of them named Joseph Frey. They opened the proceedings on January 1, 1937, by setting out from the shores of the well-known Bavarian lake, the Königsee, to make a direct assault upon the east face of the Watzmann. This face can claim precedence over every other precipice in the Alps, except perhaps the Eigerwand, for it is a sheer wall almost six thousand feet high.

In summer experienced mountaineers have occasionally reached the summit of the Watzmann by scaling this wall, and its difficulties are well known. Captain Farrar, who achieved the fifth summer ascent by this route, has spoken of the climb as "enthralling" and "requiring considerable knowledge of snow conditions". He also mentions the gaping crevasses in the enormous avalanche-banks which afford the only means of access to the series of precipitous slabs constituting the main feature of the eastern wall. The leader on this occasion took off his boots and climbed in his stockings. The only winter attempt made on this side before that of the Freys was a desperate effort by four guideless climbers in 1930. The performance lasted three days, and the men bivouacked three times in holes or caves in the wall. It ended in failure, and the editor of the *Alpine Journal* speaks of it as an unjustifiable expedition in which the survival of the party was merely due to chance.

The two Freys★ who made the second winter attempt were skilled cragsmen, but they had never been on the mountain before, and were in consequence completely ignorant of the very intricate topography of this precipice. They chose, too, to begin their adventure during a period of persistent bad weather, and everywhere the rocks were encumbered with masses of fresh snow. Anxiety for the two adventurers was first felt on the very day they started—it was New Year's Day. They had quitted their skis at the foot of the cliffs at the point where hand-and-foot climbing begins. Half an hour before midnight that night a forester chanced to see a light falling down the precipice. He hurried to the foot of the cliffs at once and shouted repeatedly up into the darkness. The falling light was a lantern that the Freys had dropped, but neither of them returned an answer to the forester's shouts. He, therefore, naturally assuming that an accident must have happened, reported what he had seen to the life-saving post, and on the morning of January the 2nd three guides were sent to investigate. But there were no signs of an accident, and the guides could see the Freys ascending the precipice, so, as the weather was getting worse, they shouted to them to

★ The Editor of the *Alpine Journal* stated that the ages of the Freys were twenty-one and nineteen years respectively, and they were hoping that a successful issue of their exploit would have qualified them for inclusion in an overseas mountaineering team, with the result of improving the living conditions for their respective fathers, aged seventy-two and sixty-two. He praised the extraordinary gallantry of the rescuers and remarked that it would be interesting to learn what the total cost of such an elaborate mobilization amounted to.

return. The climbers paid no attention to the call and continued to ascend. The fact was that this intractable couple were determined to resist any attempt at rescue, and purposely refrained from replying.

From now on, however, they were more or less continuously under observation from the village of Bartolomä until, on reaching a shelf in the face of the mountain known as the Schöllhornplatte, they bivouacked for the night of January the 2nd. On the 3rd they were again observed to be advancing over a series of great rock-steps or ledges in the face of the precipice till they had succeeded in reaching the third ledge in the series.

Meanwhile at the headquarters of the German-Austrian Alpine Club in Munich the mother of one of the two gladiators reported that she was in great anxiety because neither of the men had kept his promise to return to Munich on the 3rd. Accordingly rescue operations were set on foot by Herr Siebenwurst, who, perhaps, more than anyone else, possessed the necessary qualifications, for he had led his compatriots when they undertook the terrible search for the bodies of the four Munich climbers who had sacrificed themselves to the Eigerwand in 1936. Siebenwurst, realizing that in the thickly-falling snow rescue operations directed either from the base of the precipice or from the summit of the mountain would be equally impossible, obtained the services of a pilot with an aeroplane in the hope of being able to throw down food and clothing to the distressed climbers.

On January 4th, therefore, an experienced mountaineer who was intimately acquainted with the topography of the east wall set out in company with the pilot in the plane. They carried a load including warm clothing, solidified methylated spirit, matches, a tent-sack, and blankets. Approaching the wall at a height of about seven thousand feet, they flew as near the precipice as they dared, swooping down the face of it till they could see tracks in the snow on the fourth great ledge. Approaching a second time, they again swooped down the cliffs, and threw out a bundle—too low, unfortunately, for it lodged on the second great ledge, out of range of the climbers. So another attempt was made to get still nearer to the mountain. Steering straight for the wall, the pilot banked at the last possible moment, so that the passenger could lean out and hurl once more. This time the aim was true, and the bundle fell right on to the fourth ledge, close to the tracks. Unfortunately, however, the Freys were now seen to be above the fourth ledge, engaged in swarming up a steep crack which would give them access to the fifth ledge, and without turning back they could not reach the packet that had been thrown. So further attempts were necessary. Again and again at great risk the pilot circled nearer and nearer to the crags, until eight bundles in all had been thrown out. One load containing provisions was dashed to pieces down the cliffs, the tent-sack was dropped out of reach; but two bundles fell close to the climbers. Not till afterwards was it learnt that this dangerous work had been all in vain, and that the Freys had been unable—or perhaps unwilling—to reach any of the material provided for them.

Simultaneously with those heroic efforts in the air, a relief expedition was being organized to proceed on foot. The 100th Jaeger Regiment in Reichenhall had offered to send some good men. Altogether there were three Jaegers, nine climbers from Munich, and two from Berchtesgaden. There was indeed not a man too many; messengers were badly needed, and a code of signals was organized to operate between Bartolomä and the top of the Watzmann: by day with boards laid out on a meadow, and by night with rockets. In such weather to try to ascend the precipice in the tracks of the infatuated adventurers was out of the question. The only conceivable hope of rescuing them lay in getting to them by means of ropes from a position of terrible exposure on the very summit of the mountain. A watch, too, must be kept, in so far as observation was possible, to make sure that the two men did not turn back and make a desperate attempt to retreat by the way they had come.

Owing to its being blocked with ice, the Königsee was impassable to boats, but already in the morning of the 5th the thirteen men carrying heavy rucksacks were well on their way up to the peak, ascending by the ordinary route. They had slept at the foot of the mountain, arriving there at midnight and starting on again at six in the morning in darkness. The snow was so deep and soft that they sank into it above the hips, yet shortly after ten o'clock in that morning they had reached the top of the Watzmann and snatched a brief but much-needed rest. Some of the party then moved on over an ice-bound ridge to the middle peak, while others busied themselves on the summit with excavating a hole in the snow to serve as a shelter from the abominable weather. A grim silence reigned over the ghastly precipice at their feet, and there was no sign of the death-struggle that the unfortunate Freys were engaged in more than a thousand feet below.

In hopes of discovering the whereabouts of the Freys the rescue-party climbed on to a tower projecting from the ridge, and affording a view down the cliffs. Again and again they all shouted together, but there was no reply. For at least three hours in the bitter cold they climbed backwards and forwards along the ridge, peering into the depths in vain. Owing to the great width of the precipice it was impossible to know at what point to descend, for the Freys could not be seen, and at this juncture the situation was further obscured by the approach of a joy-riding aeroplane that circled noisily overhead and confused the attempts that were being made to communicate by signals with the valley.

Suddenly, at half-past one in the afternoon, a member of the rescue-party caught sight of the Freys, and all gathered at once at the point from which the discovery had been made. The two were seen struggling up towards the fifth ledge; they were still more than 1,400 feet below, and soon they were observed to be making preparations for their fifth bivouac on the mountain. They could not have failed to see the search-party, and though it was afterwards learnt that they were already short of food, it seems that they were still unwilling to be rescued, for they made no sign, and the incessant shouting of the large party gathered on the summit produced no reply.

Now, however, that the situation of the Freys was known, operations could be begun. For the time being the weather had cleared and there was no wind, although everywhere the rock-face was covered with snow. At two o'clock, then, the first of the rescuers was lowered over the edge of the cliff. Six ropes had been joined together, and a length of more than a thousand feet was available, but it was not enough. It added to the difficulty that as soon as the first man had been lowered for more than five hundred feet it became impossible to hear what he said, while at the same time fog enveloped the summit and made it impossible to see. The weather, too, was getting worse; it began to snow, and then, unexpectedly, from far below a faint cry for help was heard. It was the first sign vouchsafed by the Freys.

It was difficult to say which of the rescuers had the more dreadful task, those who had to descend the avalanche-swept precipice or those who, in a position of constant exposure on the summit, had to manage the ropes. The clothing and faces of the summit-party became plastered with ice, and one of them even objected to having the icicles removed from his face because, as he said, they were a protection from the freezing wind. It appeared that the Freys were now on a small ledge under a vertical cliff, about a hundred feet high and cutting them off from their rescuers, who had not enough rope to reach the position. To the hauling-party on the summit-ridge the work seemed endless as they gripped the frozen rope with their numbed hands. Finally, at a quarter to four in the afternoon, the two who had so nearly reached the Freys were obliged to abandon the struggle owing to lack of rope, and made signals to be hauled up again. The rescue work had to be broken off, and three of the summit-party hurried down to the valley to get more rope for further attempts to be made on the next day. The remaining ten spent a terrible night cowering in the hole they had hacked out of the snow on the top of the mountain. Down in the valley it was raining in torrents, and as there was not enough rope to be found there, more was sent for in the night from distant villages.

On the 6th, down at Bartolomä, a glimpse was caught of the Freys moving laboriously upward through deep snow. Nothing could be seen of the men occupying the summit, for they were hidden in the clouds flying past. An occasional rift would reveal streamers of snow being blown off the ridges to a great height in the sky. The storm was becoming more violent. On the top of the mountain, on the 6th, dawn broke with fresh snow and an icy wind from the west. Reluctantly evacuation was decided on, for no sign of life could be discovered on the east face and it was deemed impossible that the Freys could have survived such a night. In deep discouragement the party began the retreat. In the valley two brothers of the missing men awaited with anxious looks the descending rescuers. The latter could only shake their heads to them in silence.

In the meantime, however, Herr Hitler himself was stirring on his Olympus, and had called for a report. He was informed that there was no hope left for the Freys; that they must be dead. But almost at the same moment as the report was made, the news came from Bartolomä that the Freys were still alive. Watchers with telescopes had caught sight of them at work on the precipice, trying to creep still higher. Immediately the resolution that had inspired the searchers returned, and under the Führer's inspiration a new plan of campaign was hurriedly concerted. Herr Hitler promised more rope; in fact, such a quantity came that there now was enough to lower a whole party half-way down the mountain, the actual length available being more than 3,400 feet. Besides this, wind-jackets, gloves, tents, climbing-irons, and provisions were to be supplied, as well as more soldiers from the Jaeger Regiment to act as porters for carrying that outfit to the top of the Watzmann. The men who were actually engaged in succouring the Freys were to travel light and without rucksacks, so as to arrive as fresh as possible on the scene of their labours. The Jaeger Regiment also installed a wireless apparatus in the valley to facilitate communications with their headquarters.

By seven o'clock that evening a lieutenant and forty-four men were on the way to the theatre of operations. Scouts had been posted on a ridge overlooking the east wall, and these reported that owing to the violence of the storm they had been unable to see any sign of the Freys. Consequently it had not been possible to make reassuring signals to the two rash climbers, who must have been feeling that their last hour had come, for they could hardly be expected to survive another night of such harsh exposure. The expeditionary force, however, was now mobilized. From all sides came news of rain and snow. If the Freys were still alive they would assuredly not be able to escape rescue much longer. Before ascending the mountain the rescue-party lay down to get what rest they could, while the soldiers, who had arrived at the hut at eleven o'clock that evening soaked to the skin, continued for the rest of the night to carry equipment to the summit.

As early as half-past five in the morning of the 7th the rescue-party proper were on the move. It was still dark, and overhead, on the steep precipice and ridges, glimmered the lanterns of the Jaegers. The storm continued to be severe, but the rain and snow had ceased. Half-way up the mountain the party overtook the heavily-laden Jaegers and, arriving before them on the summit, set to work at enlarging the snow-shelter. A signal from the valley indicated that the Freys were now in a direct line below the top of the peak, and at the look-out post the scouts could hear their cries for help. The soldiers had already brought up the ropes, and although the provisions had not yet arrived, that fact was considered of little importance, as there seemed to be no time to eat. Indeed, so great was the haste that those lowering the rope paid it out too quickly and the man who was being lowered stumbled and fell, starting an enormous avalanche which thundered down the face. Luckily the Freys were not in its track. The man descending then climbed out on to a projecting rock, shouted and heard a faint answer from below: "Help! We are still alive."

Three more men were then lowered, and this enabled the first man who had descended to be lowered another three or four hundred feet. Here, his rope having come to an end, he shouted himself hoarse, but got no answer. A second then joined him, and they shouted together, but with no result. Avalanches of snow-dust rushed past them with the sound of great waterfalls. Everything was hidden in clouds of snow-dust, but since something had to be done, a traverse across the cliffs was tried in order to reach a point from which the missing men might perhaps be visible. At every step the rope dislodged huge chunks of snow that fell on the precariously-placed climber. He was just about to reach the position desired when suddenly to his dismay the rope swung him off his feet and began rapidly to hoist him up the cliff. Those far above him had misunderstood his movements and interpreted them as signals to them to haul. It was useless to resist or protest, for all the means of communicating with those who were at such an immense distance above him were unavailing. Irresistibly he was dragged aloft; then, as the rope had buried itself deeply in the snow and the knots caused an obstruction, the upward movement came to an end and the unfortunate man found himself back on a level with the three comrades who had descended after him. Here, on the little shelf to which they were clinging, he paused exhausted, while two more were let down to join them, so that the number of the advance group on the rock-wall was increased to six. For a few moments, while they hesitated, doubting what to do, they fancied they heard a faint reply to their shouts. Snow fell unceasingly and, after a brief consultation, another member of their small party was lowered for three or four hundred feet. It was agreed that if nothing came of this attempt the battle for the missing men would have to be given up as hopeless, for throughout the day the advance party felt continuously the gravest apprehensions whether the men controlling the ropes from the summit and exposed to the full fury of the weather up there would be able to hold out. If they succumbed, it was obvious that all who were working on the face were doomed.

Meanwhile, the leading man was lowered by his five companions and the rope ran out steadily until it stopped, and then no answer came to their enquiries. They waited, but nothing happened. Finally, in despair, they lowered another man to investigate. Again an anxious pause, and then the glad news was shouted up that the leading rescuer could be seen standing by the Freys and giving them food. The relief was extreme. It was some time before the signal came for pulling, and then the work went slowly, for three men were suspended on the rope and only five were available for hauling. However, the three were doggedly drawn up, inch by inch, and the pitiful figures of the Freys appeared. It was then the turn of the haulers to be pulled up by those who were keeping watch on the summit. In the final stage four men were actually drawn up together, a feat that may well astonish anyone who has had the opportunity of observing what alarming wear and tear the friction of the rock may inflict on the strands of an Alpine rope, even when the weight of only one man is being pulled up on it.

Hours passed, and when at last all the rescuers had been drawn to the summit they realized the appalling task of the five stalwarts who had held out so gallantly in that exposed position throughout the day with their faces and hands coated with ice, anxiously obeying what could be understood of the signals that came to them. As soon as the Freys were hoisted to the summit a tent-sack was thrown over them, but in its frozen condition the brittle fabric was torn to pieces in the icy wind, and the rescue-party employed their own bodies to shelter the exhausted couple while tea and food were administered. Nevertheless, there was no time to spare, for a long trying descent with grave danger of avalanches was still to be faced, so, after a very short rest, the Freys were roped and the retreat was begun. It was by no means too soon, if they were not to be benighted high up on the mountain. The elaborate gear was left behind, lives being rightly deemed as more important than material. The snow was up to the men's waists, and it was impossible to hurry the Freys. In the latter part of the descent two members of the party gave up their skis for the use of the rescued men, and followed at a much slower pace, floundering through the snow. By good luck and in spite of the increasing darkness all eventually reached the Alpine club-hut in safety. In the hut the floor streamed with water, everywhere wet clothes were hanging, and frostbitten feet were being doctored, while outside the storm continued. Finally, on January 8th, the transport of the injured men down the valley drew the last ounce of strength from their heroic rescuers. At two in the afternoon the ambulance was reached and by eight o'clock that evening the Freys were safely desposited in hospital. Their winter excursion on the Watzmann had occupied the two adventurers—not to mention their unfortunate rescuers—a whole week.

A severe, yet magnanimous, criticism of the Freys' exploit has been published by one of the rescue-party in the journal of the German-Austrian Alpine Club. The writer does justice to the men in admitting their audacity, perseverance, and powers as cragsmen, but rightly draws attention to their folly as well as to their inhumanity in so obstinately refraining at first from answering their rescuers' appeals. He also points out that in the elucidation of mountaineering problems brains count at least as much as bodies. Unless the heroic search-party had reached the Freys on the morning of the seventh day the wretched pair must have perished. They had clear warning of the state of the weather, even if they were not capable of forming any judgement of it for themselves; and as mountaineers they should have been able to deny themselves the summit when conditions were obviously prohibitive.

A NEGLECTED PASTIME

IF the following account of a balloon-journey seems at first
sight out of place in a book about mountaineering, I can
only say that the balloonist and the mountaineer often have
much in common, for the motive in both cases is the fascina-
tion of exploring an ideal world, the balloonist discovering
it above the clouds, in the heaven of childhood, and the
mountaineer among the eternal snows.

It is curious that the coming of the aeroplane should have
undermined the popularity of the balloon. There seems
to be no good reason for it. The invention of steam power
might just as well have ruined the vogue of the sailing yacht,
yet it has not done so. There is an analogy between ballooning
and sailing, for ballooning, like sailing, has the good qualities
of its defects. In an age of speed and frantic hustle there is a
charm in not knowing exactly where you are going or what
time you will get there, and this is always the case in ballooning. The hour and place of arrival can only be guessed at;
a balloon is no vehicle for a business man in a hurry. To
the leisurely traveller, however, who takes pleasure in con-
templation it affords many agreeable contrasts with the
ordinary means of locomotion. Instead of the thrill of speed
he experiences the ecstasy of immobility, for the rôles of the
traveller and the scenery are transposed; to the traveller in a
balloon the sensation of immobility is absolute, while the
landscape floats noiselessly past.

There is indeed no sensation comparable with ballooning, unless it be running before the wind in a sailing vessel; yet how prosaic is this bustling motion compared with the soundless progress of a balloon. Judged by ballooning standards the aeroplane, battling laboriously against the pull of gravitation, is a wretchedly noisy nerve-racking piece of machinery. In a balloon, even at hurricane speed, no breath of wind is felt. At the most, if the wind changes suddenly a faint breeze may be noticed for a moment. If an aeronaut were so insanely reckless as to risk a gas explosion by lighting a match, the flame would burn without a flicker in the windless air, for the balloon is always moving with the exact speed of the wind, which is consequently never perceptible. The rise and fall are, as a rule, as little noticed by the passenger as the speed and direction of the journey. A fall of ominous rapidity will be signalled only by a light breeze coming up from below. This possibility of misjudging speed and direction may have significance during a journey, and did in fact produce a sensational situation during the journey which is now described. Yet there is no reason why ballooning should be more dangerous than sailing, and there is certainly much less for the beginner to learn. My own adventures were almost entirely due to inexperience; an expert would certainly have made a much less erratic descent.

This balloon voyage started at Easter from Paris at the hour of sunset. There were two of us in the car, and we carried as much ballast as we thought the gas-bag could lift. Ballast is to the balloonist like money to the traveller, the more he has the farther he can go. Hoping to stay up all night and determined to go as far as possible, we carried as much sand as we could. As we climbed in, the men who were to start us gathered round, lifting off the weights attached to the outside of the basket and testing our buoyancy by half letting go. Then, as they completely relaxed their grip of the basket, we gently left the ground, hardly realizing it, so quietly did we drift into the air, while our helpers became midgets far below and the great living map of Paris began to expand under our feet. The basket rocked when we shifted our positions, but otherwise hung sedately in space like a bubble floating in a calm tide. Only careful observation of the landscape assured us that we were moving and that our direction was towards the east. The expanse of Paris and of the open country beyond was increasing rapidly, an indication that we were rising fast. In this tranquil manner we had abandoned the earth.

The stillness of the air enveloping us and the vastness of the panorama opening beneath us produced in combination a strange impression. They reminded me of a show in London in my childhood: the panorama of the Battle of Waterloo. The spectator at this show came up through the floor of a circular platform and found himself in the centre of a panoramic painting of the field of Waterloo; a realistically painted dome of sky was above, and the whole produced a curious effect of spaciousness and airlessness combined with theatrical unreality. The panorama from the balloon now gave me the same peculiar impression. It did not last, however, for the reality of the world below soon reasserted itself, as the continuous mingled sound of children shouting and dogs barking mounted to us through the still air. At half-past six we observed we were crossing the Seine in a south-easterly direction. From now onwards the journey divided itself into three phases: firstly impenetrable darkness lasting until midnight, secondly a period of moonlight, and thirdly, beginning at dawn, came the final stage, the voyage at great heights above the clouds.

During the first hours of darkness the chief source of our

anxiety was the continually alternating expansion and contraction of the gas. This was due to the instability of the temperature before night had finally asserted itself, and it caused a constant up-and-down movement of the balloon, our altitude varying between several hundreds and several thousands of feet. In our efforts to combat this rise and fall we found by sunset that we had already spent six of our precious sacks of sand. The temperature was round about 36 degrees Fahrenheit, but secure from any sensation of wind we did not feel cold. Before ten o'clock two more sacks had to be sacrificed, and this caused us some disquiet, for we knew that we should need ballast with the coming of daylight, which was expected to carry us up to an immense height owing to the sun's power of expanding the gas. For this reason a big reserve of sand was desirable, for when the gas shrank again we should need ballast for saving us from too swift a fall. Circumstances were to show that our anxiety was justified.

Although we had started with a clear sky, the weather was now cloudy and night came on with profound darkness. There was no prospect of a moon before midnight and I bitterly regretted that I had omitted to provide myself with a more efficient electric torch, our one feeble instrument having collapsed about ten o'clock. Before it had quite flickered out a reading of the barometer showed that we had risen at one time to 10,000 feet, although we were now almost level with the tree-tops. Such an altitude in thick darkness was dangerously low, and again more sand had to be thrown out. At once we rose and were drifting blindly through the inky void when a sinister vision suddenly appeared, throwing us into consternation and upsetting every guess we had been making at what was our position on the map. Dim in the darkness but surely unmistakable there appeared below and ahead of us an immense sheet of water stretching away till it was lost in the night. We strained our eyes peering into the empty blackness, and as we did so there came up a sighing sound from the dark gulf at our feet. Surely that sound could be only one thing: the murmur of the sea on the beach? We tried frantically to think out the situation and to imagine what could have happened. Since the failure of our torch we had been unable to take any bearings. Was it conceivable that we were over the sea? Such uncertainty may seem ridiculous, but it must be remembered that when travelling in a balloon several thousand feet above the earth one cannot tell whether one is becalmed or travelling at the speed of an express train, except by very carefully watching the ground. For a hideous minute or two it seemed credible that we had got into an air current that had hurried us to the coast with the speed of a whirlwind in a direction contrary to that of our departure and that we were now actually at sea. In any case there was nothing to be done. If we were indeed over the sea we must keep on travelling over it until daylight. The utter darkness added to our sense of helplessness. I had never before felt myself immersed in such a blind void. Even a blizzard on an Alpine snowfield allows one the comfort of contact with the ground. Here we were completely cut off from all connection with the solid world. Fortunately our consternation was soon over; it became clear to us after a few minutes that the water-like expanse was only a lake of mist, and the murmur of waves merely the sound of the wind in a great forest of fir trees over which we happened to be passing. We were still travelling after all on the same course as when we started, and great was our relief.

For some time after this we moved on over dim mysterious spaces, that might in the darkness have been either sea or land. At one moment, when the darkness seemed a little less

I

profound, we pulled the valve and came down nearer to the ground, hoping to see something and to let our guide-rope trail. The guide-rope is a most useful form of self-regulating ballast; when coming down too fast the speed of the descent is automatically checked by the guide-rope as an increasing weight of it rests upon the ground. A reverse action prevents too sudden a rise. On this occasion, however, the guide-rope failed in its purpose, becoming entangled in the tree-tops. Accordingly we threw out some ballast, and as we rose the wind tore us free; with a crashing of broken branches we returned to safer levels above. At last, half an hour after midnight, the moon rose and we found that we were slowly crossing moors and forests. There was no longer any temptation to sleep. During the hours of darkness anxiety had kept us alert; from now on the great spectacle of moon-lit heaven and earth kept us breathless with the splendours that it unrolled.

With the more equable temperature of night our height remained the same, a few hundred feet above the tree-tops, with the guide-rope hanging just clear of them. Unceasingly as we sailed smoothly across the moon-lit forest nightingales accompanied us with their song. Presently cuckoos were awake as well. Once we crossed an electrically lit mill beside a roaring river. Otherwise nothing but the songs of nightingales and cuckoos broke the stillness until, as we passed over a sleeping village, we heard the church clock strike two. And so the night wore on. An hour before dawn we surmised that we were passing over vineyards. A few handfuls of sand thrown out increased our elevation; we sailed over more forest to some high uninhabited moors.

The first signs of dawn appeared soon after three, as we drifted gently over a high road with a drowsy peasant plodding along it. My companion leaned out over the edge of the basket and without raising his voice asked the man where we were. He gazed up speechless for a moment as our gigantic shadow stole softly across the moon, then his answer came: "Bar-sur-Aube." We were still in highland country and apparently making for a gap or pass south of a steep, wooded summit in a range of bare hills. Some sand, parsimoniously sprinkled, just enabled us to skim the tree-tops as we floated out through the pass into the broad valley of the Aube. Far below, at the foot of the range that we had just crossed, lay the town of Bar-sur-Aube with its clocks striking four. It was quite light now and we were about a thousand feet above the river.

The sound of weirs, cocks crowing and blackbirds singing reached us. Some miles up the river lay a lake of morning mist as like a sheet of water as an African mirage. The thermometer showed 38 degrees Fahrenheit as we sailed out into the sunrise at the same majestic hasteless speed; roads bordered with poplars appeared, then more highlands. We crossed an old farm-house with a courtyard; its silence showed that the occupants were still asleep. Beyond was a wood full of song-birds, jays and woodpeckers. We were intent on the gradually widening view when suddenly our guide-rope crashed into the tree-tops, bringing the balloon up short with a series of violent jerks. For a moment it seemed likely that we should stick in a tree; and we devoutly hoped that the rigging of our aged craft would withstand these strains and wrenches. Fortunately the rope forced itself free, and thus we drifted serenely on until at four-fifty the rim of the rising sun made its appearance, lighting up the countless white may-trees in the woods underneath us.

The third and more critical phase of the journey was now approaching. We knew that when the lifting-power of the sun's rays exerted its influence upon the gas, our rise would be prodigious. The process was beginning already, and we rose steadily, but at a gradually increasing rate, until soon we were breaking through a thin layer of clouds. Beyond these we came into another world, the billowy surface of the clouds beneath us shutting out the earth and throwing up a scorching glare like the heat reflected from a snowfield. White cumulus peaks of fantastic shapes shone out in radiant glory above darker cloud masses which the sun had not yet reached. A few moments more and we were so high that the noise of a passing train and faint chimes from a village church were the only sounds that could still be heard. A curious sight now to be seen was the rose-tinted shadow of the balloon encircled by a halo which appeared on the cloud-floor under us and followed in our wake. It is a phenomenon sometimes known as the spectre of the Brocken. Through ever-rarer gaps in the clouds we caught sight of the earthly landscape looking singularly lovely in the glowing colours of the dawn.

But it was time to give thought to our direction, for since we had left Bar-sur-Aube the earth had been hidden under a sea of cloud; consequently we had only the vaguest idea of our course. Through an opportune temporary break we now detected snow lying among pine forests, and from all sides there rose the faint humming roar of mountain streams. It seemed probable that we were crossing the Vosges and that the Alps lay ahead of us. The barometer told us we were rising fast, and soon after six I observed we had an altitude of 10,000 feet. On the sea of cloud the dull red spectre of the balloon was still swimming persistently after us; we were travelling slowly as before, moving, it seemed, at the same rate and in the same direction as the cloud floor. This made it difficult to calculate pace or position. By half-past six our height was 11,000 feet and it was cold in spite of the scorching sun; some soup in a bottle was frozen.

The earth was by this time completely invisible. Nevertheless a change in the cloud formation was taking place; gradually we approached a big break in the main mass which now began to disintegrate like a polar ice-field, and for a few minutes we sailed over a wide blue gulf in the depths of which tiny towns gleamed. Here and there were pastures of brilliant emerald, with trees the size of pins' heads, and a spider's web of roads stretching far and wide. On the other side of the gulf began another great continent of massive white cumulus with a long coast-like edge realistically resembling the cliffs of an iceberg.

At about eight o'clock when the glass indicated 13,000 feet and while we were rising slowly over the new cloud-continent, we noticed for the first time that the height was making us breathless. None the less we were hungry and ate our provisions ravenously. Since dawn the rising and falling of the balloon had continued according to the variations of temperature caused by the clouds. Some of the falls had been difficult to check and we had spent more ballast than we liked. Through a temporary thinning in the layer of cloud we were able to make out that the hills underneath were increasing in size and becoming more continuous, but this was all we could learn of the world that we were cut off from; it was once more completely hidden from view. For hundreds of miles nothing was to be seen but clouds, huge castles and mountains of them, dazzling our eyes and scorching our faces with the intense glory of their reflected sunlight. Meanwhile we rose to 16,000 feet and both of us suffered from violent palpitations and breathlessness. The discomfort was more acute than when climbing at much greater altitudes in the Himalaya; we panted as if we had been running a race.

The question now before us was: had we enough ballast to justify us in attempting to cross the full extent of the Alps?

My companion, who was as ignorant of ballooning as I was, chose this moment to inform me that he had been cautioned about pulling the gas-valve at any great height, since our balloon was so old and presumably unsound, that it might become difficult to stop the impetus of a fall. We had also to consider that in coming down from a great height a big reserve of ballast is in any case necessary in order to control the descent. Although we were aware of this fact, we did not appreciate it sufficiently, as events were to prove. However, while we were arguing the point, the balloon was continuing to rise and the vast masses of towering cumulus were becoming more and more magnificent. We seemed to be no longer playing any part in the world, but to be traversing the deserts of space in some strange orbit decreed by a capricious and inscrutable fate. We were still discussing what to do when a startling revelation took place; just as we reached a height of 18,000 feet a division appeared in the far horizon of clouds, and through the opening we beheld the dazzling snows of the whole chain of Mont Blanc. The great summit itself was wrapped in a characteristic "*tourmente*", the snow-flurry known and dreaded locally as a sure sign of bad weather.

A decision was now urgent, for the idea of drifting over the Alps in bad weather in an old balloon with insufficient ballast was disturbing, to say the least of it. Unless we descended without delay we should find ourselves hanging over a boundless chaos of peaks with little chance of choosing a safe landing-place. I was in favour of attempting to hit off a solitary gap in the cloud-floor, through which at that moment one could discern open country suitable for a landing. My companion, however, still questioned the prudence of pulling the gas-valve, and in the meantime our upward movement was continuing. My arguments at last prevailed,

and a tentative pull or two at the valve-cord started us headlong
on a downward course with rapidly increasing speed.
Hurriedly we threw out ballast, and unfortunately more
than was necessary, for to our dismay, the balloon began to
rise once more. Further to add to our anxiety the gap in the
clouds had closed; below us was an unbroken veil through
which we should have to plunge without any knowledge
of the ground beneath, but in the lamentable certainty that
the ensuing condensation of gas would greatly accelerate the
speed of our fall. While we were facing this situation we
distinctly heard the dull roar that rises from a big city as the
sound came up to us through the clouds. If our choice lay
between landing in a large town or coming down in the
Alps in bad weather, the first alternative seemed preferable.
So the valve was again pulled, and this time the fall began
in earnest. As the momentum increased a breeze blew up in
our faces, a danger signal indicating too fast a fall.

Almost immediately we plunged into the sea of clouds; a
few snow-flakes flew past us, but we could see nothing else
in the dense chilly fog that surrounded us. The extravagant
speed of our fall was now so obvious that there was no need
to gauge it by the usual method of dropping paper out of the
car and observing its relative movement; we were hard at
work emptying bags of sand over the side; and while helping
in this I was also hastily preparing a basket of bottles and
provisions to throw overboard as soon as the sand had been
used up. Telescopes and cameras we would not sacrifice,
but crammed them into a wicker locker for safety when the
moment of the crash should arrive. Meanwhile the sand
flew up in our faces, for we were now overtaking the ballast
which we had thrown out.

Our fall through the clouds cannot have lasted more than
a few seconds, and now we were again in sight of the earth,

The big city that we had dreaded falling into was nowhere to be seen; we had providentially avoided it. But there was little time to realize the situation; we were falling at a very great pace towards some fields ringed round with wooded hills. For an instant I was able to observe one of many fields looking like a square on a tiny chess-board; the next moment the square had increased to a prodigious size and was rushing up to meet us at a bewildering speed. The last of our sand-bags was flung out bodily, unemptied, and almost at the same instant we struck the ground with a crash. As we clung to the rigging in a shower of sand the balloon rolled over on its side and began to drag across the field, but a strong pull at the rip-valve brought the basket immediately to rest. Several men ran up, and after trying French on them in vain we discovered that we were in Switzerland near Bettingen about six miles from Bâle. We had fallen in a field admirably adapted to balloonists, at safe distance from the city. If our barometers and cameras were broken we ourselves were unhurt. The hour was ten o'clock in the morning and a cloudy grey sky gave no hint of all the glories above it. So ended our balloon voyage; it had been a continuously enthralling adventure during sixteen hours.

As we puffed homeward in the noisy, dirty jolting train, my thoughts went back to our outward-bound journey through the sky, a journey in which we seemed to have been wafted to our unforeseen destination by enchantment rather than by the caprices of the winds. Throughout the voyage we had experienced the sensation of profound immersion and absorption in the beauty of earth and sky, as if the traveller and the world travelled in were together part of a single harmonious whole. It is the same strange and rare experience that some mountaineers are familiar with, and which is more accountable than anything else for the charm of ballooning.

A CHRISTMAS ENTERPRISE IN SAVOY

IT is strange that even nowadays travel of an almost adventurous kind is to be found within twenty-four hours of London, and at comparatively small cost.

At any rate it was in pursuit of something in the nature of an adventure that a party of travellers from England descended recently from the Rome express on to the prosaic platform of the railway station at Modane on a fine morning in December. The party, which included the writer, intended to do a little ski-ing, but its chief purpose was the more romantic task of conveying a Christmas-tree to Bonneval-sur-Arc, a remote Alpine village in the highest inhabited valley in France and thirty miles from the railway. To introduce the village children to a Christmas-tree, with its proper ritual, was a tempting enterprise, for in such an inaccessible part of the world as Bonneval the winter conditions are so severe that not only Christmas-trees, but even the commonest amenities of civilization are unknown.

In winter the mere journey to Bonneval is subject to considerable uncertainty, for the tiny village, 6,000 feet above the sea, is buried in snow to the eaves, and the forbidding steepness of the surrounding mountains, cutting off all sunshine except for two hours in the middle of the day, causes immense and formidable avalanches. These from time to time, according to the weather, beleaguer the village, roaring down across the narrow valley with a noise louder than thunder, and sometimes felling half a forest in the rush of air that precedes the onset. After recent snow, or during a thaw in spring, it is often unsafe to leave the immediate neighbourhood of the houses, and all communication with the outside world is cut off for days together. Consequently the success of the expedition depended on the weather, as it was essential to have favourable snow conditions, not only for the journey up to Bonneval, but also for returning down the valley the following day. As time was valuable, we had no wish to be snowed up at Bonneval indefinitely, and we knew that even in the most favourable circumstances the final sledge-journey from Lanslevillard, where we were to spend the night, would probably take five hours.

Meanwhile we had to get to Lanslevillard, and as we left the train, the weather conditions seemed favourable, the skis and luggage had arrived safely, and the great packing-case that contained the outfit for the tree was satisfactorily conducted through the Customs. As we came out of the railway station, the long ugly street, crammed with shabby cafés and dingy money-changers' offices, was free from snow. It must be admitted that Modane is not an attractive town, for it is the offspring of a pair of unpleasing parents, namely the railway and the Customs. In fact the affluence of Modane and its money-changers is due to its status as an international railway station at the French entrance to the Mont Cenis tunnel on the Franco-Italian frontier. Yet on this sunny morning redeeming features were visible, for just beyond the squalid street snow was to be seen gleaming among the black silhouettes of the pine-trunks, and far overhead there was a glimpse of two superb rock-peaks of the high Alps soaring into the northern sky.

Lanslevillard, our half-way stopping-place, is nearly eighteen miles up the valley from Modane, and nearly five thousand feet above sea-level; it is the last outpost of civilization on

the road to Bonneval. The first part of the journey there
is done in an omnibus driven by electric power supplied
through overhead wires. Our fellow-travellers in the bus
were peasants from neighbouring villages, returning after
a morning's shopping in Modane, and chattering good-
humouredly in noisy patois. Mostly heavy-featured men,
with huge hands and fingers, they wore the black clothes and
black felt hats that seem to be the prevailing fashion of a
region extending from Poland and Turkey to Portugal and
the British Isles. In fact, the dreary spectacle of these Sunday
suits is becoming as universally monotonous a feature of
continental travel as the colourless cosmopolitan cookery
that is found throughout Europe in all the more pretentious
hotels. Unfortunately Savoy may soon be no exception to
the general drabness, for even the local costumes of the women,
different in every village, are beginning to go out of fashion.

After rumbling along for a couple of hours in the stuffy
and overcrowded electrobus, it was a relief to emerge from
it at Lanslebourg into the bracing winter atmosphere of an
Alpine village. Since the old posting days when the international carriage-road over the Mont Cenis Pass was open
all the year round, Lanslebourg has come down in the world.
Yet although its single street is usually empty and dreary, it
is redeemed by the glorious presence of the Dent Parrachée,
a superb mountain of more than 12,000 feet, which is so
effectively framed between the houses that even at its distance
of six miles it dominates the village.

While we were admiring this beautiful peak, our friend
and guide, Pierre Blanc, drove up with the mule and sledge
that were to take the luggage up to Lanslevillard. The sledge
of the country is simply a box on runners, devoid of springs
or other luxuries, with a plank to sit on, and some hay to
keep the passengers' feet from freezing. As soon as the

luggage was loaded, we set off with as little delay as possible, for in winter the sun avoids Lanslebourg altogether, and an icy local wind that blows down from the Mont Cenis Pass was in full blast, so that there was no temptation to linger in the street.

For an hour we followed the slowly advancing sledge, listening drowsily to the creaking of the runners on the snow-covered road till we reached the comfortable little hotel at Lanslevillard. Here the fresh snow lay heavy over the whole countryside; behind us down the valley, the ice-slopes and glittering ridges of the Dent Parrachée still dominated the landscape; ahead of us, beyond the village, higher up the course of the foaming river, the mountains closed in about the road to Bonneval, as if to forbid further progress. At Lanslevillard in December the sun only shines from ten till three, merciless winter was now prevailing, and the keen air stung like a whip.

Lanslevillard has many merits besides its advantages as a ski-ing centre. As it is not a great tourist resort, there are no huge hotels to act as unventilated forcing-houses for microbes, the horrors of central heating are still a rare novelty, and most of the buildings are pleasantly warmed with stoves that burn wood. Evening clothes and fancy dress are unknown, sports are not organized, and the paradise is as yet unspoilt. That night the stars sparkled brightly, and before getting into our comfortable beds in the warm little wooden rooms, we decided to take immediate advantage of the fine weather by pushing on to Bonneval next day.

In the morning our hopes were dashed, for it had snowed heavily during the night, and all travel was for the time being out of the question. Quite apart from the danger of avalanches the snow would be too soft for sledging, and it looked as if more was coming. Evidently we must wait where we were for some days.

The inhabitants of Lanslevillard are punctiliously religious, and next morning was being celebrated as a saint's day. The sound of deep-toned church bells woke me before dawn. Later in the day as I wandered into one of the gloomy alleys that wind among the broad-eaved stone houses, there suddenly appeared a figure that seemed to belong to the Middle Ages. It was a venerable lady hurrying to mass, in a flowing black cloak with a prayer-book clasped to her heart. A close-fitting embroidered cap, from which floated at right-angles rigid wings of diaphanous black, with some of the character of an Elizabethan ruff, gave to her ascetic features a look of complete remoteness from the modern world. Lanslevillard faithfully belongs to the past, and in that lies its charm; time seems to stand still, even if the days pass too quickly.

But the weather was now improving, and we still had a long way to go. So after a delay of only three days we set out on skis accompanied by two sledges. The first of the two contained provisions for us, and hay for two mules, to enable us to spend the night at Bonneval without taxing the local resources. The second sledge was to carry the tree, and was pulled by Nina, an experienced animal belonging to Pierre Blanc.

All mules reared at Bonneval are experts at their job, for they are specially trained to deal with snow. The inhabitants buy them young, and the training is begun by turning out the foals in the snow, to play and roll about in it, so that they can learn snow-craft, while getting a good grooming in the process. Subsequently they are taught to drag sledges through the deepest drifts, by advancing in a series of deliberate leaps and bounds, with regular breathing intervals, and without getting flustered. Constant practice makes them extraordinarily clever at following the invisible track by sounding for it with their feet when they are perhaps wallowing up to their bellies in soft snow. After any particularly heavy snowfall has cut Bonneval's communications, a sledge is sent out with several mules to open the road. The leading mules unattached, flounder along, and trample their way ahead, so that the team hauling the sledge can follow in their wake, and very soon make the road practicable for ordinary traffic. In fact the mules are so good at their job, that if a sledge-driver is caught in a blizzard, it is generally best for him to leave the path-finding entirely to his animals.

After quitting Lanslevillard the road leads uphill in a series of zigzags to a bleak snow-plain. Here the Christmas-tree that we had received permission to fell a few days previously was taken on board, and lashed in an upright position on the sledge, giving it in this arctic waste some of the grace and forlorn dignity of a sailing ship navigating a polar sea. In the midst of the dreary plain that we were now crossing was the large village of Bessans, half-way between Lanslevillard and Bonneval, and the halting-place for luncheon. The hotel was almost too primitive to deserve the name. The atmosphere when we entered was like that of a greenhouse, but a greenhouse in semi-darkness, pervaded with a concentrated mixture of smells suggesting a combination of kitchen, smoking-room and farmyard. Protected by two doors, and at the bottom of a flight of rough steps was the cellar which served as the common kitchen, dining-room and dormitory. There were bunks against the wall, and from behind a curtain hung on a string, occasional snortings, stampings, neighings and bellowings showed that this remarkable living-room was also used as a stable, for in this upper valley of the Arc trees are so scarce and fuel so costly, that the inhabitants cannot afford fires for heating their houses, so that in winter they are obliged to live with their animals for the sake of warmth.

Yet in spite of the squalour of the surroundings, the wife and daughter of the landlord gave us a sumptuous meal, admirably cooked and remarkably cheap. Here, as at Bonneval, the people do not seem to dislike living with the cattle, although they sometimes complain that the stable atmosphere is rather damp. Sometimes a pen of sheep is arranged underneath the bed, as the fleeces are believed to have an absorbent and drying effect on the air. During one of my visits to Bonneval the owner of the house that I was staying in suddenly raised the hinged seat of what I had supposed to be an ordinary bench at the foot of the family bunk, and out came the heads of several ewes, quizzing us from under the bed, and evidently expecting their supper. After this had been given them, the lid was banged down again, and they were seen no more. Naturally in cold weather the warmth provided by the stables has to be jealously hoarded, so that windows are not made for opening, and doors are kept latched. This hermetically sealed existence may suit the inhabitants, but strangers don't take to it so kindly, and the moment we had drunk the land-lady's excellent coffee we were glad to escape into the fresh air and resume our journey.

From Bessans onwards the valley is nothing but a vast trench, increasingly grim and monotonous. Although there are many big peaks in this region, and although there is a fine glimpse of one of them, for the most part, the steep lower slopes conceal the summits from view. After much snow, or during the spring thaw this is the most dangerous part of the journey, and Blanc, when a boy, had a very narrow escape from death hereabouts, quite close to his home. His father had left him alone in the house for a few minutes, with strict orders not to go out on account of the dangerous state of the snow. But the old man had inadvertently left the family gun within reach, and this was too good an opportunity to be wasted. So, as soon as his father's back was turned, the boy snatched the gun, and darted out in hopes of shooting a hare. He had only reached the outskirts of the village when he heard the ominous thunder of an approaching avalanche, and, looking up, caught sight of the distant line of its surf as it curled over against the sky. By running as fast as he could, he was just able to reach a small tree and cling to it, when the appalling pressure of the deadly mass closed in upon him and shut out the daylight. He was in a frigid vice, unable to move even a finger, and consciousness faded peacefully away. Fortunately his departure had been noticed in Bonneval, the alarm was given, the church bells began tolling, and the whole village to a man turned out with their tools. With the help of so many rescuers young Blanc was discovered, dug out within a couple of hours, and eventually restored to life. He was even so fortunate as to escape without serious frostbite.

Luckily the weather had improved since our arrival, so that for us there was no question of avalanches. As we turned the last bend in the valley, and came into sight of the distant roofs of Bonneval, only half visible in the snow, a faint shrill sound came to us across the icy waste. When we realized that this was the distant cheering of the village children, we began to feel sure of our welcome. Daily, for three days, so we were afterwards told, all the boys and girls had gathered in the little snow-covered *place*, waiting every afternoon in the hope of catching sight of the long expected tree. It was an encouraging welcome, and as our pageant entered the village, it became a triumphal procession.

We found ourselves in strange surroundings, for Bonneval is no ordinary village. Smothered in snow as we saw it, it was so homogeneous with its mountain background, that it resembled one of those collections of dug-outs that were constructed in hill-countries during the great war by alternately hewing and building out of the mountain-side. Even

the roofs were half hidden in snow. A minute's stroll from
his door would plunge an unwary householder up to his
waist in a drift. The commonest luxuries of civilization were
not to be found here. At the time of our visit it was still the
custom, morning and evening, for the inhabitants to meet in
the narrow winding lanes between the houses and pass the time
of day on their way to draw water from the river, each with his
brace of copper buckets on a yoke. In spite of a multitude of
mountain torrents on every side, Bonneval had no water-supply
laid on to the houses, nor was there any electric light.

However, now that we had succeeded in arriving, there
was no time to be lost; the tree, surrounded by a crowd of
excited children, was taken to the *mairie*, the only large
building in the place. There were but two hours left in which
to get everything ready, although fortunately much of the
work had been done in advance at Lanslevillard. During
the bad weather there we had crouched round the stove in
the small living-room of the inn, drawing up lists of presents
for the children according to age and sex, and exhaustively
discussing the suitability of each article as we packed it in
coloured paper, and tied it with gilded string. Indeed, without
these preliminary labours the tree would never have been
ready in time.

I must admit that at first sight the *mairie* struck me as slightly
chilling, both physically and spiritually, for it was a mere
barrack, devoid of all fittings, and without a single stick of
furniture or even a lamp. In the centre of its vast desert of
dingy floor was a very small empty stove. We were getting
anxious, too, because it was already past four o'clock, the sun
had consequently quitted the valley after its miserably short
daily visit, and while it was evident that it would soon be
pitch dark, there was a great deal still to be done. First of
all the crowd of children had to be turned out of the room,

doors and shutters being closed against them until the show should be ready to begin. Many things had to be improvised in the short time left to us, but there were plenty of helpers. Blanc, with his son Alphonse went off to look for tools, for the tree must somehow be fixed upright in the middle of the room. Others brought wood and chopped it in order to make a fire in the stove. A ladder had also to be found, crockery had to be fetched, and a saucepan for making tea. Lighting was a problem, candles were sent for, and stuck in bottles, or fixed anywhere to ledges and crannies in the walls. Light to work by was necessary for the moment, but would not be required for long, because, when the tree was once illuminated, the unrelieved blankness of the white-washed walls would help to increase the brightness. Meanwhile we toiled anxiously by flickering candle-light in squalid gloom. As we worked we drank the tea, and tied on the toys, crackers and ornaments, or fastened innumerable coloured candles to the boughs. Hastily we read over the lists once more and checked the presents.

Outside in the deep snow and black darkness of the arctic night the crowd of children and grown-ups continued patiently assembling, indifferent to the cruel cold. Finally, when the last candles had been lit, and everything was declared to be ready, the door was flung open, and a crowd of onlookers trooped into what had been a bleak barrack, but was now transformed and irradiated by the magical glory of that superb spectacle, a Christmas-tree in full bearing. It was a moment that seemed worth the trouble, and the spectators were delightfully appreciative, young and old alike. In fact so little did any of them suffer from that failing usually known as *morgue Britannique*, that we regretted not having brought sufficient paper caps and toys for the grown-ups as well as for the children.

Like most villages in the Maurienne, Bonneval still retains the old costumes for its women, who all wore voluminous black skirts held down by thick stuff bodices, pointed in front. The men had their black felt hats; they are indeed seldom without them for "couvrez-vous" is the polite entreaty the moment one enters a house, and with reason, for the temperature of any room except the kitchen or the stable is often lower than that of the air out of doors.

Meanwhile with the help of the lists of names the presents were being handed out, while the odds and ends that adorn all respectable Christmas-trees were snipped off with scissors and distributed. Suddenly we observed that the priest and schoolmaster were making signs to silence the uproar in order that the children should be collected round the tree and made to sing an embarrassingly courteous speech in rhyme. Then, as the many candles began to gutter and die, or set fire to the tree, they were put out one by one with a wet sponge, while the company melted rapidly away. In a few minutes, before we had realized that the party was coming to an end, the guests had vanished as silently and suddenly as if they had been magically reabsorbed into the night, and instantly the frigid stillness of the mountains held the village in its grip once more. There seemed something sinister in the bareness and grimness of the deserted *mairie*, now that its temporary flicker of life had died down, and, leaving it without regret, we stumbled through the snow to supper in Blanc's hospitable house. Here we stepped from the chilly darkness of the street into what is at Bonneval an almost unique luxury, a living-room that does not depend for warmth on the presence of cattle, but is heated only by a stove. The wooden walls were hung all round with every kind of tool that a farmer, blacksmith or carpenter can find a use for, and there were some spare beds that had been got ready by Madame Blanc.

Some of the party were to sleep in them later, while the rest of us were to occupy an improvised dormitory in the *mairie*.

That night we slept the sleep of exhaustion, lulled with comfortable thoughts of the laborious progress of the tree to its triumphal climax in this Alpine wilderness. Next morning, the weather was still favourable, and we began the retreat down the valley to Modane, to catch the train home. The expedition had been more successful than we had ventured to hope.

PART II

Himalayan

EVEREST AND THE FUTURE

IT was in the early 'nineties that Clinton Dent, surgeon and mountaineer, first expounded the belief that Mount Everest could be climbed. Not long before the days of Dent, an interest in science was considered to be the only proper motive for mountaineering, and it was scarcely thought respectable to climb any important Alpine peak without at least boiling a thermometer on reaching the top. Professor Tyndall had even reprimanded the great critic and mountaineer, Leslie Stephen, for venturing to be flippant about scientific research, and Dent, in discussing the projected ascent of Everest, was careful to pay his tribute to science by welcoming the important discoveries that he believed would be made in respect to altitude, and by accepting the advancement of science as a justification of the adventure that he was advocating.

Times have changed since the days of Dent, and it is now no longer necessary to justify a taste for mountaineering by lip service to the gods of science. A fondness for mountains is nowadays considered an adequate excuse for climbing them, and although there is no longer much hope of gathering scientific fruits on Himalayan peaks, there have been during the last nineteen years no less than seven expeditions to Everest.

Certainly the facts revealed by these expeditions only confirm the truth of Dent's theory of mountain-sickness. He held that the more distressing symptoms were caused by lack of oxygen, and that the sufferings resulting from this lack and from diminished pressure could be mitigated by acclimatization. He pointed out that these sufferings would be more likely to occur in a balloon or in a pneumatic cabinet, since in neither case would there be any opportunity for acclimatization. He referred to "that grain of fact which proverbially outweighs a pound of theory", and it is evident that he would have understood more readily than modern scientists that only the most uncertain inferences are to be drawn from the results of experiments on animals in a laboratory.

Since Dent wrote his forecast, a good many fixed points in the tactical problem of the ascent have been established. The positions of the three high camps, IV, V and VI, have been settled, and are likely to remain at about 23,000, 25,000 and 27,000 feet respectively. At any rate, Camp VI cannot be much higher, and to pitch an extra camp above Camp VI, perhaps a thousand feet higher up, would be difficult, as it would immeasurably increase the problem of supply and transport.

Again, it is not likely that there will be any change in the strength of the assault parties on the last lap, for it is very difficult at these great altitudes to organize accommodation for more than two men. If it were possible to make the highest camp (VI) commodious enough to hold a reserve pair of men, such support would greatly increase security as well as likelihood of success. But the doubling of the size of the highest camp would involve an unwieldy amount of extra outfit and supplies with a consequently increased risk of casualties among the numerous porters that would be required. Nevertheless, means must be found to improve the standard of comfort at this camp, for, as one of the climbers has written, "the misery of two men enclosed in a

NORTH FACE OF MOUNT EVEREST
Showing highest point reached

tiny tent, seven feet by four, perched insecurely on a sloping ledge, so narrow that a third of the floor projects into space, may be better imagined than described".

Now the plan of attack upon Everest may conveniently be divided into two parts, the climax of the first being reached when Camp IV has been successfully established at 23,000 feet on the summit of the North Col. Access to this camp, however, is difficult, and might easily become impossible. To reach it from Camp III it is necessary to climb 2,000 feet of precipitous ice, of which only 400 feet can be ascended without step-cutting. On the way up is a vertical cliff of ice on which a rope-ladder has to be fixed to enable the heavily laden porters to ascend. Not only is this part of the route extremely awkward for the transport of tents and supplies, but in bad weather avalanches are a constant menace. Heavy snowfall, such as occurred in 1933 owing to the phenomenally early monsoon, might easily convert these steep slopes into a death-trap, and cut off the climbing-parties from any assistance. Indeed, the absence of avalanches in 1933 was supposed to have been solely due to the con-tinuous trampling of the snow by ascending and descending convoys compacting it into a relatively stable condition; surely a rather doubtful kind of security!

The camp itself, too, is awkwardly situated on the narrow crest of the col, which is terribly wind-swept, but no alterna-tive site is available, for the shelf just below the col is exposed to avalanches and therefore unsuitable for tents.

The expedition in 1933 was the first that succeeded in carrying the comparatively warm and comfortable double-walled arctic tent up to this camp, and in 1938 a similar tent was taken to Camp V at over 25,000 feet. The occupants of these tents are enabled to endure violent storms that might otherwise endanger their lives. It must not be supposed, however, that life anywhere on Everest is at all luxurious. Even at the foot of the mountain the temperature sometimes drops to below zero Fahrenheit, and in 1938, even after a hot day, the thermometer in the double-walled arctic tent on the North Col during the night showed forty-nine degrees of frost.

It is above the North Col that the second part of the attack begins, with its intervals fixed at the two highest camps at above 25,000 and 27,000 feet respectively. It is on the upper section of this route that critical difficulties are now known to exist. In the crest of the great north-east ridge of Everest there is a huge rock-step, barring the way. It has been described by one of those who have seen it at close quarters as "towering above the ridge like the bows of a battle-cruiser", enough to deter the boldest rock-climber. Mallory, in 1924, not realizing the dimensions of this obstacle, had planned to keep to the ridge during his attempts, but a reconnaissance of the great step decided later parties against this course, and in favour of Norton's route, which from Camp VI avoids the ridge in order to make a comparatively easy traverse almost horizontally across the precipices of the northern flank till the edge of the great couloir is reached. Here begins the last and worst stage of the whole climb, that is to say the crossing of the couloir, and the ascent to the summit.

A severe handicap here is the altitude, which is acutely felt, so that from Camp V upwards the climber has need for all his strength, and special rations of invalid food are provided. To the very few human beings who reach this upper region of Everest it must seem the sort of country that is only met with in nightmares. Here you must go slowly if you want to keep warm, or stop altogether if the cold is becoming too much for you. This is because the rapid panting occasioned by the slightest attempt to increase the pace induces a sensation which, according to the very few men who have experienced it, takes the form of a sort of deadly central coldness, due, it seems, to a general cooling down somewhere in the region of the lungs. To combat this fatal chilling process a special respirator has been ingeniously devised which allows the air breathed out by the lungs to warm that which is drawn in. Unfortunately, however, the apparatus is liable to be choked with ice.

Another peculiarity of these extreme elevations is that the snow is never hardened except by the wind, nor is it ever melted, for here even the Indian sun has little power. At any moment, too, out of a clear blue sky there may burst upon the startled climber a gale blowing at eighty miles an hour. In this uncanny region the influence of the seasons seems to be reversed, for the snow lies in summer and disappears in winter. This is because in winter the ferocious northerly squalls strip the rocks of snow until the coming of the warmer southerly monsoon winds loads them up again. It is during the rare intervals of calm weather between the onsets of the opposing winds that the climbers must hope to find the rocks free enough from snow to justify an attempt.

As to the quality of the climbing on these upper slopes of Everest, it seems that up to the last stage, as far as the great couloir, it is for the most part easy enough for experts in full possession of all their powers. On the other hand, unfortunately, the rocks on these slopes resemble layers of slates on a roof, and they lean outwards at an awkward angle, so that even an expert, if exhausted, might be tempted to delay progress fatally by stooping to help himself with his hands, instead of relying on his balance or on the grip of a single boot-nail in the normal manner of practised climbers.

At the great couloir, however, the situation changes, and the most serious of Everest's defences are concentrated against the attackers. At the entrance to the couloir the precipice steepens formidably. The climbing here is now recognized to be difficult, even by strictest Alpine standards. There is the same roof-like formation of the rock, so that on these smooth repellant slabs a covering of snow half an inch thick becomes a prohibitive obstacle, and any false step may hurl the climber to destruction down the immense northern cliffs. It is at this point that every attempt has failed, and always must fail, unless fine weather happens to create favourable conditions both of rock and snow.

Indeed, all hopes of success on Everest must depend on fine weather, and on the progress made recently in the technique of high climbing, especially in regard to acclimatization. Veterans whose powers are already known stand in a class by themselves; as for the others the leader must observe their performances, and classify them accordingly, either as fast or slow acclimatizers.

Unfortunately it appears that simultaneously with the process of acclimatization a gradual deterioration of stamina takes place, and this has a disastrous effect in diminishing resistance to fatigue. In order to give some idea of the two processes, Dr. Greene, writing as medical officer in 1933, explained that an unacclimatized man is a fit man under difficulties, whereas a man who is both deteriorated and acclimatized is an unfit man with his difficulties greatly reduced. Major Hingston, medical officer to a previous expedition, has supplied an ingenious analogy; he compares the interaction of acclimatization and deterioration with the interaction of a drunkard's increasing toleration of alcohol with a concomitant undermining of his general health.

This whole subject, however, is still insufficiently explored, and although it seems to be the rule that quick acclimatizers are quick deteriorators, and that slow acclimatizers are slow to deteriorate, it is too soon to dogmatize. In 1933, at any rate, the season was cut short so early by bad weather that it was impossible to test the slow acclimatizers very thoroughly, while the seasons of 1936 and 1938 were even more unfavourable. At the same time the significant fact must be remembered that in no expedition so far has any member ever been fit for a second attempt on the summit, and none of the high climbers have got off scatheless. In 1933 one of the climbing-parties suffered from slight frostbite, and another was discovered to have slightly strained their hearts. It is unfortunate that no method is known of testing beforehand a man's capacity for acclimatization. The fact is that authorities differ as to the time required for getting the best results. Some say that at Camp IV a few days are enough, even for slow acclimatizers. On the other hand, two former leaders have agreed that in the case of exceptional individuals three weeks at each stage would be satisfactory, were it only possible.

Opinions differ, too, as to whether the delays caused by the storms in 1933 resulted in excessive deterioration, and whether the time spent on the North Col was not longer than was desirable, so far as the fitness of the party was concerned. Four of the climbers actually endured the hardships of this camp at 23,000 feet for as long as eighteen days. These men certainly suffered in condition, nor is it surprising that another climber, after inhabiting Camp V at over 25,000 feet for eight successive days, "stood in considerable need of medical attention". There is no doubt that above this height mental as well as bodily powers decline, and there is great danger that the climber may not have sufficient mental concentration to enable him to check a slip that at normal elevations he would be able to control without any difficulty whatever.

Yet despite such severe handicaps the altitude records have

147

been remarkable enough. In 1924 four men reached 28,000 feet, and the same height was reached in 1933 in conditions that were much more unfavourable. In 1933, indeed, an early monsoon, accompanied by serious storms, left only thirteen days during which it was possible to work, often only for a few hours a day. Nevertheless not only did the climbers reach 28,000 feet, but eight of the porters were able to carry loads to an altitude exceeding 27,000 feet, and would have gone higher if required. In 1938 the climbers did almost as well in weather that was very much worse.

Of course in estimating the chances of a successful ascent the question of pace is all important. It is thought that a climber must achieve more than 250 feet an hour if there is to be any hope of his getting to the top. Norton, in 1924, in the long ascending traverse across the face of Everest on his final day's climb, when he attained 28,000 feet, only accomplished 1,300 feet in six hours. It is as if a party on the ordinary route of the Matterhorn were to take sixteen hours instead of the usual four or five in climbing from the Swiss hut to the top. On Everest in 1933 Smythe was three hours in ascending his last 600 feet. In his case, it is true, the conditions were bad, and every year improvements in method tend to accelerate the rate of progress, so much so, indeed, that it has even been thought possible to keep up a rate of 500 feet an hour throughout the final stage. This would mean that the top of Everest might be reached from the highest camp in four hours, a reasonably safe time-table, since it would allow an ample margin for the return journey, even if the anticipated three or four hundred feet of extremely difficult ground greatly prolonged the time. It is at any rate encouraging to reflect that in 1933 Smythe and Shipton accomplished a phenomenal improvement in Everest speed records by climbing from the North Col to 24,500 feet at the surprisingly fast rate of a 1,000 feet an hour. It was only later in the season, as they began to suffer from deterioration, that their rate of progress declined.

In 1938 the expedition deserves notice in respect of an important innovation, for it was the first *small* expedition to attempt the ascent. Unfortunately the bad weather, as in 1936, was once more prohibitive. Wind and cold were continuous until the 5th of May, when snow began to fall in quantities. From that date for the rest of the brief season the mountain was never in condition for climbing. Yet in spite of the weather the high camp was pitched and slept in at an altitude of 27,200 feet, and such results seem to justify the enthusiastic belief of the leader in small expeditions for the future. Apart from this innovation, procedure in the coming years is not likely to differ from that in 1933. No doubt to begin with, just as in 1933, the slow acclimatizers will be employed in making the great ice-slopes below the North Col accessible to laden porters, and will subsequently be expected to establish Camp IV on the col. The fast acclimatizers should then follow, ready to make the first attack as soon as they are in condition. There is no likelihood of any attempt to persevere after the monsoon period has begun. If oxygen is taken it will probably be in its dilute form for use on the last lap only. In the earlier stages reliance on delicate and intricate apparatus, rather than on acclimatization, would, it is believed, be dangerous.

Finally, at least three consecutive fine days must be available, and at least four men must reach the top of their form simultaneously. Unfortunately the chance of fine weather lasting for as long as two days in succession instead of merely for twelve hours is comparatively slight.

However, if the weather is propitious and the campaign proceeds according to plan, the fast acclimatizers should be in position to attack the summit in the second half of May, while the slow acclimatizers would be ready in the first half of June. With our increasing knowledge of Everest, and the progress made in the persevering siege of the mountain, the odds against a successful ascent in any given year have slightly diminished. Mallory once estimated them at fifty to one against the success of any single expedition, and Shipton, who led the successful reconnaissance party in 1935, has agreed with him. Ruttledge, the leader in 1933 and 1936, has expressed the opinion that five to one would now be a fairer calculation. No doubt, some day, as Shipton has put it, the top of Mount Everest will be reached, but the victor will be like a sick man climbing in a dream.

Yet in any case it is true to say that each expedition stands on the shoulders of its predecessors, so that, apart from the terrible uncertainty of the weather, the conditions become slightly more favourable every year.

A TRAGEDY ON NANGA PARBAT

THERE is no doubt that the popularity of mountain-climbing is increasing in the Himalaya as well as in European mountain ranges. All over Europe, the new fashion of 'hiking' and the improved facilities for travel have drawn attention to the hills. Moreover, since the novelty of the Alps is said to be exhausted, adventurous climbers are more frequently turning their thoughts to the Himalaya. So intense, in fact, is the keenness of the rising generation that in the case of the great Himalayan peak, Nanga Parbat, over 26,000 feet high, and situated in a district where difficulties of supply and transport compel the authorities to limit rigorously the number of expeditions approaching the mountain, there is frequently a waiting-list of several climbing-parties clamouring for permission to attack.

Nanga Parbat has killed more mountaineers than any other Himalayan summit has done, and it may seem strange that so formidable a mountain should be so much sought after. The fact is that a peak that is suitable for record-breaking purposes must exceed 26,000 feet, and it happens that the supply of such peaks is limited, ten of them being in the forbidden territory of Nepal. Of the remainder that are available, Everest is very far away, and can only be approached after delicate negotiations with the Tibetan Government.

Kangchenjunga, although it has been repeatedly attempted, is more terrible than Nanga Parbat, and the giants of the Karakoram are not only remote, but are said to be no easier to climb. Consequently the ambitious mountaineer must content himself with Nanga Parbat. Yet, if Nanga Parbat is less redoubtable than Kangchenjunga, it is still in many respects the most imposing summit in the Himalaya. It is not merely the tenth highest mountain in the world, but it occupies a position of superb isolation, without a rival within fifty miles. From its summit the crags and ice-walls of the southern face fall almost sheer to the floor of the Rupal valley for 14,000 feet, forming the greatest precipice in the world. The north face is almost equally abrupt, and the spectator, only fifteen miles away, on the banks of the Indus, sees the supreme peak soaring to all but 23,000 feet above his head. There is nothing in the world to compare with such a spectacle.

It was in 1934 that the late Herr Merkl's expedition met with its shattering repulse. Accounts published by the survivors enable us to study in detail one of the greatest tragedies in the history of mountaineering, and it is a story that contains many lessons for climbers. The previous history of the mountain is brief. The first expedition that attempted the ascent was British and took place in 1895. In that year the famous English mountaineer, Mummery, after climbing unsuccessfully to 20,000 feet on the desperately difficult north-west face, left the rest of his party and, accompanied by two Gurkhas, set out to make a short cut over the Diama Pass (20,000 feet) to see if an easier route existed on the other side of the mountain. When the remainder of the party, travelling by the valleys, reached the appointed meeting-place, there was no one there, and it was evident that Mummery and the two Gurkhas, in descending the pass, must have been swept away by one of the numerous ice-avalanches that thundered down its north-eastern slopes.

After this fatality thirty-seven years passed without any attempt being made; and then, in 1932, Herr Merkl took out

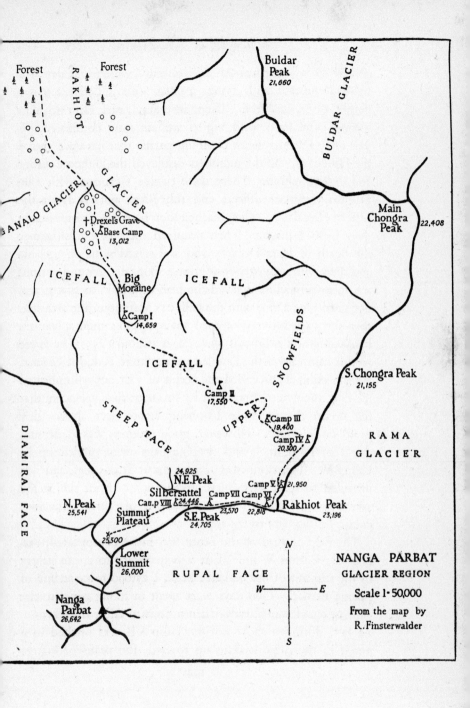

Forest RAKHIOT Forest

Buldar
Peak
21,660

BULDAR GLACIER

GLACIER

BANALO GLACIER

Main
Chongra
Peak   22,408

†Drexel's Grave
△Base Camp
13,012

ICEFALL   ICEFALL   Big
Moraine

S. Chongra Peak
21,155

△ Camp I
14,659

ICEFALL

UPPER   SNOWFIELDS

STEEP FACE

△
Camp II
17,550

△Camp III
19,400

Camp IV 20,300 △

RAMA
GLACIER

DIAMIRAI   FACE

24,925
N.E. Peak

Silbersattel
Camp VIII △24,446

Camp V △ 21,950

Camp VII Camp VI
△   △
23,570   22,818

Rakhiot Peak
23,196

N. Peak
25,541

Summit
Plateau

S.E. Peak
24,705

X
25,300

Lower
Summit
26,000

RUPAL FACE

N

W   E

S

Nanga
Parbat
26,642

NANGA PARBAT
GLACIER REGION
Scale 1·50,000
From the map by
R. Finsterwalder

a very strong German-American party, which was defeated by bad weather and coolie troubles after it had reached a height of 23,000 feet. Then, in 1934, came Herr Merkl's second expedition with which we are now concerned. It was one of the strongest climbing-parties that has ever visited the Himalaya, and the members displayed the highest courage and determination. There were twelve Germans with two English transport officers and thirty-five porters from the eastern Himalaya. They reached their base-camp in seventeen days from Srinagar. Then occurred their first misfortune: the death of Herr Drexel, who was seized with pneumonia and died within twenty-four hours. This disaster and various transport difficulties delayed the plan of attack, so that it was not until June 22nd, with the help of continuous fine weather, that the expedition succeeded in equipping their advanced base-camp at a height of 19,521 feet (Camp IV). The route to this camp from the base led up the huge Rakhiot Glacier. As the climbers ascended the series of vast and complicated ice-falls, they were threatened by immense ice-avalanches that fell down the precipice towering 10,000 feet above their heads on the right. However, good progress was made, and stores of food, fuel, and sleeping-bags were carried up to Camp V. This camp was at a height of 21,965 feet, and was intended to serve as the last 'strong-point' from which the assault-party could set out to establish the three remaining camps on the way to the top.

The next section of the route was more complicated, for, between Camps V and VI, it was necessary to climb nearly to the summit of the Rakhiot Peak, a 23,000-foot satellite of Nanga Parbat. Two days were spent in fixing ropes to the cliffs to enable the heavily-laden porters to effect the traverse. At last, during a snow-storm, Camp VII was pitched in a notch in the ridge leading up towards the peaks of Nanga

Photo: Schneider

SUMMIT OF NANGA PARBAT (26,660 ft.) FROM CAMP 6 (22,835 ft.)

Parbat. The site was at 23,328 feet, and had to be laboriously hewn out of névé, hardened by the wind. On the evening of their arrival the weather cleared, but a sea of cloud lay below, concealing Camp IV and the rest of the world. The climbers seemed as if marooned on some vast iceberg in a polar sea.

According to Herr Schneider, the route above Camp VII is "mostly difficult and especially very long". On the climbers' left is an abyss, 10,000 feet deep, its depth increasing as the climber gains height. In the bottom of the tremendous gulf, through gaps in the cloud-floor, could be seen from time to time glowing patches of green meadowland, glimpse of another world. The route follows a soaring ice-ridge to the Silbersattel, a depression lying at a height of 24,464 feet, between the two eastern peaks of Nanga Parbat, and giving access to a great plateau of névé, hitherto unvisited. Across this lofty snow-plain the way ascends gently for nearly two miles up to a minor summit of the mountain, 25,800 feet high, and then down into a final depression, from which a steep shoulder in the ridge has to be climbed before the highest peak can be reached. So far, at the immense height at which they had been travelling, the weather had remained fine. Yet a sinister feature was the constant sea of cloud that cut the climbers off from the rest of the world below, and—had they only known it—down at Camp IV a storm was raging daily. They fondly hoped that beneath the clouds at their feet Müllritter was busy stocking Camp VI with food and fuel to cover their retreat from the top. They little knew that this work was completely held up by constant heavy falls of snow. At their own camp it was only towards the evenings that the clouds used to rise threateningly round the tents and smother the ridge along which they had to travel.

At last, on the morning of July 6th, the five Europeans and eleven porters who had hitherto held out against mountain-sickness and exhaustion, emerged from Camp VII. It was to be the day of fatal decision. On that very morning an experienced Swiss mountaineer happened to be gazing at the celebrated view of Nanga Parbat from the summit of the distant Chachor La. He noted the ominous black clouds that were being driven by the wind against the great cliffs of the mountain. It was evident that the weather had broken, and the solitary watcher could see that a severe storm on Nanga Parbat was only a question of hours. Indeed, Bechtold, who was deputed that morning to escort two sick porters down to the advanced base at Camp IV, was caught in the snow-storm that was raging at the lower levels, and only reached safety with great difficulty. It is said that it required much persuasion to prevent the remaining porters from evacuating Camp VII and following the invalids.

But at any rate the Europeans in the party at Camp VII had no thought of danger—yet. Lured by the blue sky above them, they decided to set out on what they hoped might prove to be the final stage of their pilgrimage. At first all went well. The Austrians, Aschenbrenner and Schneider, went ahead to cut steps up the steep slope leading to the Silbersattel, and gained height at the rate of 650 feet an hour—an extraordinary speed for such an altitude. They even crossed the great elevated snow-plain lying beyond the saddle and began to mount the ridge towards a snow dome of 25,971 feet. At a height of 25,280 feet they halted, for the main body behind them was coming on with increasing deliberation. Evidently all was not well with the porters; yet waiting for them on the highest plateau in the world was cold work in such a violent wind. The two Austrians felt that they were temptingly near the end of their journey, for the supreme peak, 26,620 feet high, was only 1,000 yards away and only 1,380 feet above them. However, it presently became obvious that the main body could go no farther that day, and the two leaders were reluctantly obliged to retreat and rejoin their companions in order to fix one more camp, close to the Silbersattel, at 24,935 feet. At this highest camp some soup was cooked for an evening meal—it was as much as they could eat—and all were now confident that the summit of Nanga Parbat was at last within their reach. They cheerfully assumed that the wind which raged across the high plateau on the edge of which they were camped was a constant phenomenon at these extreme heights.

Nevertheless, on the morning of July 7th their hopes were dashed, for a tremendous roaring snow-storm burst upon them, and the blizzard was so fierce that it was impossible to breathe in the open. "The driving snow was blown horizontally in broad sheets," wrote Schneider; and by ten in the forenoon perpetual darkness seemed to gather about them. All day they lay in their sleeping-bags in the tents, while the storm raged. It was impossible to cook, and only once could a little snow be melted, enough for half a cupful of tea apiece. Snow fell unceasingly, and the occupants of the tents felt that they were being buried alive. The night that followed was the worst in Schneider's experience. The tent-poles were broken by the violence of the gale, and the tents could not be erected until next day. Sleep was almost impossible, and headaches were common.

When dawn broke on July 8th there was no improvement, and living in the tents had become nearly unendurable. At eight o'clock, therefore, Wieland struggled into the tent occupied by Aschenbrenner and Schneider for a council of war. Finally it was agreed by all that the attack must be written off as a failure, that the whole party must descend to Camp IV; and when all were ready, Aschenbrenner and Schneider were directed to start ahead of the rest with three porters to break the trail, leaving the main body of eight porters under Merkl, Welzenbach, and Wieland behind them to follow in their steps. As the advanced party started, the visibility was ten yards, and the task of making tracks in the deep, fresh snow was terribly fatiguing. Moreover, just as they were embarking on the descent of the steep slopes below the Silbersattel, the gale blew one of the three porters out of his steps. He was saved by means of the rope, but his load, which consisted of the double sleeping-bag and india-rubber mattress belonging to Aschenbrenner and Schneider, was blown off his back and was never recovered. The porters had their own bags to sleep in, but the two Austrians were now without protection for the night, and it was therefore imperative that they should reach the shelter of a camp before dark.

As the advance-party descended, exhaustion from exposure, starvation, and mountain lethargy began to overcome it; every thirty yards the five men sank down to rest in the snow. In turns, first Schneider, and then Aschenbrenner, were almost overwhelmed by weakness. All the time the storm continued. When they reached easy ground, it was agreed to remove the rope, which was now felt by the whole party to be an encumbrance. Unfortunately the result of this manœuvre was that near Camp VII the three porters dropped behind, and were lost sight of. The two leaders, however, pushing on alone, and after passing over the very top of the Rakhiot Peak, came to Camp V, where they were able to find some food, although the tents must have been fast disappearing under the enormous accumulations of snow. At length, in the late afternoon, they arrived at Camp IV, confidently expecting that their three porters would shortly rejoin them, or be picked up by the main body which they believed to be close behind. When no one turned up it was assumed that the whole party must have halted at Camp V. Meanwhile, at Camp IV they found Bechtold, Müllritter, and Dr. Bernard, who were weather-bound and had been trying repeatedly, but in vain, to reach Camp V. Normally it was a steep, easy climb of three hours, but the weather and the fresh snow had made it almost impossible. That night half a metre of snow fell, and the storm continued as it had done at this level all the week; but on the morning of the 9th, the clouds lifted momentarily, and the inhabitants of the camp saw a number of men at a great height, coming down the mountain. The gale must have been terrible at the higher levels, for snow streamers a hundred yards long were blowing off the Silbersattel. A solitary figure could be seen following the others; it was probably Wieland, for, as was afterwards learned, it was at about this time that he died. As they stared in astonishment, the men in camp realized to their consternation that the main body was still on the far side of the Rakhiot Peak, and had not even reached Camp VII.

That evening the sky cleared with a raging gale, and four porters were suddenly observed descending the Rakhiot Peak. The occupants of Camp IV hurried out to meet them as they approached, and helped them into camp. All four porters proved to be badly frostbitten and had to be sent down to the base for treatment. For those at Camp IV, day after day passed in increasing anxiety. Repeated attempts were made by the garrison to carry help up the mountain, but, after a first attempt, the porters in camp were all too exhausted to follow their leaders, and the latter often wallowed up to the shoulders, helpless in the masses of fresh snow. The conditions that now made even the relatively easy task of the descent so difficult, became prohibitive when it was a question of forcing a way uphill. Twice they tried to reach Camp V, but only once did they succeed.

All hope of finding their comrades alive had now been wellnigh abandoned, when, on July 15th, an astonishing incident occurred: a single figure appeared, coming down the glacier, and the porter, Angstering, alone, exhausted and badly frostbitten, staggered into the camp. He had been a whole week on his way down from the highest camp (VIII), without food or shelter in the raging storm, and this is the terrible story that he told: it appears that soon after Aschen-brenner and Schneider with the advance-guard had started down on July 8th from Camp VIII, Merkl, Wieland, and Welzenbach with the main body of eight porters set out, as arranged, to follow in the tracks. The storm, the deep snow, and the prolonged exposure at extreme altitudes soon began to overwhelm them, so that they collapsed before reaching Camp VII, and passed the night in the open on a tiny shelf of snow, just below the Silbersattel: Merkl and Wieland sharing a sleeping-bag, while Welzenbach, who, it seems, had lost his bag, lay out among the porters, who presumably had bags of their own. During the night a porter died, and on the morning of the 9th only three Europeans with four of the porters were strong enough to start; Angstering and two other porters were so ill that they remained lying where they were. Of those who were able to continue, Welzenbach, in spite of his night without a sleeping-bag, seemed to be the strongest, and was even able to fix a rope to an ice-axe, upright in the snow, in order to give security to the party on their way down to Camp VII. It was just as they were reaching this camp that Wieland sank down quietly in the snow and died. Unfortunately only one tent was now habitable, and, as there was not room for all in it, Merkl told the four strongest porters to push on down to the next camp (VI), not being aware that the tents there were by now buried out of sight in the snow. The four porters that were sent on subsequently overtook the stragglers from the advance-party, these having lost their way on the Rakhiot Peak. Of this combined group of seven porters, three succumbed before they could rejoin Aschenbrenner and Schneider at Camp IV.

In the meantime, the party that remained at Camp VII passed another terrible night; the sleeping-bags had filled with snow-dust, and Merkl was seated with Welzenbach, outside the tent, and apparently semi-delirious. In this state, without food or shelter, Merkl's party remained from the 9th till the 11th, when they were rejoined by the porters with Angstering and Gaylay, who had succeeded in creeping down from the place where they had been lying out in the snow since the 8th, and where they had left a dead comrade. The reunited party then stayed at Camp VII for the whole of the 12th, and during the ensuing night Welzenbach died. On the 13th, Angstering made a despairing effort to escort Merkl and Gaylay down to Camp VI, Merkl using two ice-axes as crutches. When further progress became impossible, they scooped a small hollow in the snow and crouched in it till the 14th. The weather then began to improve, and they tried again to move down, but were too weak to continue. At last, on the 15th, Merkl told Angstering to try and fetch help. Angstering accordingly set out once more on his miraculous journey, and succeeded, as we have seen, in reaching safety. His two companions must have died soon after his departure. Thus ended the greatest mountaineering disaster that had hitherto occurred in the Himalaya.*

* *Nanga Parbat Adventure.* Bechtold (John Murray).

In 1937 a still greater disaster occurred to another strong German party on Nanga Parbat. Owing to abnormal weather conditions an avalanche overwhelmed one of the camps during the night, killing the seven Germans and nine Sherpa porters who were sleeping there.

In 1938 another German expedition made further determined attempts which were frustrated by the terrible weather.

As to the conclusions to be drawn from the study of the catastrophe in 1934, it is possible to learn more from the story of Merkl's gallant failure than from the example of an expedition that has never come near to disaster, and it is likely that several general principles will be evolved for guidance in the future. Firstly, climbers will recognize the danger in an expedition of making the final assault "top-heavy" by allowing too many members to take part in it, for the example of Merkl's campaign has shown that by taking so many Europeans to the higher camps, not only are the porters that have to establish the camps given more work than they can perform efficiently, but the number of mountaineers in reserve at the advanced base, and available for emergencies, is dangerously depleted. Secondly, in respect to tents, strength of canvas and poles will not be too rashly sacrificed to lightness. Thirdly, leaders will not push forward assault parties until every camp in turn has been adequately organized. Finally, we may assume that Himalayan storms will be treated with greater respect, even to the point of abandoning an apparently hopeful attempt at the cost of deliberately submitting the personnel to the subsequent fatigue and tedium of repeating every phase of the attack from the very beginning.

If such principles as these are observed in future, the tragedy of Nanga Parbat will not have been in vain.

NEW PASSES IN THE HIMALAYA—I

JUDGED from a mountaineering point of view, every mountain range has a golden age in the history of its exploration. It is the period before the peaks have been climbed, when the topography of the passes is still a subject for delightful speculation. Can that alluring gap in the skyline be reached, can it be crossed, where will it lead to, and what is to be seen on the other side? Such are the fascinating problems that occupy the explorer in almost every valley.

In the Alps where all the peaks have long since been repeatedly climbed by almost every conceivable route, there are, of course, no new passes left. In the Himalaya, on the other hand, the golden age still flourishes, and new passes are plentiful. So numerous are they indeed that the explorer who has noted a new pass can afford to leave it unattended to for years without much risk of its being interfered with.

The Bhagat Kharak Pass was an instance in point. It is a gap in the range of high peaks which surround the three sacred sources of the Ganges in Garhwal. The pass is a conspicuous feature to anyone exploring the Bhagat Kharak Glacier. This glacier, which is about ten miles long, has its origin in a wilderness of savage peaks varying between twenty and twenty-three thousand feet in height. Shipton says of these mountains that he has never seen grimmer precipices, and till 1912 they had never been explored.

Attention was first drawn to the Bhagat Kharak Pass by the writer in 1912 after visiting its summit and exploring the surroundings during a journey through British Garhwal in the same year. Since then almost thirty years have elapsed, yet no one has attempted to make an honest pass of this gap by crossing it and descending it on the other side. Strictly speaking, therefore, as it has never been made into a pass, it should still be described as a gap or saddle.

The making of passes is certainly the most enjoyable part of Himalayan mountaineering, being quite unlike the desperate death-struggle involved by assaults on major peaks. The man who is driven by an overwhelming urge to attempt what is often called the "conquest" of one of the greater Himalayan mountains, must expect more pain than pleasure from the enterprise. The explorer of passes, on the other hand, while he experiences less of the dubious excitement that is to be got from battling with a vastly superior adversary, and encounters fewer hair-breadth escapes, has a mind free to enjoy all the gentler pleasures of exploration. It was to these delights that we were looking forward on the Bhagat Kharak Glacier in 1912.

When I first made acquaintance with the pass, or let us say the gap, I was camping on the glacier, accompanied by the Savoyard guides, Pierre Blanc and his brother, Justin, together with a party of Bhotias from the village of Mana, about ten miles distant. We were looking for any passes that might serve as exits from this great ice-valley, and at the same time link together the three sacred sources of the Ganges by affording communications between Badrinath (the village we had come from), Kedarnath and Gangotri. One of these routes, we hoped, might take us over on to the great Gangotri Glacier, which is believed to be the biggest ice-field in the central Himalayan chain.

It always seems a pity to spoil a new pass by visiting it without crossing it, for thus one deprives it of most of its

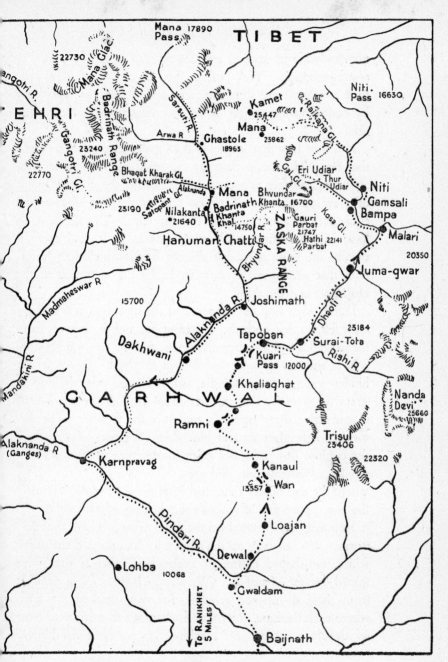

SKETCH MAP OF THE APPROACHES TO KAMET

················· Indicates Author's Route

novelty without making sure that it will serve as a means of communication. Very often the excuse is that neither time nor food are sufficient, and one would risk starvation by endeavouring to get down to civilization on the farther side.

It was in July that we decided to make an attempt to reach the gap. The camp that we occupied on the glacier was about 14,000 feet above sea-level. From the climatic point of view an altitude of 10,000 feet in the Himalaya is the equivalent of about 5,000 feet in the Alps. The air seems to have just the same exhilarating sparkle in it, and there is usually the same agreeable absence of flies, including horse-flies, that sometimes in summer make life a burden in the Himalaya and the Alps.

During that July the influence of the monsoon was making itself felt, so that both the scorching sun and the breezes from the ice-fields had lost their fierceness, and the day-temperature was as mild as summer weather in England. Down in the hidden valleys towards India, warm clouds were waiting in strata till a renewal of the monsoon-wind in the south-west should drive them upwards and over the frontier to be dissolved in the thin air and blue skies of Tibet. Everywhere the copious flow of water from the melting snow was like a rapidly advancing tide, and great lagoons lay near the camp, where the day before there had been fields of snow. During the hot, oppressive afternoons the roaring of avalanches was so frequent that it resembled the noise of an incessant thunderstorm. On our way up the glacier we had noticed the many white, fan-shaped chutes of avalanche-fragments that were spread out on its surface. We always kept as far as possible from these ill-omened remains, for they marked the areas where each flanking gully was discharging from time to time its deadly contents of tumbling stones and ice-blocks.

BADRINATH PEAK 23,420 ft., NORTH FACE (See page 167)
Position of Saddle or Pass marked by arrow-heads

Photo : A. Heim

Occasionally we were startled by the terrific spectacle of these formidable avalanches shooting out from some hidden ravine on to the level reaches of the glacier with the speed and suddenness of an express train rushing out of a tunnel.

The gap that we hoped to cross was situated on the skyline to the right of Badrinath Peak, shown in an illustration to this book and conspicuous enough to be an irresistible lure to any climber. The obvious route to it marked A A A in the illustration, and leading up the full length of the big glacier that is tributary to the Bhagat Kharah would, however, have exposed us during several hours to being bombarded by ice-avalanches falling from the series of tremendous ice-cliffs that guard the whole of this face of Badrinath Peak. Consequently we voted that this route was out of the question. Fortunately there seemed to be a way round, for it was probable that by getting on to the small hanging glacier marked D D D in the illustration, we should be able to cross the low ridge at the head of it, and thus arrive on the upper levels of the big tributary glacier well above the danger zone.

Accordingly on the 9th of July we moved camp an hour lower down the Bhagat Kharak Glacier, establishing ourselves for one night on a grassy moraine opposite the junction of the big tributary with the main ice-stream.

Next morning at twenty minutes past three we left camp for the new pass. The ice-fall of the big tributary glacier has a peculiarity that is characteristic of Himalayan ice-formations, for it is broken up to an extent that is out of all proportion to the very moderate slope of its bed. However, as I have already explained, the route up the course of this glacier was the dangerous direct approach that we intended to avoid, and so, instead of following it, we climbed one or two rock and snow couloirs that led up on to a little hanging glacier opposite our camp. After walking across this small glacier, a minor and very easy pass took us over into the upper basin of the big tributary, well above the danger zone, just as we had planned. Thus we had triumphantly turned the enemy's defences without incurring any risk.

On this upper plateau the slope was fairly gentle as far as the *bergschrund*. A *bergschrund*, it may be explained, is a rift or chasm that occurs in the glaciation of all great mountains, and forms the dividing-line where the immense weight of the lower mass of ice breaks away by gravitation from the upper slopes. To the mountaineer, the *bergschrund* is the moat that defends the enchanted castle, and beyond this last defence is the purpose of his pilgrimage, the supreme heights, aloof and rigid in their celestial armour of unyielding ice.

Above this *bergschrund* the angle steepened so that in some seasons the snow might be avalanchy and dangerous, perhaps forcing a climbing-party to take to some rock-cliffs on the right. As usual in the Himalaya, the angle turned out to be much steeper than a distant view of it had led us to suppose, but with increasing eagerness to see the unknown country ahead, we raced panting up the final slope. Suddenly we found ourselves on the top of the pass, and a thrilling spectacle was revealed. All difficulties had disappeared, and to our intense relief, beyond the smooth snow-saddle on which we stood, we could see below us an immense glacier, without a ripple on its vast surface, flowing gently and evenly down an arctic-looking valley, and vanishing out of sight in what must have been the direction of Gangotri. Surely such an enormous glacier could be no other but the great Gangotri Glacier itself? As far as we could see, this side of the pass was much easier than the way up which we had come. Anxious to learn more, we pushed on, without pausing on the watershed, and continued in a horizontal direction, for a quarter of an hour towards the south, above some rock-ridges, till we were able to make out an easy way down to the flat ice of the great glacier far below us. From our outpost was now revealed the wonderful precipice of the western face of Badrinath Peak, with a gully in it, plunging without a kink in its course, from the top of the mountain to the level glacier at the bottom, a distance perhaps of 7,000 feet.

There was no time to go farther, and so, returning to the pass, we built a cairn on a prominent rock-tower. Westward from it was a wonderful view of one of the Satopant peaks, about 22,000 feet, and reminding us of the Weisshorn, but even more sublime and inaccessible in its appearance. Behind us on the Tibetan frontier, blocking the middle distance, was Kamet, 25,450 feet, lording it over his great satellites and the surrounding country.

Again to-day I was struck by the fact that Himalayan ascents are not merely much longer than climbs in the Alps, but are steeper and more difficult. The alternation of fiercer heat and cold not only weathers the Himalayan mountains into sharper shapes, but accounts for the almost incredibly steep hanging glaciers that astonish the spectator with what seems a defiance of the forces of gravitation. One of the peaks above our camp, for instance, not only compared in the boldness of its outlines with that amazing rock-pinnacle at Chamonix, the Grépon, but, unlike the Grépon, it was sheathed from head to foot in glittering ice. Even Badrinath Peak, 23,420 feet, that resembled in shape the placid outline of Mont Blanc, and dominates this part of the valley with its massive ice-fields, would be dangerous to climb, for, although it does not look difficult, its slopes are exposed to devastating avalanches.

The total time that we had taken for the ascent to the pass from the camp was about seven hours, and our delight in our discovery might have been absolute, had time as well as provisions enabled us to complete the crossing. As it was, the new pass, although it was only suitable for mountaineers, was nevertheless satisfactorily easy for as far as we had been able to see down the unknown glacier, and if this glacier was not the Gangotri, it must at any rate be an important tributary. Indeed, it seemed certain that we had discovered a direct route connecting the sacred sources at the villages of Badrinath and Gangotri.

Reluctantly we turned, and began to descend by the way we had come. At first the very steep snow had a disagreeable tendency to slide away in small avalanches that revealed ice underneath. Lower down, the surface was more secure, and the Bhotias amused themselves by learning to do standing glissades. The art of glissading down hard snow in a standing position resembles ski-ing, but differs from it in one important respect. In the soft snow met with in ski-ing, the nervous novice can always stop himself by sitting down promptly, and he constantly does so to save himself from being run away with. In a standing glissade, on the other hand, it is generally disastrous to slip backwards, for all control is lost, and the unfortunate performer, unless he has learnt how to get up again while still on the move, shoots down helplessly on his back at an increasing speed, and if the slope is long and steep, he may be very seriously hurt when he reaches the bottom.

I was, therefore, rather reluctant when, after we had got down to the small dry glacier, Pierre, who has a passion for short cuts, suddenly announced that he would make one by glissading down a narrow snow-couloir below the snout of the glacier, and enthusiastically invited us all to come with him. For my part, I had no hesitation in refusing, for not only was this gully revoltingly steep, but I had noticed on the way up that the middle of its course was interrupted by a waterfall. However, Bhotias are always ready for anything, and, on Pierre's announcing that he was sure the waterfall would not give any trouble, two of our gallant followers volunteered to accompany him. Thereupon, glissading at a great rate, all three of them rapidly disappeared down the grim funnel of the forbidding couloir. Pierre, as instructor, went in front, while his pupils, in fits of laughter, ignoring the possibility of danger, and with absolute confidence in their professor, constantly shot on to their backs, to be duly fielded by Pierre, who had in fact preceded them for that purpose.

Bhotias are, of course, born cragsmen, and even on snow, of which they are usually quite ignorant, have no sense of fear; so hardy are they, too, that it is difficult to persuade them to carry any food for themselves while climbing. They will scornfully protest that having had breakfast before starting, it would be absurd to eat again before nightfall. However, even a Bhotia is noticeably the better for taking a little nourishment with him on a climb, and eventually he learns the advantages of doing so.

As it happened, there was no occasion for any anxiety over Pierre and his two companions, for, late in the evening, when I got back to camp, I found that they had already arrived, and were sitting round the fire waiting for me.

NEW PASSES IN THE HIMALAYA—II*

THE next problem in our programme was to discover a direct
route from Mana to Niti. Each of these villages is situated at
the foot of an important pass over which trade is carried on
with Tibet every summer. The inhabitants are exclusively
Bhotias, and the idea of crossing over the mountains from
one village to the other appealed very strongly to our Bhotia
followers. This was natural enough, for the ordinary journey
from Mana to Niti takes about a week, and involves a laborious
détour by the rough mountain paths that serve as main roads
in this country, down one long valley and up another. As
an improvement on this long way round, we hoped to make
a short cut across the continuous ice-fields extending from
Kamet to the Parbat group. This watershed separated the
village of Niti from our camp at Mana, and, if we could
find a pass, we had hopes of doing the journey in only three
or four days.

Now in the Alps, when it was still possible to find new
passes, a mountaineer who discovered one usually prided
himself on its difficulty; in the Himalaya, on the contrary, it
is only the easiness of a new discovery that commends it, and
this is natural, for here the prowess of the discoverer is less
important than the utility of what he discovers.

On this occasion the prospects of finding a useful pass
seemed favourable. We had been exploring the head-stream
of the Ganges that flowed down from the Mana Pass to the

* See sketch map on page 165.

village of Mana, and at the head of the first tributary glen on the east side of the valley was a glacier with an attractive-looking gap in the sky-line behind it. There was a tradition among the Bhotias that a dog had once come over this gap from Niti, and it only remained for us to see what lay on the other side.

There were evidently various possibilities. The gap might be useless, and merely connect us with a glen that would bring us back to the valley that we had started from. Or, on the other hand, it might at once lead us in triumph into the upper valley of the Dhaoli, where Niti was. There was also a third possibility that the gap might give access to the Thiapap glen. In that case, although, if we were to follow the downward course of the Thiapap River, it would only lead us back to the Ganges below Mana, there would still be a chance for us if we travelled upstream, because the Thiapap glen is connected with Niti by a pass at its head known as the Bhyundar Khanta, and this pass we might use as a sequel to the dog's gap in order to get us to Niti.

The first thing to do was to get back to our base at Mana, and collect stores. On the way down to the village from the Bhagat Kharak Glacier, Pierre went off with his rifle to scale the vast precipices north of the valley in search of fresh meat, for the Bhotias said there were thar to be found in that very formidable country. Pierre took several Bhotias with him. He afterwards told me he was amused by their considerately offering him a helping hand in difficult places, and showing surprise when the offer was not accepted. After shooting five thar, Pierre returned full of amazement at the extraordinary agility of these animals, and the tremendous size of the precipices that they frequent. With a wide experience of both chamois and ibex he had come to the conclusion that on really difficult rocks thar were as superior to ibex as ibex were

THE BHOTIAS

to chamois. Anyone who has seen chamois bounding at full gallop across the face of an Alpine precipice will appreciate the significance of such a testimonial. As human food, however, and from a gourmet's point of view, thar were less admirable; in fact, after a meal off them, I needed no naturalist to tell me that they belonged to the same genus as the goat. But we were short of fresh meat, and not a scrap of the five carcases could be wasted.

According to Sherring, the Bhotias inhabiting Mana and Niti were a race that is not purely Tibetan, but comes of a Tibetan stock. They speak the hill dialect of their neighbours, and have forgotten their own language, for they have been partially Hinduized. Some of them belong more to the Tibetan race than to any other, and the worship of Tibetan deities is included in their religion. They are traders from childhood, and all through the summer are busy carrying merchandise over the Mana and Niti Passes into Tibet on the backs of pack-sheep. They have the monopoly of this trade because their religious views permit them to eat with Tibetans, although from a fastidious dislike of the dirty habits of the average Tibetan they are sometimes unwilling to do so. Their trade is mostly in Tibetan borax, salt and wool which they exchange for grain, sugar and piece-goods from India.

The Bhotias of Mana and Niti certainly form the most admirable raw material for making mountaineering porters. They are delightful to deal with, and only require training for work on snow and ice, for they have little to learn as cragsmen. They are intelligent, willing and infinitely superior to their neighbours, the ordinary hillmen; in fact I have never come across a bad Bhotia.

Our camp at Mana was pitched on close-cropped grass in a wilderness of scattered boulders. There were no trees anywhere in the neighbourhood, although the valley is here only 11,000 feet above the sea. In the village that night there was much social activity, and at dusk a Bacchanalian procession danced past the camp, carrying in triumph an old man half naked and wholly drunk, who was intending to sacrifice a goat, a fact, I think, that made him very popular. The dancers who accompanied him advanced with gigantic strides in single file through the camp with a swinging serpentine follow-my-leader movement that revealed both grace and strength. As they went by they snatched brands from the camp-fire and waved them round their heads in time to the dance. Then, the whole procession, with its whirling torches, swept rapidly down the valley and was gone into the darkness as quickly as it had come.

A few days later there was a festival for all the village children, beginning at five in the morning, and likewise culminating in the sacrifice of a goat. The children looked particularly charming; like all the clansmen they wore frock-coats and drawers of undyed sackcloth, with bright red forage-caps, and their long black hair came down to their shoulders. Many of them from four years old upwards spent the whole day close by the camp, clambering about happily, and without any supervision, over a steep and jagged rock-pinnacle which projected dizzily above the river that foamed and roared in the bottom of the gorge, hundreds of feet below. A false step on the part of any one of these tiny children would have hurled him to destruction, but not a single parent paid the slightest attention to them.

On the 17th of July we were up long before dawn. Not a star was visible, and the big rains had been announced to have started on the previous day, but as it was not raining at the actual moment we set out at twenty minutes to six, after sending off some camp-followers, who were to go round by the valleys, and meet us, we hoped, at Niti.

At first we ascended the long valley leading up to the Mana Pass on the frontier. A thin crumbling track wound its way along a precipitous gorge at the bottom of which rolled and thundered the torrent that fed the head-waters of the Ganges and is here known as the Sarsuti. From the cavernous recesses of the gorge there rose always the dull booming sound of boulders rolling over each other along the bottom of the furious river. We crossed lush, rain-soaked pastures, our boots decorated with the torn and dripping petals of innumerable flowers, and then blue sky began to appear.

There were fourteen Bhotias accompanying us, and they seemed to enjoy carrying their heavy loads. The truth was that these men of Mana appreciated a trip to Niti, just as a Londoner might enjoy a holiday in Paris. They hoped, too, that by accomplishing the journey in half the customary time, they would cause a considerable sensation when they arrived at Niti.

To-day one of them, by name Bonia, was lagging, a fact so inconsistent with his character that rumour had it that he was ill, but when he eventually turned up, stolid and taciturn as usual, he repudiated the suggestion. He was a most reliable youth, one of the most gallant of our porters, with a handsome impassive face, his only trouble being, according to Pierre, that he was "affreusement bête." Pierre, however always suffered fools—if not gladly—at any rate kindly, and he knew that in spite of the taciturn manner, Bonia was as strong as a mule, and always willing. So, indeed, were all the Bhotias, and one of Bonia's colleagues, Shyamu, whom we had made into a sort of extra head-man, not only throve on the strenuous work of carrying heavy loads at these altitudes, but was even growing visibly fat on it.

Soon we turned off from the main valley, and climbed the

steep entrance of the Kulhia glen, virgin soil, for all we knew to the contrary. All the upper region of this glen was filled with glacier, and early in the afternoon we pitched camp half-way up its true right bank, building the usual memorial of our passage in the form of a massive wall round the kitchen fire-place. Over it we put an awning supported on a sort of gallows, and this completed the building.

After an early dinner by daylight in this comfortable shelter, with subsequent night-caps of brandy, hot water, lemon and sugar, we began to think better of the weather, the rains seemed to be holding off, and lovely apricot-coloured clouds hovered for long in the place of the departed sun.

On the 18th of July, although alarum-watches woke us at three, the mountains were so much hidden in mist that we waited till five o'clock before starting. The climb turned out to be merely an easy walk over smooth névé to the gentle depression that was our pass.* On the far side of it there was little to be seen, only clouds boiling in a great cauldron of rugged crags, with the occasional gleam of an ice-field coming through the mists. Looking back down the glen up which we had come, we admired the magnificence of Kunaling, the peak standing sentinel at the entrance of the Bhagat Kharak valley, with a panoply of sharp ice- and rock-*arêtes*. For only a moment, while the clouds parted, we saw the huge bulk of Badrinath peak with its glittering snow-fields, and another peak beyond it, big, black and forbidding. It was situated behind and to the right of a conspicuously steep pass at the head of the Bhagat Kharak ice-valley. In a

---

* The ice has altered so much since the date of our crossing that Smythe, in 1938, found there was a steep slope on this side which would convert this easy walk into a mountaineering expedition.

photograph of Heim's* it is shown as one of a number of nameless peaks. Probably it was Satopant, a mountain of more than 23,000 feet, only recently mapped by the Indian survey. The Himalayan Journal for 1939 reports it as often wrongly identified by explorers.

But now, driven on by tormenting anxiety to sample the descent, Pierre and I raced ahead in a series of standing glissades, leaving Justin to follow with "les enfants" as the guides always called the Bhotias. We suspected that if we descended directly into the valley that we saw beneath us, it would turn out to be the Thiapap glen, leading back as we had foreseen, to the Ganges below Mana. We therefore tried, as well as we could, to avoid losing height, and to traverse the upper slopes without going down to the river, hoping in this way to reach the pass at the head of the glen, in the expectation that it would be the Bhyundar Khanta, a second gateway for us on our road to Niti. On our left descended an *arête* towards a big glacier far below in the valley, and we began to feel more certain that the glacier must be the Thiapap. Crossing the *arête* by a minor pass in it, we continued traversing slopes high above the valley-floor in rain and mist. There was now no view at all, apart from the glimpses of a glacier above us of unknown magnitude, and it occurred to me that stones might fall from it at an uncomfortable velocity. It was difficult to find space for a camp, but there was now little doubt that we had struck the right valley, and that the big glacier below us was the Thiapap ka Bank, flowing down from the Bhyundar Khanta, the pass that was to get us to Niti.

I was accordingly anxious to go down farther and camp by the Thiapap Glacier, but Pierre argued against this plan,

* *Thron der Götter*, by Heim and Gansser, Morgarten Verlag, Zurich and Leipzig.

as he still feared it would cause us to lose height unnecessarily. He still hoped that we could get on to the upper part of the Thiapap Glacier much nearer the Bhyundar Khanta, by crossing one more ridge that we could see farther along the hill-side. Opposite us, we could dimly make out through the clouds, the huge ice-bound precipices of the Parbat peaks rising to more than 22,000 feet.

Eventually we camped miserably in the rain on an uncomfortable slope, at an altitude perhaps of about 14,000 feet. From where we were we had a fine view of the massive ice-stream of the Thiapap ka Bank, 2,000 feet below. Our clothes and the tents were very wet, and when I knelt on the floor-cloth of my Whymper tent to search for something, the water oozed through to my knees.

However, the rain did not last without a break, and in a momentary interval screams and shouts from the Bhotias announced that a musk-deer had been sighted, so Pierre went off in pursuit. It was perhaps just as well that the deafening din made by our followers had effectually put the quarry to flight, for musk-deer are very strictly preserved, and killing one without permission would have made us liable to a heavy fine.

As there was little view from the camp, I had the futile inspiration of strolling farther along the grass- and stone-slopes of the mountain-side in the direction of the Bhyundar Khanta in the hope of getting a view from the next ridge beyond us. The result was discouraging, for I found that not only were there countless steep ravines and ridges to be crossed, but in several gullies there were waterfalls that proved very awkward obstacles. At any rate I learnt that we should be obliged to go down to the glacier, for further progress by continuing the traversing of these interminable ravines and ridges was out of the question. So I returned to camp in heavy rain. With such dense clouds hiding all the mountain-tops, it was impossible to make out the lie of the land, but presumably the multitude of flowers round the tents was consistent with the belief that we were in "the valley of flowers", as the Thiapap valley has been called.

We had wisely chosen the camp-site very carefully, on the most prominent ridge available, uncomfortable enough, it is true, but, as far as we could make out through a curtain of mist, it was out of range of projectiles from the unknown glacier that lurked somewhere threateningly above our heads. During the night we appreciated the importance of this precaution, for in spite of our comparative security, we were frequently awakened by the thunder of avalanches, and in one instance the uproar was so terrific that we all came tumbling out of our tents in alarm in the middle of the night. It was a demoralizing situation, for, whether by day or by night it made no difference, the enemy was only audible, never visible. It seemed indeed as if all the surrounding mountains were on the move, giving us the disagreeable impression that we shared in this general impermanence.

The next two days were gloomy and uncomfortable, for we were held up where we were by the monsoon weather. Partridges appeared near the tents, and twittered at us in astonishment, till five of the imprudent birds were shot by the guides and added to the larder. As we wanted some fresh meat, two of the Bhotias were sent with six rupees to buy some mutton from the shepherds who, we heard, were somewhere down the valley beneath us, pasturing their flocks near the glacier. Our men eventually returned with a sheep and one rupee, so that the purchase cost six shillings and eight-pence. Subsequently the whole party of Bhotias spent most of the night singing round a smoky fire in the rain, in a state of exhilaration produced by fresh meat. Later they discovered a cave which was better shelter than the leaky tents. The shepherds, they reported, had come from Niti by the Bhyundar Khanta, and would now, by using the pass we had crossed—the Kulhia Khanta seemed the best name for it—be able to trade directly between Niti and Mana. Niti was even said to be only four sheep-marches from our camp, that is to say sixteen miles, a considerable understatement, as we afterwards found out.

Meanwhile snow had fallen as low as 15,000 feet, within a thousand feet of camp, and opposite, across the valley, it was still falling on the 22,000-foot peak of the mighty Parbat group, which was almost completely hidden in cold ghostly clouds. Below the Thiapap Glacier the lower reaches of the valley could be seen, bright green with grass and beautifully wooded. At one moment a patch of leaden-blue sky appeared in the south-west, over the Indian plains. The mountains on the near side of the blue were an angry purple, and above them floated heavy cumulus clouds. In addition to the ice-avalanches caused by the mild temperature of the monsoon season, rock-avalanches were constantly roaring and thundering, everywhere set in motion by the copious rain. The rain had also found its way under the kitchen awning, and the boulders which formed the fire-place had begun to drip in the most inconvenient and unexpected places. Underneath the hearth-stone a brisk little brook was bubbling cheerfully, and the whole of the kitchen enclosure was a swamp. The cold and damp were chilling for those who had suffered recently from frostbitten toes. Moreover the fire smoked abominably.

During the second night of our detention it poured incessantly. For the last four days indeed there had been scarcely any intermission. Finally, on the 21st, judging that the situation had become intolerable, we decamped and descended two thousand feet, through flowers and juniper bushes, or knee-deep in the soaking grass, till we reached the moraine of the Thiapap Glacier. There we camped opposite the influx of a big tributary glacier coming from the base of the western precipices of Hathi Parbat. We were now on the Bhyundar Khanta sheep-track, which here diverged from the glacier in order to rejoin it later, farther up its course. Here, even more than elsewhere, the hugeness of the scale was overwhelming; even the moraine loomed above one like a mountain. Juniper was abundant, and emptying the water from our boots we made an immense fire for drying tents and clothes.

The rain was actually stopping at last. Beds of juniper were laid underneath the tents, and, as night came on, the moon appeared in a cloudless sky. Too often this Thiapap valley is packed with cloud, for it draws the monsoon currents right up it, and deflects them to some extent from the neighbouring valley of the Ganges. Consequently the Thiapap valley is rich in woods and pastures, but above all in the prodigious luxuriance of its flowers.*

Glaciers in this country are extensively covered with stones. On the Bhagat Kharak, for instance, we walked for hours over stones of every variety of dimension, from the size of a pea to that of a cottage. It was curious to see that in many places a surface of grass had grown over the stones underneath which the ice lay hidden. The lateral moraines were often well covered with grass or juniper, and between moraine and mountain-side there were often sheltered grassy plateaux which formed convenient camp-sites.

The morning of the 24th of July was the first day since the 18th that had been sunny enough to dry the tents and bedding.

---

* See F. S. Smythe's *Valley of Flowers*. (Hodder & Stoughton.)

While I sat luxuriously on a circular air-cushion on the ground, with my back against the conveniently sloping outer wall of a Whymper tent, in a position that is as ideally comfortable as is possible anywhere, I tied up a damaged finger for Narain. Like Bonia he was a handsome youth, who seldom spoke to us or to his fellow-clansmen, and as I attended to him he watched me with his usual air of sleepy scornful indifference. As is the case with many Bhotias, his smooth slender features had something of feminine charm which belied the toughness and robustness of his character and constitution.

In the inhabited parts of Kumaun and Garhwal the doctoring of the country-people is an important part of a traveller's obligations. Many of the sick are obstinately determined to consult a white man, however ignorant of medical science he may be. They often have more confidence in an untried European than in one of their properly qualified Indian practitioners. Sometimes a villager would even seek advice for an absent friend who was either too ill or too busy to apply personally, but I was always obliged to draw the line at prescribing in a language of which I was sadly ignorant, for a patient I had never seen, who was probably suffering from some disease I had never heard of.

Some of the patients used to puzzle me a good deal at first, for they would proudly bare their stomachs to exhibit terrible scars, sometimes only partly healed, and at first I assumed that these must be the ravages of some unheard-of skin disease. Later I discovered that the trouble they were complaining of was *inside*, and that these strange external phenomena were merely the ghastly results of the ruthless cautery that was the favourite remedy for most illnesses. Once I came across the operation in actual progress by the roadside. An unfortunate victim of dysentery or cholera lay on his back on the ground with stomach exposed, while a friend crouched over him, industriously puffing at a piece of red-hot charcoal placed on the naked skin.

While Narain was being disposed of the guides were organizing a gymkhana, and two teams were chosen for a tug-of-war. A brisk altercation soon ensued, and I eagerly took part in it. It is curious that after a long stay at high levels the temptation to join in any quarrel should be so irresistible. Later in the evening peaceful darkness brought the proceedings to a close, and while the shadows grew and spread from the depths of the valley, the peaks on either side became slate-black against the fading light. High on a few hill-sides the green of the forests still shone in the setting sun, and a brilliant rainbow mingled with the cloud-girt ice-cliffs of the great hanging glacier on the Parbats. When the highest clouds parted for an instant, a glorious rock-pinnacle emerged far up in the sky, amazing us with its unearthliness.

As night drew on, the Bhotias sat chanting in a circle round their roaring fire of juniper-wood, and the moon came out from behind the dark mountain above us, shedding its soft light on the monsoon-mists that floated gently up the valley. The songs droned on with a fascinating and hypnotic mono-tony; they seemed to have no end and no beginning. Some were prayers for a successful passage over the Bhyunder Khanta, while others were odes celebrating the feats of mountain-travellers in the past. From time to time one man sang a monologue, and was answered by the rest in chorus. As I lay in my sleeping-bag, this music that seemed to me so exquisite, just a lot of men singing through their noses, went on long into the night, and lulled me into a blissful sleep.

On the morning of the 23rd of July it was pouring with rain once more, but the Bhotias, on being asked whether they would like to try the Bhyundar Khanta, all voted for making the attempt at once, and so keen were they that as soon as we had started, they began to set the pace. Always good-humoured, they were specially so at the moment, and promised that they would dance for us on their arrival at Niti, for they said there was a good *maidan* there.

Setting a course for the pass, we ascended the true right bank of the Thiapap Glacier, and soon crossed a big tributary glacier coming in from the north. Some easy broad rock-gullies brought us out above overhanging cliffs. We then traversed southwards, skirting the brink of the cliffs till we were close to the beautiful Thiapap ice-fall, and here we breakfasted in the sun. A stream poured over some purple rocks, and there were myriads of primulas. The air was fragrant with flowers. Behind us farther down the valley was a magnificent little peak of 18,000 feet. Peaks of this height count as small in the Himalaya. Tourists in Switzer-land sometimes ask incredulously whether Himalayan moun-tains really look bigger than the Alps. There can be no doubt that they do; nor is the fact surprising when it is considered that the Himalayan range rises to such much greater heights, not only above sea-level, but also above the snow-line. It must be remembered that in the Alps, as a rule, a mountain rarely looks thoroughly big unless it reaches a height of 12,000 feet, and that the highest Alpine peaks—excepting only Mont Blanc and Monte Rosa—never exceed this altitude by more than about 2,000 feet. In the Himalaya, on the other hand, a peak need only be 20,000 feet to seem gigantic and there are many well-known Himalayan summits that exceed this elevation by heights varying between five and nine thousand feet. The difference in scale, therefore, between the two ranges is enormous, and it is not surprising that the Himalayan giants give an overwhelming impression of boundless immensity.

The final ascent to the Bhyundar Pass, 16,000 feet above sea-level, was a long plod over soft snow under a blazing sun. From the top there was an impressive view of the great rock-peak, Rataban, 20,000 feet, with a massive cupola of snow and ice, that gave it some resemblance to the Zermatt Breithorn.

We were glad to have escaped from the Thiapap valley. Although it was warm and beautiful, it was too full of monsoon clouds. It was easy to see from the vantage-ground of the pass how the great height of these mountains detains the monsoon on the Indian side of the range, and prevents it from affecting the climate of Tibet. One could also observe how the passes let the bad weather through from valley to valley, for the clouds could be seen trying to creep through the gap in which we stood. Obviously the monsoon had not yet penetrated thoroughly, for the mountains towards Niti and Tibet were still free from the fresh snow that was so conspicuous on the heights from which we had come. The landscape, too, towards Tibet had a different appearance, for it was much more arid, and its outlines were much more rounded. On the Niti side of the pass the gorgeous flora which we had admired on the western slopes no longer prevailed.

The descent eastwards was a tedious tramp over the dreary brown waste of stones covering the Gal Glacier. At first we roped, but soon we were able to avoid the glacier by descending the moraine at its side. Below the glacier a good deal of jumping from boulder to boulder had to be done in order to cross a torrent that flowed down from a side-valley. The heavily laden Bhotias insisted on following us reckless of the risk of drowning, till Pierre headed them off to a better crossing-place. We passed the night at Thur Udiar, a good camping-ground only six miles from the village of Ghamsali, which is in the valley of the Dhaoli, and is an easy day's march from Niti.

With our arrival at Niti, the crossing from Mana over the Kulhia and Bhyundar passes was completed. Probably the whole journey—granted fine weather—might have been done in three days of energetic travelling. The only difficulty on the way had been due to the monsoon. Our Mana Bhotias were therefore triumphant, and the tribesmen at Niti gave them the welcome that they expected. They danced and sang, and ate and drank to their hearts' content, for they were honoured guests and their adventure had been crowned with success.

A PILGRIMAGE TO KAMET*

I—THE FOOT-HILLS

It was on the eve of the Great War, and I was making my third voyage to India to attempt the ascent of Kamet, the Himalayan peak on the Tibetan border of British Garhwal, 25,450 feet above the sea, and at that date unclimbed.

On April the 12th, at three o'clock in the morning, I suddenly awoke with the sensation of lying in a warm bath. The darkness was profound, but, just outside the cabin, a deafening clamour of Hindu mail-sorters throwing mail-bags about the deck signified that the P. & O. liner in which my guide Pierre Blanc and myself had been travelling, was at the end of its journey, and at anchor off the port of Bombay. The oppressive dampness of the heat, and the noises of our arrival made further sleep impossible, the lethargy induced by the sea-voyage began to disappear, and we hastened to go on board the tender that was to take us ashore.

I suppose I was already elated at approaching the Himalaya, the object of our pilgrimage, perhaps I was beginning to experience what—to borrow from the terminology of religious conversion—I can only describe as a change of heart. It is the change created by the double spell of those two most potent magics, the snow-mountains and the East. A mountaineer who has experienced the delights of this metamorphosis, so subtle and yet so profound, keeps an undying longing to recapture the happiness that it brings. I think that most of those who

* See sketch map on page 165.

189

have been fortunate enough to pay more than one visit to the mountains of Asia will know what I mean.

I might compare this mental state with a condition, possibly more common, in which the intensity of the feeling induced is rather similar. Proust has described this condition as a sudden exhilarating uprush of intuitive happiness, brought about as a rule by a chance combination of trivial circumstances. In his view these circumstances evoke memories that have been dormant since early childhood, a time of life when the capacity for happiness is at its highest. From the similar intensity of the mountain-lover's bliss we may perhaps infer that in him this capacity, instead of becoming atrophied in childhood, has been prolonged into adult life, and that he is not therefore under the necessity of fishing for his happiness in the reservoirs of his infancy, but can derive it from a source that is always available.

Another experience, too, invites comparison with the mountain-lover's in respect of the peculiar kind of felicity that it excites; I refer to mystical experience. There is, however, this difference; that the great mystics believe themselves to enter into direct communion with the absolute itself, while to the mountain-lover the sense of communion is not as a rule direct.

It will perhaps be objected that the material aims of an expedition aspiring to break records by ascending an unclimbed peak higher than any that had been previously conquered, accords ill with the sort of spiritual frame of mind that I have ventured to lay claim to. On the other hand if we consider that thought possesses no vitality until it has been welded into action, and that philosophers find an ever-increasing difficulty in dissociating the material from the spiritual, I may well be allowed a little common thread on which to string the pearls of experience.

Photo: C. F. Meade

APPROACHING THE KHAIAM SADDLE IN 1910
Our first sight of Kamet

But these reflections are by the way. There was no time for them in Bombay, where much shopping had to be done, and, as our train was to leave at nine-thirty that night, we dined early under the whirring fans of the tranquil and spacious Taj Mahal Hotel. By contrast, the immense, dimly lit Colaba railway terminus seemed an inferno, for it was seething with heat, turmoil, uproar, and palpitating with all the excitements of oriental travel. We had to thread our way in semi-darkness across acres of platform, through countless Indians, either patiently encamped amid piles of luggage, or else surging in hordes towards the trains. One man I noticed squatting on the ground with a smart new gladstone-bag on his lap; suddenly he rose to his feet, extracted from the bag a pair of trousers, and put them on with an air of great composure before climbing up into his railway-carriage.

Pierre and I were lucky in securing a compartment with a bucket of ice to ourselves, and as we travelled through the night, the suffocating mugginess of Bombay gave place to the scorching heat of the Indian plains. So fierce was it that in the early morning the hot blast of air coming in through the open window caused Pierre to wake in panic under the impression that the train was on fire. As we passed Muttra, the thermometer registered 113 degrees Fahrenheit in the shade, and it was strange to reflect that within a very few weeks we should probably be experiencing temperatures below zero.

Eventually, shortly before eleven o'clock on the third morning after leaving Bombay, the train from Agra began to toil up the incline, where the Indian plain slopes gently upward, as it approaches the foot-hills of the Himalaya. The little railway terminus of Kathgodam lies at the base of the range, which stands up with the startling abruptness of a wall. The slower snorting of the engine indicated that the

smooth surface of the plain which we had so long been crossing was no longer level, and as we gazed through the carriage
window at the distant blue wall, it gradually took shape as a
dramatically steep barrier of wooded foot-hills.

It must be admitted that in travelling out to the Alps from
England there is a certain amount of disappointment, for at
no particular moment can the mountains be said to begin;
one reaches them by imperceptible degrees. In the central
Himalaya, on the other hand, the foot-hills rise from the
plains with a suddenness that takes one's breath away. In
the Alps only the approach across the Piedmontese plain gives
such an impression of startling abruptness.

At the foot of this barrier, then, we got out of the train to
prepare for the forty-nine-mile drive up to Ranikhet, the
hill-station from which the march on foot was to begin. The
air was filled with the fragrance of flowering trees. Wild
peaches were in bloom, and crimson rhododendron-trees
covered the hill-sides, everywhere shedding their petals, so
that the ground in the shade glowed with the colour of rubies.
It was a pleasure to see the gradually increasing number of
pine-trees, with their suggestion of the nearness of high
mountains. Presently we broke the long tonga-drive by
stopping at an hotel, half-way up the mountain-road to Ranikhet. The tonga, it should be explained, was the predecessor
of the motor-car in these hills, and was a dog-cart usually
pulled by a pair of wizened ponies, yoked to a pole. The
seats were hard and the ponies galloped, so that the jerking
and jangling of the motion often caused minute fragments of
the steel from the pole to fly into one's eyes. A few hours
in a tonga generally sufficed to give one an aching behind,
as well as most of the symptoms of a congested liver.

At Ranikhet we lodged in the dak-bungalow. Dak-
bungalows or rest-houses usually consist of two or three

living-rooms each containing chairs, a table and a bedstead, with windows and doors opening on to a verandah. Tin baths are to be found in grim little cells at the back of the building. The bungalow at Ranikhet was 5,000 feet above the sea, with a smooth green lawn in front, and surrounded by steep pine-clad slopes. A river ran 2,000 feet below, and, opposite, across the valley, stretched a range of foot-hills, 7,000 or 8,000 feet high. A temperature of only 69 degrees Fahrenheit seemed refreshingly cool after the experiences in the train.

A curious characteristic of these foot-hills is the bewildering difficulty of the topography. The details of the landscape are vague and complicated, so that it is often puzzling to keep any notion of the courses of the rivers or the whereabouts of the passes. Anyone who is familiar with the Alps will notice that the scale of the country in the foot-hills is distinctly Himalayan in character. The hill-tops, although they are mostly wooded, are high enough to be considered mountains rather than hills from a European point of view, and the valleys seem more spacious than in the Alps.

As is usual at this time of year, there was much dust-haze, and smoke from forest fires often concealed the distance. On every side sounded the weird twittering cry of kites, but perhaps the most characteristic note in these wildernesses is the uncannily mechanical call of a species of cuckoo. He has four different notes which he repeats without any variation in the same sequence, day and night. The words "I am fed up, I am fed up" are supposed to represent his endless refrain, and have earned him the name of the fed-up bird.

There is a prevailing air of sadness in the scenery here that is in keeping with the melancholy crying of the birds; in spite of the unlimited forests, the country before the coming of the rains has a parched appearance, streams are rare, there is little grass, and even the aromatic scent of the pines seems stifling.

The immediate neighbourhood of Ranikhet could, I suppose, be described by an estate-agent as residential; well-kept paths wind in and out among attractive-looking private bungalows, buried in woods, yet there is a quality of smugness in these half-tamed jungles, and the dusty hot-weather atmosphere is totally lacking in the exhilarating sparkle of Alpine air. It is owing to the contrast that it affords with the stifling hot weather of the plains rather than to any other merit that the summer climate of the hill-stations is so popular. Ranikhet is as high as Zermatt, but there can be no comparison between the two climates. Nevertheless the monotonous and melancholy beauty of the foot-hills is leavened by the proximity of the greatest mountain-range in the world. From the arid forests above Ranikhet, the pilgrim on his way to the sacred sources of the Ganges can refresh himself with a nearer view of the home of the Gods than he can get from the plains. Above Ranikhet on a clear day a vast panorama of snows is visible, culminating in the gigantic twin summits of Nanda Devi, and the superb ice-peak of Trisul.

Hindus have always recognized the divine attributes of mountains. For thousands of years Nanda Devi, the destroyer Goddess and Trisul, the trident of Siva, have been venerated by countless pilgrims, toiling slowly on their endless marches up the footpath along the holy Ganges to where the sources of the river issue from the eternal ice in the home of the Gods. It was near our destination in these mountains that the Hindu God, Badrinath withdrew himself finally from the world in his search for Paradise, when his quest came to a triumphal end in the high valleys of Garhwal. Perhaps the modern mountaineer in his explorations can claim to be a fellow pilgrim seeking the same goal.

At Ranikhet we had spent several days examining stores and repacking them, for from this point the journey on foot began. Captain Slingsby, who was carrying out another of his attempts on Kamet, was also staying here and making up loads for his party. We had several talks together, and I tried in vain to convince him that the west side, which he proposed to attack once more, was impossible, as Eastern Ibi Gamin, a neighbouring peak of 24,000 feet would cut him off from the summit of Kamet.

On the day after our arrival a party of half a dozen Garhwalis who had served us as permanent coolies in previous years marched up to the bungalow. With affable smiles and hands politely clasped, they demanded to be engaged at once, and graciously promised to ascend to the very summit of Kamet with us, provided we would immediately give them boots, stockings, puttees and sweaters. As a matter of fact trousers struck me as their more urgent need, but in any case I did not expect that they would accompany us very far, for, from a mountaineering point of view, Garhwalis can only be said to be a good deal better than Kumaunis, and that is not saying much. However, when we told them that we should promise them nothing at all, but that they could come on the daily pay-roll for the time being if they liked, they all seemed delighted. The fact is that Bhotias are the only inhabitants of the country that are worth engaging for mountaineering, and they are in a class by themselves.

Shortly after the arrival of the Garhwalis there turned up to our great satisfaction a party of the Bhotias themselves. One can feel nothing but admiration for these men. They are as hard as nails, good-natured, energetic and always laughing. It is true, however, that their fondness for tobacco is almost a failing, and—when they can get it—they show an inordinate enthusiasm for strong drink. The government allows them to distil their own spirits, but I never succeeded in drinking any, because one sniff at the bottle was always enough to give me too vivid an idea of what the taste must be. The Bhotias' craving for tobacco is sometimes a trial, since prolonged halts are necessary to allow them to indulge in it. The stuff is lit in a hole in the ground, and a tiny tunnel is ingeniously constructed through which the whole party in turns inhale clouds of pungent smoke in a series of spluttering gasps. The process seems to refresh them, and until it is completed it is difficult to get them to go on again.

The appearance of the men is most picturesque; their black, well-combed hair is worn long to the shoulders, and the small bright scarlet forage-caps are a pleasant contrast to the drab colour of the sackcloth frock-coats and drawers. The features of the Bhotias are obviously Mongolian, and their complexions are of a light copper shade, often fairer than those of southern Europeans. The women are frequently pretty. The men lead a nomadic existence, being occupied all the summer in trading across the immensely high passes into Tibet, and carrying their merchandise on the backs of great herds of sheep and goats. They are afraid of the heat, and don't usually venture so far down as the Indian hill-stations, except in winter.

At last on May the 1st we got off on the first stage of the hundred miles or so that was to be done on foot to the frontier of Tibet. We now heard no longer the characteristic twittering of kites, but were soothed by the monotonous cooing of innumerable wood-pigeons inhabiting the sun-warmed pine-forest through which we passed. In the limpid atmosphere of a fine day the village of Almora, twenty miles away, looked deceptively close. Before our enchanted eyes, as we followed the path through the trees, there appeared an incredible portent, the mighty ice-peak of Trisul, apparently floating

Photo: C. F. Meade

KAMET FROM THE KHAIAM SADDLE, 1910
The small peak on the left is Eastern Ibi Gamin

in the sky. The dust-haze, banked below the eternal snows, had the same grey-blue tint as the sky above, so that the great mountain seemed like some phantom ice-island poised in space, utterly cut off from the world of men.

The boundless wilderness of foot-hills was mostly burnt brown by the sun, except where the forests covered a carpet of pine-needles. As it was the dry season, there was a depressing absence of springs or running water. Ever up and down, the path led along or across the wooded ridges, plunging into valleys, and climbing through forests, to cross into further valleys beyond. All the time the vision of Trisul remained motionless in the heavens, never changing a single line or shadow of its mirage-like beauty. As we approached the bungalow of Mujkhali, where we were to spend the night, our thirsty eyes were refreshed by the sight of a tiny trickle of water flowing down to join the parched river. In a pool, so small that it seemed scarcely more than a puddle, a dark object projected. It moved and I saw it was the snout of a village buffalo enjoying its siesta under water, with only its nostrils exposed to the air. On the verandah that evening Pierre sat and mended his boots, with the squirrel eyes of all the Bhotias fixed intently upon his every movement. Rooks raised their evening clamour, and I wrote my diary with a towel over my head to keep off flies.

It was our third visit to the Himalaya, and it was evident that Pierre had completely won the hearts of the Bhotias. Even in their speciality of cragsmanship they recognized him as a master, and they always obeyed him instantly in everything he wanted them to do. Perhaps, indeed, some men are born to influence others, and this may explain why, long after the only two watches that we had with us on the expedition had completely lost touch with the correct time, it was always by Pierre's watch that I set my own.

As we now flattered ourselves that we were old travellers, we derived a smug satisfaction from practising various tips and wrinkles we had learnt from previous experience. All the loads, for instance, were not only conspicuously numbered in large figures, but in the case of boxes these numbers were marked on each of the six faces, so that when the loads were stacked in a heap, it was quite easy to read the numbers at a glance. Loads were also painted different colours, as an indication of their contents; petrol and paraffin were scarlet, groceries yellow, altitude equipment blue, and the various cases containing the cash, in bags of rupees, were black. Each of us carried a master-key for the cases, and an index of their contents.

Our head-man was Alam Singh. He was the most distinguished-looking of all his fellow-tribesmen, and his appearance fulfilled my idea of a cross between an Italian nobleman and a Red Indian. It was an act of considerable courage on Alam Singh's part when, at the end of our journey in 1912, he ventured to come as far as Bombay to sample the horrors of civilization. Motor-cars, the ships in the harbour, and the lift in the hotel may have caused him as much surprise as his unusual appearance certainly did to the sophisticated inhabitants of Bombay. But if he did feel much astonishment, he was too dignified to show it.

Alam's versatility was most remarkable, whether on the march or in camp, or as valet, cook, butler, Alpine porter, or general manager. When we started in the morning, usually not later than dawn, it was he who saw to it that each coolie-load was accompanied by a ticket, with a corresponding number on it. On arriving in camp each coolie would then hand over his load, give up his ticket and receive his pay. Owing to this method, the men knew that they would not be kept waiting for the arrival of loitering comrades, but would each be paid instantly at the end of the march. Consequently there was no inclination to waste more time than was necessary on the way. The tickets we manufactured at Ranikhet by cutting up biscuit-tins into squares and punching the numbers on them by means of a hammer and nail.

Another device for securing comfortable travelling conditions was to employ two privileged porters to accompany us with light loads, usually ahead of the coolies, so that when the camping-ground was reached, a change of shirt was available, and a small awning was put up, under which food could be heated over a fire. In this way we avoided the tedium of waiting in pouring rain or blazing sun for dilatory coolies to arrive with long-expected food and tents. We also found it advisable to expedite the arrival of the more essential requirements by dividing up as far as possible such urgently needed loads as tents, in order to make them lighter to carry. It was obvious that the prompt arrival of one's personal luggage was not of much use without a tent being available to unpack it in.

In the matter of cookery, too, we had our own system. Camp cooks, like camp interpreters, even if not allowed to do marketing, may be ruinously corrupt and oppressive in their dealings with the people of the country, and may have a disastrous effect on an expedition. A case in point was the story of a party of explorers who were ascending one of the greater Himalayan glaciers with a long and imposing procession of their innumerable camp-followers, while on the opposite side of the same glacier, within the hollow formed between the ice and the lateral moraine, a steady, but less conspicuous stream of porters carried away the choicer goods of the expeditionary force for the disposal of the head-man and his friends.

In our own case, rather than engage some unknown cook from the bazaar, we taught two of the Bhotias the simple cooking that we required, and the arrangement was most satisfactory. As Bhotias do not attach excessive importance to etiquette or caste distinctions, it was always possible to sit over the camp-fire with them, and supervise their efforts. I noticed that when the cooking was done by these men, the health of the party was always excellent. Diarrhœa, that can be such a curse in the hills, never troubled us at all, except when we employed job-cooks whose caste restrictions kept us from interfering with their methods. The only explanation that seems likely is that hill diarrhœa is due to some infection produced by careless or dirty cooking above a certain altitude. At any rate the disease, if taken in time, seems to be curable, either by descending to the plains, or else by eliminating the professional cook.

In dak-bungalows, also, it is as well to be cautious about the food. Curry has been praised from a medical point of view for its power of stimulating appetites that are jaded by life in the tropics, but it is also well to remember that from the dak-bungalow cook's point of view curry is a most effective disguise for stale meat.

The third march from Ranikhet took us from Sameswar to the tea-estate of the Troup brothers at Kausanie. Beyond Sameswar the hill-sides were covered with forests of the magnificent *Pinus longifolius*, which the government were doing their utmost to preserve. Old residents, however, regarded the forest policy of the government with misgivings. Formerly villagers were allowed to burn the undergrowth, and did so, freely, every year. Recently, however, the government had penalized the burning with the idea of preserving the timber and inaugurating local industries. Critics declared that the old system of frequent periodic burning gave perfect satisfaction because it allowed grass to grow under the trees for the village cattle, and was not drastic enough to destroy the tree-seeds. The new system was alleged to be disastrous on two grounds: firstly, that it deprived the peasant of a right that he had always valued, and secondly, that when after a long interval forest fires broke out accidentally, the destruction of trees that had not been subjected to yearly burning was often disastrously complete. In the past, no doubt, scientific innovations introduced by a paternal government have not always produced the results that were anticipated. The native plough, for instance, was a small wooden implement that merely scratched the soil. On the initiative of a paternal government, deep-working modern ploughs were introduced into the hills for the edification of the peasants, but with disconcerting results. The modern implements cut up the land so effectually that when the trains came, the soil was washed bodily off the steep hill-sides, and nothing but stones remained.

The dak-bungalow at Sameswar is only 4,000 feet above sea-level. We set out from it in the early morning, and followed the cart-track leading to the head of the valley in order to reach the ridge on which Kausanie is situated. The river was reduced to a mere trickle this year, and there were no big fish left in it; in the fields the reapers were already gathering the ears from the corn, leaving the stalks standing, so that cattle could be turned in to graze. Ahead of us up the valley lay terrace on terrace of rice-field and corn-field, streaks of mellow colour, green and gold, hazy in the softness of the summer morning light. Finally, coming to the head of the valley, we climbed through armies of rhododendron trees to the depression or pass in the wooded ridge from which the Troup bungalow confronts the snows of Kumaun and Nepal.

II—THE SNOWS

At this point of the journey, on Kausanie ridge, 7,000 feet above the sea, the first phase of the approach to the snows may be said to end, for at last we had finished with the foot-hills. Indeed we were standing at the actual threshold of the great peaks, for it is at Kausanie that the first near view of the prodigious Nanda Devi group bursts on the traveller with dramatic splendour. Through the trees we now gazed down into the depths of another valley, new to us, built on a vast scale and containing a maze of minor hills, laced with a silvery network of rivers entangled in sombre masses of dense forest. Across the uneven floor of this great valley there rippled a myriad of cultivated terraces, and the whole richly variegated expanse lay like a softly tinted map at our feet. And yet, for the moment, we could have no eyes for the glory of that valley, for there, before us, dominating every-thing else, and drawing the attention irresistibly, rose the great Hindu Goddess, Nanda Devi herself,* crowned with glittering ice. On her right was Trisul, and on her left the eternal snows stretched into the far distance. The beauty of the names rang in our ears. Nanda Devi, the destroyer Goddess, Trisul, the trident of Siva, Panch Chuli, the five fires, Nanda Kot of the perfect shape, with the mysterious Api and Nampa, almost lost in the distance of unknown Nepal.

The valley, indeed, seemed a symbol in miniature of the whole world, containing apparently a universal variety of things: rivers, forests, fields, villages and hills. In the fore-ground the tall flowering rhododendron-trees and pines, beyond them the great depth and breadth of the valley, backed by double and triple ranges of blue foot-hills culmin-

* Nanda Devi is 25,645 feet and is the highest peak in the Empire.

ating in the supreme splendour of the snows. In spite of the
majesty of the peaks and the vastness of the valley, there was
none of that savagery of desolation that for some people
mars the beauty of many Himalayan landscapes. Kumaun
and Garhwal in this respect resemble the more thickly wooded
scenery in the high Alps. Comparison with the Alps is
inevitable, but comparison can only emphasize the difference
in scale. After my last visit to Kausanie, with a vivid recol-
lection of its never-to-be-forgotten view, I travelled directly
from India to Switzerland, visiting Riederalp to look at the
Weisshorn and the Matterhorn. To me, fresh from the
experience at Kausanie, these imposing Alpine giants seemed
to have diminished in stature, dwarfed as they were by
comparison with the mighty Nanda Devi group.

Size in mountains is certainly not a quality to disparage.
Some critics may prefer their mountains small, but they are
by no means justified in depreciating what they sometimes
refer to as "mere size". Mere size, on the contrary, can
have a considerable æsthetic value. Admittedly British
mountains do contrive to produce a remarkable impression
of size, in spite of their different order of magnitude. Nevertheless a visit to Himalayan peaks ought to convince us that
the far greater scale of these giants is more than proportionately
effective. The advantage of size is that when a traveller who
is only familiar with smaller mountains comes to the Himalaya,
he is swept off his feet, so that he tends to look upon Himalayan
heights and depths as utterly immeasurable, symbols in fact
of infinity, and æsthetically considered, it is as a symbol of
infinity that Himalayan magnitude has its value.

As we stared and stared, bewildered by the grandeur of
the scene, we noticed that to leeward of the summits of all
the great peaks white streamers were showing against the
blue sky, proof that hurricanes were raging along the heights,

and tearing the snow from them in clouds. And yet here below it seemed a perfect summer day, the air was clear as crystal, and every detail of those superb shapes shone with that cold, hard, merciless radiance that is so impossible to paint and so enchanting to behold.

The urgency of absorbing what one could of so much beauty was almost oppressive. There was a primer of Himalayan geology in my luggage, but it always remained unopened. In the paradise of the Gods geology seemed a desecration. Face to face with Nanda Devi, who would dare to look at her teeth or ask her her age?

Along this wonderful ridge a level path led us for a quarter of a mile to Messrs. Troup's bungalow. In so remote a wilderness, it was a surprise, on turning a corner, to come upon a venerable, white-haired Englishman, resting on a garden-seat, and peacefully contemplating the view. It was Captain Colin Troup, Mutiny veteran, and hospitable joint owner, with his brother, of the Kausanie tea-estate. A few yards farther along the ridge, snugly situated amid smooth lawns and brilliant flower-beds, stood the bungalow with its broad verandahs commanding the same majestic panorama that we had been admiring. Indoors there prevailed the perfection of civilization and comfort under the auspices of the magnificent old grey-bearded Mahomedan butler, an impressive model of the most dignified deportment imaginable, but cruelly handicapped in my estimation by the fact that Captain Troup persistently referred to him as "Cock-robin".

The Kausanie estate was peculiar in one respect, for the tea grown on it was the China variety. To me, who had never tasted China tea in the country of its origin, it tasted better than anything I had ever drunk. Unfortunately after it had been cultivated for fifty years or so, the growers

Photo : C. F. Meade

KAMET FROM THE GHASTOLE GLACIER, 1912

began to discover that the plants were gradually deteriorating, and the enterprise was eventually abandoned.

Captain Troup's courtesy to a guest was so considerate that he even apologized for inflicting on me—so he expressed it—"such a quantity of old stories about the Mutiny". It would probably have gratified the late Lord Kitchener to have known what pleasure an army-order of his had once given to this old gentleman living in so remote and lonely a district. Captain Troup, who was a highlander, told me that suddenly, one morning, at Kausanie, he heard the music of the pipes coming nearer and nearer to the bungalow. Scarcely believing his ears, he hurried out and found to his astonishment a company of a Scotch regiment at his front-door. The officer in command explained that, being on a route-march, he had brought his men to call, for, by Lord Kitchener's army-order, any military unit that happened to be in the neighbourhood of a Mutiny veteran was to make a point of at once paying their respects. It can be imagined with what delight this hospitable old soldier entertained his unexpected guests.

After Kausanie the itinerary to Kamet passes through the tea-estate of Messrs. Nash at Gwaldam, and changes direction in order to circumvent the tangled mass of peaks and glaciers composing the Nanda Devi group and reach the head waters of the Ganges. The route eventually follows an eastern tributary stream, and terminates at a point beyond its source among the distant glaciers of the Tibetan frontier.

As we set off in the early morning, the pine-trees were dark against a white sunrise; already we heard the staccato shouts of the ploughmen urging on their little oxen; below us among the tree-tops there still lingered streaks of cool night-mist, almost as blue as wood-smoke. The air was fresh as water, and I drew deep draughts of it, before beginning the plunge into the stifling depths of the valley. We had to descend to the level of the river, past the village of Baijnath, and then in the afternoon climb for thousands of feet through the woods to Gwaldam. As we descended, I remembered how the previous year at Baijnath I had stopped to listen, fascinated by the singing of a row of women weeding in a field, accompanied by a man with a tom-tom walking up and down the line, bending over each individual in turn as she toiled, while he beat time to the work and led the singing.

Down by the river golden orioles were flitting in the thickets, and rocket-magpies with tails that reminded me of children's kites. At Gwaldam is the bungalow of the China tea-estate of the Nash brothers who entertained us with the hospitality that had made them so well known to travellers. The bungalow is in a perfect situation. It cannot be compared with the bungalow at Kausanie, because, although the view is in its way equally beautiful, there is not such an immensely wide panorama. The height above sea-level is about 7,000 feet, and there is a terrace of green lawn in front of the verandah, with flower-beds full of roses, petunias and sweet-peas. Rhododendron forest surrounds the garden, and below is the prodigiously deep gulf at the bottom of which are the rapids of the Pindari River. Soaring above tier on tier of towering forest-clad hills, and facing the verandah across the abyss of the river, the ice-peak of Trisul rises to a height of 23,000 feet. It is only fifteen miles distant, and between the level of the river and the summit there is a difference of 20,000 feet.

Tigers are rare as far up in the hills as at Gwaldam, but a wandering tiger is sometimes heard of. Before the Nashes had settled here, a party of natives was once following in single file the woodland path to the village. There had been rumours of a tiger in the neighbourhood, and the leader of the party was in the act of brandishing an axe, and explaining to his companions exactly what he intended to do to the animal if it should venture to show itself. The words were hardly out of his mouth, when a tiger jumped out at him from the bushes, seized him, axe and all, and ran off with him into the woods, disappearing as abruptly as it had come. Only a few of the man's bones were ever discovered.

In connection with tigers I remember a macabre fragment of conversation I once overheard in a rest-house. "Yes," said a voice from behind the thin partition of the next room, "the forest officer shot her; he sat up all night over the woman." The information, so tantalizing in its briefness, intrigued me, and I discovered afterwards that Kumaun had been infested with man-eating tigers owing to a tigress with the propensity having successfully instructed her children in her methods, and the last of these, a female, had been accounted for in the manner described. It is remarkable that the most notorious man-eater in Kumaun was a leopard, the celebrated man-eating leopard of Almora. It was credited with having killed more than a hundred and eighty men and women.

The most convincing tiger-story, however, was told me by my host. In the middle of a hot, sleepless night he suddenly heard the unmistakable snort of a tiger snuffing the air just outside the open window, and after daybreak he found the great pug-marks in the flower-beds. He was following them up, and had just discovered that the tiger must have made a complete tour of the house during the night, when his butler rushed up shouting that the brute was at that moment devouring the best buffalo from the compound, not a hundred yards away in the jungle. Without an instant's hesitation, and feeling nothing but the most reckless indignation, Nash snatched a loaded rifle from a rack in the hall, and dashed off in hot pursuit, crashing noisily through the undergrowth without the slightest feeling of apprehension. Suddenly, however, his heart stood still, and so did he. From the bushes close in front of him, invisible, but dreadfully menacing there came a low, long-drawn, blood-curdling snarl.

"Heavens," I exclaimed, "what did you do?"

"Well," replied Nash, "I started walking on tiptoe, *backwards*, as quickly and quietly as I could, and I never stopped till I got out of the jungle. I left that tiger alone with his buffalo, and never saw either of them again."

Leopards, unlike tigers were very common, and had even been shot from the verandah. Nash lamented that he had had to give up keeping dogs, as leopards always caught them sooner or later. One Scotch terrier, Jock, had been the only survivor, but only because he never strayed far from his master's side. Even this dog, however, had at least one narrow escape, for it had once raced on rather far along the garden path ahead of Nash, and the latter suddenly came round the corner to find the innocent creature enjoying a playful romp with a leopard. The romp might have ended badly if the dog's master had not been at hand.

At Gwaldam we were close to Kim's country, and were shortly to follow in the lama's steps when he travelled towards Badrinath and Kedarnath, the great peaks near the sources of the Ganges. This is a country where the miracle of Purun Bhagat would surprise nobody. A holy man appeared here on one occasion on his way from Badrinath village, wearing only a loin-cloth, and living on berries or food brought to him from time to time by villagers. He was well educated, and spoke excellent English. His father was a Calcutta school-master, and he had taken a degree in engineering. He explained that religious principles and dislike of sedition had driven him into the wilderness. He was willing to work for his keep in order to be able to stay in the hills, as only in the hills did he find contentment. Another fakir, the previous winter, used to sit stark naked, covered with snow-flakes, meditating in a trance, without noticing the food that admiring peasants brought him.

As I sat in the verandah of the bungalow, I listened to the choir of cicadas hissing in unison till their rhythm seemed a fever simmering in my blood. Cuckoos, too, were most persistent in the surrounding woods. There was the ordinary cuckoo, familiar in England, and another kind that I loved. This bird's deep gentle hooting on four short monotones made the woods throb with an enchanting melancholy. Another plaintive sound was the call of the fed-up bird. It was the last sound heard as one fell asleep, and as consciousness returned in the morning, there it was again. No doubt anyone who disliked this sort of country as fervently as I happened to delight in it, might be driven almost distracted by these incessantly repeated refrains.

In Nash's library I had found Sherring's book, and once more I read in it the Hindu text so comforting to the complacency of the Himalayan traveller:—

"He who thinks on Himachal, though he should not behold him, is greater than he who performs all worship in Kashi (Benares). And he who thinks of Himachal shall have pardon for all sins, and all things that die on Himachal, and all things that in dying think of his snows, are freed from sin. In a hundred ages of the Gods I could not tell thee of the glories of Himachal, where Siva lived, and where the Ganges falls from the foot of Vishnu, like the slender thread of a lotus flower."

The sun was setting, and I shut the book in order to watch Trisul emerging from layers of tranquil cloud. Slowly the snows became crimson in the after-glow. The forest grew bluer and darker as night came on, and as I waited for the tremendous spectacle to end I counted five tiers of ridges, and watched while each in turn was plunged in darkness, till one isolated golden pinnacle on the final ice-ridge remained alone in the sky, and then in its turn faded from my view. Later, the constant calling of the fed-up bird drugged me to sleep.

III—THE INNER SNOWS

The departure from Gwaldam marked the beginning of the third phase in our pilgrimage, the journey through the remote region of the inner snows, which equal the outer range in magnificence, but lie behind it so that they are invisible from the Indian plain. The first stage of the journey was a flanking march along the west side of Trisul. From the verandah at Gwaldam there had been ample opportunity for studying the route through glasses, for it led straight up a hanging valley exactly opposite the bungalow, and only divided from it by the profound gulf in which flowed the Pindari River. The hanging valley was covered with countless miles of rhododendron forest, and descended steeply from a wooded pass about 10,000 feet above sea-level, to empty its river into the rapids of the Pindari, 4,000 feet below the verandah.

At a careless glance, a mountaineer with experience limited to European ranges might have allowed no more than a good day's march for reaching the pass. In point of fact, no less than three camps were required, and the allowance was by no means excessive. The landscape was indeed everywhere so vast that it was difficult to judge distances. Even the sort of ravine that in the Alps might be expected to be of bridgeable size, may in the Himalaya necessitate more than an hour's détour over some steep and stony path.

As usual our departure took place at dawn. On the second

day's march up the hanging valley we camped at Loajan, a delightful site, a high grassy promontory, lying at right-angles across the valley, with a flat top commanding a magnificent view southwards towards the plains of India. Eastwards a heavily forested glen soared towards the snows of Eastern Trisul. Towards India we could look back to Kausanie, nestling on the shoulder of a foot-hill of 11,000 feet. West of us was a great hill—in such a country it cannot be called a mountain—known as Dunghia Bokhial (pronounced Bokiawl), a fine pasturage for sheep. Even accustomed as I now was to Himalayan standards, it was a surprise to learn that the summit of this pasturage exceeded 13,000 feet.

On a little shelf in the hill-side, a few feet below the level of the table-land on which we were established, the Bhotias' tent was pitched. In the evening Alam Singh stalked up and down the terrace above his followers, or stood sentinel over them, as Pierre said, much as an old buck-chamois might guard his does. All night the eerie crying of the fed-up bird resounded through the boundless wilderness of rhododendron forests.

In the morning the more active among the new coolies made a dash as usual to seize the smallest loads. This was a tragi-comedy that always ended in the bitterest disillusionment, for the smaller loads being made of tightly packed jam-tins, were much the heaviest to carry. On this occasion Alam Singh soon restored order, and we set out on one of the pleasantest marches of the journey, to an ideal camp-site at Wan. Here the tents were pitched on a natural lawn under the shade of giant cypresses, at the head of a valley, about 8,000 feet above the sea, and at the foot of the final ascent to the wooded pass that we had scrutinized from the far-off verandah at Gwaldam. Hitherto occasional thunder-showers, and the practice of rigorously shutting up the tents during the day had afforded us the only escape from flies, but now we were at an altitude where flies were becoming scarce. In the woods were brilliant scarlet birds, as decorative as goldfish, and in shape partly finch, partly swallow, with dark wings, heads and backs. I was also delighted to hear the pathetically monotonous little song of the Tibetan ruby-throat, with its six staccato notes in a minor key sung in a descending scale, and reminding one of a very small and rather sad child trying to whistle through its teeth. I had previously only heard it at Mana, a village more than 11,000 feet above the sea, and comparatively close to Tibet.

All that evening the camp was crowded with villagers, needing medicine or medical advice. One old man who complained of illness and begged for medicine to cure it, subsequently invented more illnesses in order to get more drugs. When the medicine gave out, however, he was delighted to receive gifts of used packing-paper. Old petrol tins of course were highly esteemed.

On the following day, having decided to walk up one of the summits of Dunghia Bokhial, we left camp by moonlight, at four in the morning. A rifle was a welcome addition to our equipment in the cane-brake before dawn, for on the previous day we had seen traces of a leopard which had been sleeping curled up on the path, and there were also bears about. One of the local coolies went in front, bare-footed and bare-legged. The danger of travelling exposed in this way through jungle in the dark, did not strike me till I saw him suddenly leap backwards in alarm at a dead branch that he had mistaken for a snake. A few minutes later, in a clearing of the jungle, there glimmered through the early morning mist an apparition so dazzling that it took us some moments to realize that what we saw was a pink rhododendron tree in full bloom, lit up by the first rays of the rising sun, so that all its thousands of flowers shone like jewels.

Nameless peak   W. Ibi Gamin, 24,200 ft. | Kamet, 25,447 ft.   Mana Peak, 23,860 ft.

E. Ibi Gamin, 24,170 ft.

Photo : C. F. Meade

KAMET GROUP FROM THE WEST

Higher up among the trees there were plenty of manol pheasants, and bear-tracks appeared in the winter snow that still lay along the ridge of the hill. Pierre used to spend a good deal of time shooting these pheasants. His peculiar method was to use a rifle, for he declared the birds were so cunning that they could judge the range of a shot-gun to a nicety, and their amazing aptitude for sprinting enabled them to keep out of reach. A rifle, so Pierre said, flustered them and upset their calculations, although admittedly it required an expert to hit a manol pheasant with a rifle bullet once the bird was on the run.

With daylight, progress became more rapid, and as we emerged from the trees and rose higher, a great panorama was gradually revealed. Below, the valley was still filled with the mists of dawn. Beyond and above Wan, the west face of Trisul confronted us at impressively close quarters, overshadowing everything with the nearness of its immensity, but I was surprised at the small extent of glacier appearing on this side of the mountain.

As we approached the top of the hill we broke into a run, so anxious were we to see the view towards Kamet in the north. Surely that must be Kamet, a glorious peak, isolated like the Matterhorn, but far more dazzling to the eye, for it was much more richly laden with snow and ice. However, we soon discovered it was Nilakanta, the loveliest mountain in Garhwal, but, compared with Kamet, merely a minor peak of 21,000 feet. Later, the real Kamet revealed himself in full majesty, towering above all his fellows.

It was disappointing that although we had been travelling towards Kamet for more than a week, and were fifty miles nearer to the great mountain, another fifty miles still lay between us, so that we were too far to be able to identify details satisfactorily. Indeed, Kamet hardly seemed any nearer than it had appeared to be when we had last caught sight of it, a hundred miles off, from the hills above Ranikhet.

In less than three hours we ran down to the pass that separated Wan from the next camping-ground at Kanol. It is the first of the three passes between Gwaldam and the small town of Joshimath in the upper valley of the Ganges. As the village of Visp in the Rhone valley is to the distant Matterhorn, so is Joshimath in the Ganges valley to Kamet. Similarly, as Zermatt is to the Matterhorn, so is the Bhotia village of Niti to Kamet, for, although the mountain is out of sight, Niti is the nearest village to it.

The grassy plateau on the divide was like a park, with tall rhododendron-trees, crimson, pink, mauve and white. Unfortunately we found, when we reached Kanol, that the chuprassi, to suit his own convenience, had pitched the camp in the very smelly neighbourhood of the village, on a site where there was little air and an abundance of flies. Worse still, he had prudently vanished from the scene of his crime, on the plea of finding coolies for the next stage, and he was now safely out of reach. Probably it was the annoyance caused by this misfortune that now detonated a fierce quarrel between Pierre and myself. There is no doubt that altitude acts as a powerful irritant to the temper, and the Indian climate probably contributes to this effect. In the Himalaya any discussion, however innocently begun, may end in a violent altercation. For this reason the ideal companion for Himalayan mountaineering is a friend like Pierre with whom one can quarrel furiously without causing disastrous results.

It was thirteen miles from Kanol to Ramni, and that seems a long march in India. The camp at Ramni, however, was a refreshing contrast after the horrors of Kanol, and the Bhotias soon pitched it on a series of charming grass terraces under shady trees, while the guilty chuprassi, embittered by the failure of his effort at Kanol to obtain the appreciation that he had apparently expected for it, made unkind but unsuccessful attempts to disparage the delights of our new home.

Camp life was always interesting, for there was always plenty to observe. Bhim Singh, for instance, a chubby young man, the *doyen* of our Garhwalis, was entertaining to watch. His originally exuberant spirits were abating noticeably as he got nearer to the snows, but he still derived enjoyment from his position in the camp hierarchy, which secured him authority without responsibility. The grandeur and haughtiness of his manner were particularly impressive. A suppliant would approach him with the utmost humility in order to beg his intercession in an application for a job. Obviously Bhim Singh had never set eyes on the man before, but for some minutes he would stand frowning with folded arms, as if plunged in the deepest thought. At length he would rouse himself from his *rêverie*, and grant the petition with a scornful nod. Then, turning courteously to me he would testify fervently to the virtues of his new *protégé*. It is one of the many merits of the Bhotias that they never perform these curious antics.

An Indian Wesleyan pastor lived at Ramni, and owned a Tibetan mastiff, a charming animal, like a big, thick-set, blunt-featured collie-dog, with a chow's tail. In spite of a misleading appearance of age and dignity, he was really quite frivolous, and was only eighteen months old. His master rather eagerly offered to lend him to us for our journey, and I felt tempted to accept. A mongrel terrier that we had once borrowed during a previous expedition had been a great success. He had a predilection for Europeans, and when we went off with a light camp to climb a peak of 20,000 feet on the Tibetan frontier he refused to be left behind. The last day of the climb it seemed cruel to take him any farther, as he had to be tied on to the rope most of the time on account of the danger from crevasses. So we left him fastened up inside the tent. However, some time after we had started, we looked back and saw that he had succeeded in breaking loose. He soon caught us up and accompanied us to the summit. Perhaps at that early stage of Himalayan history (it was in 1912) this action of the gallant animal may have won him the dogs' world-record for altitude.

The pastor kindly brought us some potatoes which we exchanged for jam, and he gave us some local honey which Pierre exposed in the sun in order to drain it away from the numerous foreign bodies in it. Meanwhile Tippu, the mastiff, romped ponderously among the tents. His deep bark boomed through the camp; in fact it boomed so incessantly, and with such deafening effect, that we resolved to elude the generous efforts of the owner, and leave the gentle monster behind us.

Tibetan mastiffs, when full grown, have a great reputation for ferocity, and their rôle is not that of the ordinary European sheep-dog, but they are kept exclusively for defending the flocks against bears and leopards. They wear heavy collars bristling with spikes, and during the day they are often yoked together to a stick in pairs. Whenever we happened to meet them, the shepherds in charge hurriedly snatched at the yoke, and held on to it as tightly as possible till we were out of sight. At sunset, when the sheep are driven into the circular stone folds, the dogs remain at large outside. It is said that two of them are capable of tackling a leopard, and there is a story of an Englishman visiting a village near Ramni, and finding two dogs guarding it in the absence of the inhabitants. The dogs attacked immediately, and the Englishman, with the only cartridge that he had in his gun, shot one of the pair, but had no time to reload before the survivor flew at him and killed him.

Next day we started for Kaliaghat at four-thirty, just as dawn was beginning to break. It took us an hour and a half to walk up to the pass, which is the second of the three passes between Gwaldam and Joshimath. The march was one of the longest in the whole journey. It began with a climb of 2,000 feet to the pass, then came a descent of 5,000 feet into a very hot valley, and a long tramp up again of 3,000 feet to Kaliaghat, in all amounting to a grand total of 10,000 feet up and down during the day. To achieve an equivalent performance in Switzerland, it would be necessary to start, say, from the Riffelberg, walk up to the Gornergrat, and descend to Zermatt, before finally strolling up to the Schwarzsee for the night. No doubt it would not be more than a fair day's exercise for a good walker, but in order to appreciate a Garhwali coolie's point of view, the good walker would have to carry somebody else's portmanteau on his back.

The pastor saw us off from Ramni, and came with a lantern to show us a useful short-cut behind the camp. As we climbed, we could see lights moving in the village and in the deserted camp, where one of the chuprassis was still hunting for reluctant coolies. Alam Singh had been left behind to load and despatch the men as soon as they turned up. Having posted himself on a hillock, he was calling repeatedly into the night to the surrounding villages, and his forlorn cries of "Coolie, coolie, coolie" came up to us out of the darkness.

At that date one of the conditions of land tenure was the obligation to carry travellers' luggage. Consequently the various villages of the neighbourhood had to take it in turns to supply coolies. One of the two chuprassis accompanying travellers warned the lambadar overnight of the number of carriers required, while the other chuprassi was already on his way to make arrangements for the stage that followed. The fee paid to a coolie varied between fourpence and eightpence, and on these terms a peasant might have to carry a heavy suit-case, a fifty-pound tent, or a chest full of jam-pots across country for any distance up to fourteen miles. On the longer marches even the small present of an extra penny was much appreciated. The system must often have inflicted great hardship, and has since been abolished.

We passed many smooth lawns among the rhododendron-trees, ideal sites for camps. In one of these clearings we found the Bhotias busy smoking, having stopped to gather the bark of a sort of yew tree that they mix with their tea. I noticed that to start their pipes was just as laborious a job as lighting a stove, and a burning rag had to be applied to the tobacco before it would catch fire. The native tobacco-smoke has a peculiar smell, and, sickly though it is, I have often longed for the reek of it, for it is vividly associated in my mind with memories of starlight nights by Himalayan glaciers, with the Bhotias singing and smoking in a circle round a roaring blaze of juniper branches.

Farther on we had a view of the notorious Goonar Lake, in a distant valley, a brilliant jade-colour, and set in dense pine forests that covered all the surrounding slopes. The lake had been produced by a mountain sliding down into the valley, and blocking the river. As the water gradually rose higher behind the huge natural dam, the government engineers got to work, and laid a telegraph line down the valley below the lake. Twenty-four hours before the dam burst, orders were telegraphed all along the line to evacuate every village in the danger-zone, and when the flood came not a life was lost.

The track leading down to the pass wound through endless woods, brilliant scarlet birds darted among the trees, and gorgeous manol pheasants scuttled away over the pine-needles into the shadows. Frequent refreshing showers mitigated the intensity of the heat as we descended to the bottom of the gorge to cross the river before beginning the long climb to Kaliaghat.

At Kaliaghat the camp was soon crowded with villagers. Some wanted medicines, but most of them came from curiosity. One old man touched my heart by producing potatoes for us from every fold of his voluminous garment, and firmly refusing to accept anything in exchange. The old lambadar, who had a voice like a lion's roar, and the appearance of a bear, came to see that his people brought the customary wood and water. Like most hillmen he wore a dingy tunic of undyed sackcloth, twisted round his legs to form loose drawers. Slung across his shoulders he carried a sickle. Nearly all the men carried distaffs, which they skil-fully kept spinning as they talked.

In spite of the rain Pierre as usual went out shooting for the pot, and climbed most of the surrounding crags. Evidently there had been plenty of shooting in this neighbourhood, for the Kuari district is popular with sportsmen, who have a tendency to believe that where game has once been found in abundance, it will remain abundant indefinitely. The Kuari district illustrates the fallaciousness of this theory.

From Kaliaghat the path is all uphill to Dakhwani, where the camping-ground is far from any village and at an altitude of about 10,000 feet, in fact only 2,000 feet below the summit of the Kuari Pass, the third, last and highest of the passes on the way from Gwaldam to Joshimath. For me the Kuari Pass always seemed to mark the border-line limiting the foot-hills that surround the high peaks of Kumaun, cutting them off from the still more mountainous province of Garhwal in the Tibetan frontier region.

We pitched the tents on a little stream near a fine mountain torrent that rushed out of a rocky gorge. The higher grass-slopes shone in the sun with the colour of brass, where the herbage had only recently been released by the melting of the winter snow. Near us were huge rhododendron-trees, with trunks so vividly red that they almost matched the crimson of the flowers. I lay across the door of my tent in my sleeping-bag, listening drowsily to the sound of the stream. In my dreams I seemed to hear another sound like the humming of a tuneful bluebottle, and rousing myself, I discovered a Garhwali, a few yards off, squatting on the ground, strumming pathetically on a tiny home-made guitar. He must have cast a spell over me, for I listened and listened until the sun set, the stars came out and darkness fell. Finally Pierre insisted on breaking off the concert for us to go to supper.

The Kuari was the most mountainous of the three passes that we had to cross on our way up-country. Joshimath on the other side of it is only thirty miles from Kamet, and nearer still to the magnificent Parbat group and the mighty Nanda Devi. In spite of a cold in the head, a blistered heel and the constant rain-storms, I was in the best of spirits. The mountain air was irresistibly exhilarating, and seemed to contain a breath of life from the glaciers.

At break of day Pierre and I, starting in advance, pushed on hurriedly to the top of the Kuari Pass, 12,300 feet above sea-level. Walking fast in an easterly direction up the ridge in which the pass is situated, we reached a small peak of about 15,000 feet. We were hoping for a view, and suddenly, while we waited, there appeared through a rent in the clouds a glittering snow-field hanging in space. Nothing more wonderful than this could we imagine, but after a moment, at an astonishing height above it, the clouds parted again, and something shone like silver, infinitely far up in the sky.

For a moment we were spell-bound. Then, as the vision took shape, we realized that it was no mirage which we had before us, but the sunlit crest of Badrinath Peak. After a few minutes the curtain of cloud descended again, and we saw no more. Only the massive snow-bound crags of Hathi Parbat appeared fitfully through heavy banks of cloud. The Kamet group did not vouchsafe an appearance.

We walked down over hundreds of acres of winter snow to the camping-ground at Kulara, which we reached in pouring rain, there to spend a wet and chilly night. The headache that seized me was probably caused by travelling too fast up to 15,000 feet earlier in the morning—no uncommon experience. Just as we arrived, Pierre went off to shoot a bear, and as I walked in to camp, the 23,000-foot peak of Dunagiri, swathed in icy mists, peered down at me for a moment, ghostly and immense—and then vanished.

Next morning we had a lovely walk to Joshimath. This large village with its temple, situated in the heart of the high Himalaya, is a sort of metropolis for this part of Garhwal. It is perched high up on fertile slopes, overlooking the Ganges which flows along the valley-bed, 3,000 feet below. The path led through smiling woods, with springs and running water. The sound of cow-bells reminded me of the Alps, and as we approached the village the deep murmur of the Ganges sounded from far down in the gorge. Temple bells were ringing, and the narrow village street was gay with the red caps of numerous Bhotias, some of whom had come in from Mana and Niti to meet us.

Soon after we had established ourselves in the dak bungalow, I found that some of the many Bhotias were Captain Slingsby's men, and that Slingsby himself was here on his way to Badrinath and Mana for his attack on Kamet from the west. I had a talk with him and again argued that further attempts from the west were hopeless, but I failed to convince him. The reason for his incredulity was that from the highest point he had reached in the previous year, he believed he had seen what he described as "a carriage-drive leading right up the mountain", and nothing would shake this conviction. This year he had contracted dysentery, but, undismayed by this formidable handicap, he was determined to push on, and resumed his journey soon after our arrival. He promised, however, that if he was unsuccessful, he would come round and join us on the east side of the mountain.

The position of Joshimath makes it seem quite at the end of the world; there is no visible exit, and the vast steep mountains that surround the valley appear to meet on every side. Opposite, a wall of gaunt brown crags reaches up to the clouds, and higher up the slopes behind the village, glimpses are got of snow-patches above the brown mountain-wall at unimagined heights. In the Alps I know only the valley of the Vénéon in the heart of Dauphiny, or the valley of the Visp below Zermatt, that can at all compare with this landscape for savagery and grandeur.

The bungalow was comfortable, and seemed luxurious after tent life. It had just been redecorated with a new kind of paint, which was said never to lose its freshness. Unfortunately there was a disadvantage in this perpetual freshness, for we found that it came off perpetually on our clothes.

While I was at Joshimath I made anxious enquiries about the movements of the Rawal Sahib, or high priest, as the date was approaching for his annual migration from Joshimath to Badrinath, near the sacred source of the Ganges. I knew that for this trek he usually required the services of three hundred coolies, and so I had reason to fear a shortage of labour. One year I had met the procession on the march, straggling in endless single file along the narrow mountain track that wound its way up and down through the river gorges. At the head of the procession walked three attendants wearing sashes and carrying maces; then came a man blowing a trumpet, closely followed by four coolies supporting the Rawal Sahib in a carrying-chair, while on either side of him, men brandishing great white yaks' tails, fanned him whenever the path was wide enough to enable them to do so.

This year, however, the move had not yet taken place, and a ceremonial visit at Joshimath was indicated, with an exchange of gifts. Accordingly, watched by a dense and silent crowd, we met on the verandah of the high priest's house, a building that was not unlike the home of a prosperous villager in the Italian Alps. Attendants put wreaths of flowers round our necks, and a desultory conversation took place with the help of an interpreter. A traditional and rather cruel religious ordinance prescribes that the Rawal Sahib must always be a native of Madras. This fact, I suspect, accounted for the air of home-sickness and disillusionment that pierced the poor man's courteous but apathetic demeanour. I had already met him on many occasions, and now, as always before, there was an unsolved mystery about his appearance. How did he so invariably manage to look as if it was exactly three days since he had last shaved? Daily the bristles on his chin showed exactly the same degree of promise to within a fraction of an inch. It was not till long afterwards that the solution of the enigma came to me by inspiration in the night. In a flash I realized that it was not a question of a razor at all, and that he did not shave, but used a pair of scissors every morning. The mystery was solved!

But to return to the ceremonial visit: during the conversation I noticed that a faint gleam, which I failed to account for, came into the high priest's eyes, as he roused himself to put a question to the interpreter. The latter listened carefully, and then turned to me:

"Rawal Sahib says 'why do travellers want to go to the tops of mountains'?"

This was a poser, for I knew that whole books had been written to supply the answer to this question, and had failed to do so. Finally, I could think of nothing better than to say: "Probably because the tops of mountains are very near to God." I watched with some anxiety while this pretentious remark filtered its way through the interpreter to the Rawal. I saw the gleam in his eyes increase and develop into a broad cynical smile; then back came the answer, half-volley:

"That explanation is not a sufficient reason."

For an instant the high prest looked almost happy, but soon sank back again into his habitual lethargy.

That evening, in the stormy yellow light, the impending mountains were coal-black, and their crests were shrouded in threatening clouds. Far below in the depths of the valley, the Ganges could be seen issuing from the narrow gorge through which it poured from Badrinath, and the river's grim gateway looked more than ever forbidding. In the distance I could see a gossamer thread zigzagging across the hill-side in a patch of dying sunlight, and vanishing into the blackness of the gorge. It was the famous pilgrim-route which follows the course of the Ganges from the plains to the ultimate sacred source in the mountains above Badrinath. The pilgrims bring with them every kind of infection, plague and cholera included. During cholera epidemics the disease travels at the pace of the pilgrims, and its progress up the valley can be reported daily to Badrinath by telegraph. Every precaution is taken, and along the pilgrim route it is advisable to plunge all knives, forks, spoons and crockery into boiling water before each meal.

As it was necessary to spend some time in Joshimath to see about stores and coolies, I devoted part of one day to accompanying the district engineer who was inspecting one of his bridges in the bottom of the valley. Bridges in this country are a great anxiety, both to those who build them and to those who have to cross them, for the destructive power of the rains in these enormous mountains is overwhelming. The descent into the bottom of the valley was like a plunge into the tropics, for the climate 3,000 feet lower down was very different from that of Joshimath. On the path beside the river we found ourselves in contact with the pageant of the pilgrimage, always on the move, and as relentless in its hasteless progress as some primæval tide. There were people from all parts of India, some even from Ceylon, and their clothes showed every variety of fashion and colour. To judge from the pathetically advanced age of some of the pilgrims, they seemed to have put off the task until it was too late for them to have much hope of reaching the goal alive.

IV—THE TIBETAN BORDERLAND

As we left Joshimath we began the fourth stage of our journey, for from here we were to ascend into the precincts of the Tibetan Tableland, and to feel the influence of the Tibetan climate. This year, having abandoned the western route, we were to approach the mountain from the east, and instead of following the Ganges to Badrinath and Mana, we were to branch off to Niti. Niti, like Mana, is a Bhotia village, more than 11,000 feet above the sea, and only inhabited in summer. As the monsoon currents seem more inclined to follow the main stream of the Ganges to Badrinath and Mana, the climate of the tributary valley of the Dhaoli where Niti is situated, is drier, and consequently pleasanter during the rains. Moreover, although the main river flows through magnificent scenery, the valley of the Dhaoli far surpasses it in the grandeur of its incomparable precipices.

At last, when our business was all finished, we started off on the path up the Dhaoli valley on a gloriously clear morning with a gentian-blue sky, and all the distant snows shining in the sun. We were pleased to think that the north wind which blew through the camp at Tapoban that night came from Kamet and the plateaux of Tibet. We now seemed to have definitely emerged from the sweet but sometimes oppressive dreamland of the foot-hills. Nevertheless, although we did not know it, we were not yet out of harm's way, for, as the camping-ground at Tapoban was much used by shepherds, the water-supply was suspect, and probably the water for tea had not been properly boiled. At any rate we were due to suffer for it a few days later. In this country besides the faculty of resisting microbes and malaria, one of the most important qualifications for exploration work is the capacity to digest the excessive proportion of grindstone in the flour of which the indigestible native chupatty is made. By carrying one's own flour, by always boiling the water in inhabited districts, and as far as possible dodging mosquitoes when passing through the lower valleys, there is little risk of illness. But unfortunately these are counsels of perfection.

The following morning we overslept, in spite of much praiseworthy coughing and fidgeting on the part of the zealous Bhoties outside the tents. The result was that we did not finish breakfast and get packed up till after five. The meal, I remember, consisted of spaghetti and cups of chocolate; sometimes we even breakfasted off semolina pudding made with condensed milk, but an unusual regime seemed natural enough in circumstances where appetites never needed stimulating.

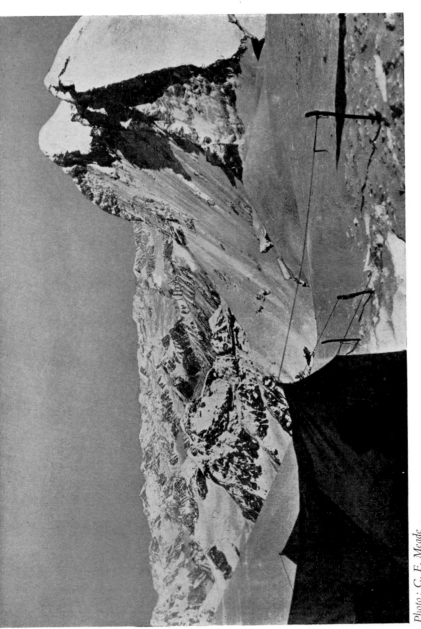

Photo: C. F. Meade

WESTERN IBI GAMIN FROM ABOVE SLINGSBY'S SADDLE

Note ridge descending left from chief summit. It had appeared easy when seen from below

As we started, the Bhotias rather proudly drew our attention to a distant summit, declaring that it was the Mana Peak.* This was a mountain that we had originally introduced them to, and they had very properly adopted it as one of the glories of their wonderful country.

It was a long nine miles' tramp uphill to the camping-ground of Samedi. We advanced slowly through many processions of sheep, goats and half-bred yaks, conducted sometimes by pigtailed Tibetans whistling shrilly to their flocks through their teeth. Pure-bred yaks were not so frequent. With their sumptuous flowing coats, and vast bushy tails, they were far handsomer than the half-breeds. The Tibetan goats, with pelts like polar bears, resembled the wild goats of the Rocky Mountains.

Northwards over Tibet, the sky was always blue. It was only behind us in India that rain was falling, and here the rocky path was still deep in dust. It was encouraging to see that we were rising all the time. The precipices overhanging the river were becoming more and more magnificent, and we caught an inspiring glimpse up a side-valley of the glorious ice on Dunagiri's southern *arête*, glittering in a gleam of sun. Unfortunately it was threatening to rain, even here, and letters from India suggested that the big rains had already arrived, although it was only the middle of May. If these anticipations were to prove correct, any attempt on Kamet would be out of the question.

When we got to Jumar Gwar, two days later, we found that the camp was charmingly situated in a pine-wood, above the banks of a torrent that flowed down from a tributary valley. It was just as well that the site was agreeable, as we had to stay here a week owing to the fact that Pierre developed dysentery. The cause, no doubt, was the water at Tapoban.

* 23,860 feet.

Treatment was a problem. There was not much encouragement to be got from the medical handbook I had with me, as the only forecast it gave was the bald statement that in severe cases death might be expected to take place on the eighth day. Ipecacuanha was the only remedy indicated, but this, it was stated, usually caused vomiting, presumably without effecting a cure. I hoped, however, that if I kept the patient absolutely still with a hot-water bottle in his sleeping-bag, he might succeed in keeping some of the drug down, and what little remained inside him might do some good. In any case, if the treatment failed, I did not possess any of the other remedies that the book recommended. Fortunately results developed as I hoped, and a few days later we established Pierre as a convalescent, lying in a hammock under the trees.

It was most opportune that the postman now brought us some French Alpine periodicals, for we were running short of French books. I had been contentedly reading *Les Indes Sans les Anglais* under the impression that the subject was *Les Indes* Sous *les Anglais*, but we had nothing in reserve. Pierre, who usually had an almost unlimited susceptibility to the charms of good literature, used to complain of Balzac that "on commence à lire, et puis on ne sait plus ce qu'on fait; c'est vraiment trop abrutissant". By now, however, he had exhausted our stock of Balzacs, and had been reduced to a volume of Victor Hugo's love-letters with which he was dallying rather coldly. In fact, the Revue Alpine came as a godsend.

There was very little to be got now to eke out the provisions that we carried with us. No eggs, milk or chickens were obtainable. Yak-butter sewn up hermetically in skins, was beginning to be available in the valley, but there were no villages in reach of where we were. Yak-butter is very rich, and has to be melted and strained to get rid of the dirt in it. For tinned foods we were quite well off. Each provision-load was supposed to contain food for Pierre and myself for five days. The only drawback to this arrangement was that there was a tin of herring-roes in each load, and hitherto, when after every five days, I opened a tin of roes, it invariably burst like a bomb. It was apparently a mistake to bring herring-roes through the Red Sea.

As regards picnic food for taking with us on the march, Utam Singh always accompanied us carrying a light load. Utam was by birth a Garhwali, but for practical purposes a naturalized Bhotia, for he lived with the Bhotias of Mana. His fascinating combination of stupidity, conscientiousness, enterprise, and sense of humour were endearing. He would greet one in the morning with a profound salaam, join his hands in attitude of supplication, suggestive of intense humility, roll his eyes, and then, concluding that his antics had gone far enough, and were becoming ridiculous, he would burst into an irrepressible guffaw.

After a week to make sure of a cure, I judged that it would be safe to leave Jumar Gwar. It was the 23rd of May, the day, we afterwards heard, on which Slingsby had moved up from Mana to his base camp, preparatory to attacking the mountain from the west. One of our men had just come down from Niti, and reported meeting no rain on the way, whereas we had had quite a deluge, lasting for three or four hours. Every step nearer to the frontier evidently takes one into a drier climate, and with every mile that we advanced, the landscape became more Tibetan in appearance. Every day, too, the air was becoming more stimulating. Only the two chuprassis failed to respond to the stimulus, but according to Pierre's theory about chuprassis this was to be expected. As he said: "Il ne faut jamais les garder après quatre mille mètres, l'altitude les gâte absolument, et ils deviennent tout de suite moisis." I think his theory was approximately correct.

Malari was now the only village between us and Niti, the scent of pines and junipers was growing stronger, and the characteristic fragrance of Niti was already noticeable in the air, the heavenly smell of sweetbriar. Down by the river there was wild lavender. On our right the track leading to Dunagiri village disappeared up a forbidding-looking side-glen, with a tremendously precipitous cleft at its entrance through which poured the turbid torrent-water coming from the Bagini Glacier. Somewhere up that glen, too, must be the mysterious 23,000-feet peak, triangulated, but unnamed. Certainly the most astonishing feature of the terrific landscape was the colossal scale of the gorge scenery, the incredible precipices at impossible angles towering into the clouds above the river and the path. The latter was sometimes carried on logs pinned to the face of the cliff. For 4,000 feet the walls of the gorge rose sheer, and then receded into the clouds into the region of perpetual snow; it was a scene that might have been a dream of Gustave Doré.

After working our way through this grim canyon for several miles, the valley opened out, and we began the ascent to Malari. Here, at a height of 10,000 feet the camp was pitched on a tableland lying across the valley, and overlooking the lower reaches which were clothed with deodars. Pierre, always indefatigable in supplying the larder, now shot a marmot. It was a young one, but I ate it rather unappreciatively, and it struck me that the meat resembled inferior rabbit.

Starting next morning on the final stage to Niti with a cool air blowing and a blazing sun, in a few hours we reached the village, which is situated in a bleak high valley carpeted with thousands of acres of pink and white sweetbriar. Some of the houses with two stories and balconies were quite Italian in appearance.

Near the camp, edelweiss was plentiful, and on every side the immense knees of great rounded hills that were covered with stones or grass, projected above the skyline, permitting no view of the snows, or of the long glen leading over the Niti Pass into Tibet. Having emerged through the imposing gateway of the Malari gorge into this different landscape, we felt that we could disregard the frontier, and consider that we were at last really in Tibet, at play on the roof of the world, in a magic atmosphere that enchanted and intoxicated the climber, but was sometimes so rarefied that to breathe it could be fatal.

Here then we had reached the last inhabited outpost on the way to Kamet, and the plan for attacking the mountain had now to be put into action.

V—THE FINAL MARCHES

Above Niti the main valley again grows narrower and steeper, but in spite of innumerable stony ravines and rock-shoulders, the hills on either side still maintain the general character of gigantic downs. The important Tibetan trade-route that zigzags laboriously across the vast slopes of these mountains is nothing but a straggling sheep-track. During one long day's march, until we diverged in order to ascend the Raikana valley, it was to be our road.

Our first act, however, was to send an advance party of twenty men up the trail to deposit loads at a place that we had named Bridge Camp. Next day, with forty coolies, we set out on the long march to this camp. Ascending the hill-side above Niti, we were soon looking down on the roofs and

courtyards. Warm mists drifted past us and revealed patches
of blue sky. Below, poised on the cloud-surface above the
floor of the valley, floated a strange phenomenon, a rainbow-
coloured disk like an archery-target. To each of us his own
shadow appeared in the centre of concentric circles.

Hoping that this peculiar portent might be favourable,
we continued to wind our way upwards round the immense
flanks of the hills, across an endless series of desolate ravines,
till we were several thousand feet above the torrent. As we
rose, the slopes became more thickly clothed with grass.
Behind us, Dunagiri, emerging magnificently through a
filmy curtain of cloud, pierced the heavens like a sword of
ice, and glittered dazzlingly in the sun. Towards the frontier
the sky remained serenely blue, and the warm vital air around
us was fragrant with the scent of wild-flowers and of aromatic
juniper. Perched on the high shoulder of a hill opposite, a
forlorn and solitary little wood was visible. Ahead, a bird's-
eye view of the upper reaches of the valley confronted us,
and extended as far as the confluence of the tributary torrent
coming from the great Raikana Glacier, which was the route,
as yet invisible, that was to lead us to Kamet. Doubtless it
was the mysterious charm of that bleak and empty land of
Tibet that transfigured even the most commonplace features
of the landscape. It was a relief, too, to feel that we were
no longer overshadowed by the overwhelming precipices
of the gloomy Malari gorges.

The site of Bridge Camp was still far below us in the
bottom of the upper reaches of the valley. On the way down
to it Pierre made a long détour, inspired by the tranquil
passion of marmot-hunting. This was a pastime that was
usually too slow to suit Pierre's impetuous temperament,
for the marmot-hunter's method is to sit dozing near the
mouth of a burrow in the hope of waking at the moment

Photo : Pierre Blanc

WESTERN IBI GAMIN FROM THE 23,000 ft. SADDLE

when the marmot chooses to come out. Marmots seem scarcer in this part of the Himalaya than in the Alps, probably owing to the great number of birds of prey; near Mana we never even saw a burrow.

In camp that evening the Bhotias who were to accompany us on the mountain had their equipment given out to them. It consisted of blankets, shirts, drawers, sweaters, puttees, white sun-hats, snow-spectacles and woollen Balaclava helmets. Boots had already been supplied. The Balaclava helmets were so much appreciated that long afterwards, during the return journey, the proud owners insisted on wearing them in the villages, even in the tropical heat of the lower valleys. However, our followers' manner of wearing their new finery effectually counteracted any tendency it might have had to Europeanize their appearance. They wore the shirts outside their trousers, with the shirt-tails flapping in the wind, and they contrived to give a curiously coquettish appearance to their new headgear by pulling down the lining of the hats so that it raised them a few inches off the head. Altogether our private army presented a very striking appearance.

The next two days, the 30th and 31st of May were fully occupied in erecting the bridge that caused us to give the camp its name. Close to the tents a bed of winter snow had spanned the torrent; later in the year the snow would melt, and in order to provide for this contingency, we proceeded to put up a rope-bridge, an easy job at that moment, since the snow, as yet unmelted, would serve us as a scaffolding while we were fixing the ropes. The structure was really nothing but a rope-ladder with wooden rungs, and was secured to heaps of boulders at each end. The only way to cross it was to crawl on all fours. On the bed of snow under the bridge we noticed the tracks of a snow-leopard.

The following day three men were sent down the valley to Niti and beyond to fetch a further three days' supply of potatoes, onions, salt and dates for the coolies. Meanwhile the rest of us started up the Raikana valley on our way to the Raikana Glacier. It was a delight to breathe really high mountain air again. As we toiled over an interminable waste of stones, and advanced on to the glacier, the brilliant pallor of the first rays of the morning sun lit up the domes and towers of the arid range of mountains that formed the Tibetan frontier overhead on our right. Yet the moment of stepping on to a Himalayan glacier is by no means always a dramatic experience, for very often, as on this occasion, it is difficult to know whether one is walking on glacier or moraine, as everywhere there stretches the same undulating sea of stones. Gradually, however, as the sun climbed higher, the dark green of the juniper nestling in the waste of boulders took on a brighter colour, and the sky assumed a deeper, kindlier blue, that made me think of Italy. As the light grew stronger, the barren rocky range on our right reminded me of those desolate red mountains that border the coasts of the Red Sea; it formed a striking contrast with the shapely and heavily snow-laden summits that we had left behind us in India.

Eventually a camp that we called Cascade Camp was pitched between the moraine and the cliffs on our right, from which there descended a fine waterfall frozen completely solid. Soon after our arrival, while the sun was setting, Pierre and I strolled from the tents to a moraine-hillock from which we could see down the valley towards India, and watch the play of light and shadow on the great Kalanka-Changabang-Dunagiri group of snow-peaks. That night we sat over the camp-fire after supper, drinking brandy-punch and discussing plans for the climb. We were calculating

for camps at nineteen, twenty-one and twenty-three thousand
feet. Subsequently we abandoned this scheme, and established camps at sixteen, twenty and twenty-three thousand
feet. I have little doubt, nevertheless, that the first plan was
the best, for the stages that we subsequently decided upon
were too long to allow satisfactory acclimatization. Later,
as usual, the evening ended with the Bhotias singing in a
circle round their fire, and smoking the communal pipe. I
lay listening in my sleeping-bag as long as I could keep awake,
and when I could listen no longer the sounds went on in my
dreams.

The topography of the eastern approaches was now beginning to reveal itself. From Cascade Camp we could see to
the west three big glaciers flowing at an easy angle towards
us, to unite and form the main ice-stream of the Raikana, a
mile or two above the camp. These three great glaciers all
resembled the Mer-de-glace or the Aletsch Glacier in type,
and consequently afforded plenty of easy walking. The right-
hand glacier was the principal glacier of the three, the Raikana
proper; it had an easy pass at its head, leading into Tibet,
and Justin Blanc had explored it in the previous year. The
central glacier of the three was a tributary, and came from
the foot of the 24,000-feet peak, Eastern Ibi Gamin. It might
well be named Strachey after its discoverer. Behind Eastern
Ibi Gamin could just be seen the white brow of Kamet. The
left-hand glacier was also a tributary; it rose out of sight
behind a long minor spur coming from Kamet, and its source
was in the upper snows of Kamet itself. It was none other
than the Kamet Glacier, and it was the clue to the ascent of
the mountain.

Fortunately for us barhal were already making their way
up the Raikana Glacier at the same time as we were. Pierre
had long ago come to the conclusion that rarefied air affects

the trajectory of a rifle-bullet, so that he always modified his aim accordingly, and certainly with excellent results, for we feasted daily off a constant supply of the best fresh meat.

Meanwhile, as we camped higher and higher, progress became slower, for we were constantly sending down for more stocks of provisions and firewood in order to mass them in dumps farther up the glacier. Moreover, time was getting on—it was now the 3rd of June—and we estimated that by this time Slingsby, on the other side of Kamet, must be well above the saddle named after him, and probably more than 23,000 feet above sea-level. We could not know till long afterwards that he had already made one of his determined attacks upon the mountain, and had reached a great height above the saddle. Eventually, being forced to retreat, he had an acute collapse, which was to disable him for the rest of the season.

Unfortunately ever since we had left the Niti valley the weather had continued to be bad. The air was cold, though there were occasional gleams of scorching sun. Every day threatening clouds and mist crept up from the direction of Niti and the Indian plain. The climate on the Raikana that June was very different from the warm, misty, sunny days of the previous July.

We had decided that if the weather was not too bad, we would continue our journey up on to the Kamet Glacier on the 7th of June. We hoped to be able to choose a site for a high base-camp somewhere on the long, narrow upper course of the glacier. Peeping out of my tent at six that morning, I saw nothing but mist, and crept back into my bag again. At eight o'clock, waking with a jump, I discovered that it was a gloriously fine day, and we must start at once. Hurrying through breakfast, we had soon packed the tents and were off. As we came to the little green lake which last year had reflected the three lovely ice-peaks of Mana in its water, we found that it was completely snowed up, and more or less invisible. Alas, as we branched off from the Raikana on to the Kamet Glacier, the weather began to go bad again. Nowhere, however, was there any difficulty, and eventually we found a good camp-site at about 16,000 feet, about half-way up the Kamet Glacier. This would do for our high base-camp.

Next day and during the fortnight that followed we remained here weather-bound. Daily there was Scotch mist or rain, and often there was snow. We could only wait and hope that the weather would get better. Whenever it was clear enough to see anything, we could admire the beauty of our situation, for, close opposite to us, Mana Peak with its ice-precipices, 8,000 feet high, and massed in vertical tiers, shone through the clouds at intervals. The landscape indeed had completely changed since we had left the Raikana Glacier, for our course had taken a bend away from the neighbourhood of the Tibetan frontier, slight in regard to distance, but sufficient to alter again the whole character of the scenery. The peaks that here surrounded us no longer displayed the rounded outlines of the Tibetan mountains, but towered above us with all the uncompromising severity and startling beauty of the Indian Himalaya. All day long we heard the thunder of avalanches among the precipices of the Mana Peaks, and from time to time the melancholy piping of a ramchocor resounded from the crags behind the camp. Ramchocor are giant partridges, less good to eat than English birds, and harder to shoot on account of their keen sight and the astonishing speed at which they can race uphill.

In the base-camp here it was easy to forget that we were living at a thousand feet above the altitude of the highest mountain in the Alps. Yet the fact is, as Brigadier Norton has pointed out, that even an acclimatized traveller can notice a difference after reaching a height of 15,000 feet. An accelerated pulse and breathing are common to most people at this elevation, and I sometimes felt the worse if I completely satisfied a mountain appetite that had not yet succumbed to altitude. Certainly tempers get worse the higher one goes.

If the altitude and the weather affected our tempers, at any rate the delay caused by the badness of the weather gave us time to make improvements in the camp, while we amassed enough firewood and provisions to last the whole party for a month. We even indulged ourselves with such luxuries as baths, hot-water bottles and parasols, besides a paved causeway that led one dry-shod to the sleeping-tents, and a dining-room with kitchen adjoining, both built with solid stone walls.

Yet although the camp was comfortable we soon found that it lacked one amenity, for it was by no means as safe as we had supposed. We had pitched it in what appeared to be an absolutely sheltered position; nevertheless, one afternoon, when there happened, fortunately, to be no one in the kitchen, a slab of rock, about the size of a tombstone, came spinning down the mountain-side, and crashed through the roof, tearing a great hole in the awning. Another more disagreeable mishap occurred in the middle of the night. One evening it had begun to snow heavily, and owing to the fact that all firewood had to be brought up the glacier on men's backs, we had gone to bed early, in order to economize fuel and keep ourselves warm. As we had brought all our luxuries up to this camp, we always slept in pyjamas, and it was consequently a shock when I woke up about midnight in my comfortable sleeping-bag, and found that my tent had collapsed on to me under the weight of snow on the roof. There was no alternative but to creep out into the night, barefoot and shivering, dig the tent out with my hands, and laboriously set it up again.

Fortunately the bad weather did not detain us here for more than a fortnight. But now, however, as the time has come to describe the actual climbing on the mountain, I must first of all say something about the previous campaigns that had taken place on it.

VI—KAMET

The great Himalayan summit, Kamet, known to Tibetans as Kangmen, a name signifying "huge grandmother of the sacred snow-chain", was not discovered till 1848. In that year the surveyor, Strachey, measuring the peaks in the tangled panorama of mountains visible from a view-point near the hill-station of Naini-Tal, found that one among them, a hundred miles away, was more than 25,000 feet high, surpassed all its neighbours by more than a thousand feet, and was only inferior by a couple of hundred feet to Nanda Devi herself, the highest mountain in British territory.

The peak was given the name of Kamet, and twenty years later, the German brothers Schlagintweit, pioneers far in advance of their time, attempted to climb it, approaching from the northern side in Tibet, and reaching a height of 22,239 feet. It is a curious fact, only discovered some forty years later, that this remarkable feat, brilliant thought it was, had not really taken place on Kamet at all, but on Eastern Ibi Gamin, a neighbouring peak of 24,170 feet, which the climbers had not realized lay between them and their objective. It is curious, too, that several subsequent parties should have made exactly the same mistake.

The next explorers after the Schlagintweits were Longstaff,

Bruce and Mumm with Alpine guides. They came from the Indian side in 1907, and reconnoitred both the eastern and western approaches. The result of their researches was that the great thoroughfare of the Kamet Glacier, affording the only means of access from the east, was condemned as dangerous on account of the ice-avalanches which appeared to fall right across it from both sides. Judging by the map, therefore, a western glacier, named Khaiam, now seemed to offer the most hopeful alternative.

Accordingly in 1910, with Pierre Blanc and the Italian guide, Alexis Brocherel, I reconnoitred this glacier, hoping that it might provide a level highway, and afford a safer approach to the citadel than the route up the Kamet Glacier was said to do.

Well I remember the sanguine hopes with which we set out to ascend the glacier, after camping below it on the river flowing from the Mana Pass. Our camp was only a couple of marches above Mana, which is the last Indian village on the west side of the mountain, and 11,000 feet above sea-level.

But the Himalaya, unlike more sophisticated ranges, provides constant surprises for its explorers. We found that the glacier that we were ascending, instead of affording us the easy, gradual approach that the map had encouraged us to hope for, not only turned out to be short and steep, but was shut in at its head by a ridge about 20,000 feet high, which prevented us from seeing any farther. As there was a depression in the ridge that was obviously accessible, and looked like a convenient pass, we pushed on hopefully. After walking half-way up the glacier, we could at first see nothing beyond the ridge that formed the horizon above our heads, but as we approached the supposed pass, there gradually rose above and beyond it the rocky dome of what was evidently a very big peak. Could it be Kamet? When at

amet—

Photo : C. F. Meade

KAMET AND EASTERN IBI GAMIN FROM THE EAST WITH THE HIGH
SADDLE BETWEEN THEM

length we reached the gap there was no longer any doubt. The big peak was indeed Kamet, but unfortunately it was three or four miles from the saddle on which we stood, and in addition, it was cut off from us by a vast gulf, two or three thousand feet deep. In the bottom of the gulf an enormous glacier, not marked on any map, and coming from the foot of Kamet, flowed smoothly away out of sight in the direction of the Ganges and the Indian plain.

This *dénouement* closed our proceedings for 1910. The great unknown glacier that we had discovered appeared to be the missing highway that we had hoped to find, for it came from the actual foot of the peak. It was falsely shown on the map as quite a small ice-stream emerging into the Mana valley near a camping-ground called Ghastole. If the map had been correct, this Ghastole Glacier (as it might be called) should have been enclosed at its head by a semi-circular mountain-range completely cutting it off from Kamet.

However, the mystery of this glacier was soon to be cleared up. In the following year, 1911, I was not in India, but Captain Morris Slingsby made an attempt on Kamet, and, acting on my advice, travelled up the Ghastole Glacier. As was expected the map was wrong, the glacier was twice as long as indicated, and the journey up the ice led Slingsby right round the actual foot of the mountain, ultimately enabling him to climb to a height of more than 22,000 feet.

In 1912, the Blanc brothers, Franz Lochmatter, Johann Perren and I followed in Slingsby's footsteps, and in our turn had the satisfaction of realizing our anticipations. After walking up the first four miles of ice, as shown on the map, we reached the point where the map marked a *cul-de-sac*. Here, looking round a corner of the mountains north of us, we saw as we had expected another four miles of unmapped glacier emerging from behind the foot of the huge precipitous pyramid of Kamet, towering 7,000 feet into the sky. So the facts had conclusively contradicted the map, and these upper reaches of the glacier, where we were standing, were the same that we had looked down upon from the Khaiam Saddle in 1910, and as we had supposed, here was the hoped-for highway that led to the foot of the mountain. Whether the latter could be climbed or not was another matter.

To clear up this point it was necessary to camp higher up the Ghastole Glacier, near its head. One long march took us up its entire length, and we pitched an advanced base-camp at 18,000 feet. To get to this camp we had to circumvent the foot of a great spur that descended from Kamet, and was crowned with jagged minor summits that were heavily snow-clad. Behind this spur we found ourselves in the innermost recesses of an arctic landscape built on a colossal scale, and entirely cut off from the every-day world like that wonder-fully isolated "Jardin" in the upper region of the Mer-de-glace at Chamonix. Our position was close to the base of a wide and lofty rock-wall or curtain of precipice uniting the main mass of Kamet with the superb double-headed rock-peak of Kamet's principal satellite, Western Ibi Gamin, 24,200 feet high, and like Kamet, situated on the Tibetan frontier. The depression between the two mountain-masses appropriately came to be known as Slingsby's Saddle, for it was the point that he had reached and passed during his attempt in 1911.

Our world, however, as is so often the case among these vast mountains was a world of illusions. For instance, for anyone in search of a route up the satellite, Western Ibi Gamin, there appeared to be a magnificent, easy rock-ridge ascending in one continuous sweep from the level of the glacier right up to the summit of this peak. Again, another great *arête* ascended from the point where the curtain of precipice was joined to the main mass of Kamet; apparently it led right to the top of the latter mountain with hardly a break anywhere. Half-way up this inviting *arête* a single rock-tower seemed to be the only obstacle, and to climb over it or cross its face looked feasible. It was this *arête* that Slingsby, encouraged by the convenient approach up the Ghastole Glacier, had chosen for his attempt on Kamet the previous year.

Yet the fact was that the friendly appearance of each of these two great ridges was utterly deceptive, and neither Western Ibi Gamin or Kamet was accessible in the way that we supposed. The attractive route up Western Ibi Gamin, as we subsequently discovered when viewing it in profile, was intersected by a huge vertical step, at least a thousand feet in height, and, in the case of the other ridge, the rock-tower that we took to be a mere tooth on the way up Kamet, was in reality the other great satellite of Kamet, namely Eastern Ibi Gamin, a peak 24,170 feet high, at least a mile distant from the greater mountain, and completely cutting us off from it.

Slingsby still believed after his attempt in 1911 that Kamet could be climbed by this route, but after my party had made two attempts by it in 1912, one of them failing at a height of 23,000 feet in bad weather, we became convinced that any attack on the mountain from this side would either involve us in the hopeless task of crossing the intervening summit of Eastern Ibi Gamin in the way, or else in the equally hopeless effort of traversing horizontally the precipitous face of this peak. Actually, both Slingsby's party and mine had been repeating the original mistake made by the Schlagintweits in their ascent more than forty years previously, and it is a remarkable fact that none of the attacks on Kamet from this side ever took place on the mountain, but all came to an end on the slopes of Eastern Ibi Gamin. It must be admitted that even a long experience in the Alps is insufficient to prepare one for the bewildering vastness of scale and complexity of topography that is characteristic of the Himalaya.

Later in the same year, when we realized the uselessness of making further attempts on the west side, we crossed the range to Niti, in order to investigate Kamet thoroughly from the east. It was only then that we explored the easy eastern approach up the Kamet Glacier, and discovered that the route which had been rejected, was by no means as dangerous in respect of avalanches as had been supposed. In fact there could be no doubt that the Kamet Glacier was the key to the ascent.

Such, then, were the reasons that had caused us to return to the east side of Kamet in 1913, and to find ourselves once more on the Kamet Glacier, established in our advance base-camp, as I have already described.

It was the 20th of June. The bad weather had come to an end at last, and that morning a blazing sun drove us out of our tents at half-past six. There was evidently a prospect of a day or two of fine weather, so we busied ourselves packing loads for a move to higher camps. To have started at once would have been useless, as the fresh snow everywhere had not yet had time to settle. To wade up the glacier through unconsolidated snow would have been prohibitively exhausting, and higher up, where the slopes were steeper there would have been danger from avalanches. That evening we went to bed in broad daylight to the accompaniment of the Bhotias' singing. As we lay listening in our sleeping-bags the concert was interrupted by the roar of a big rock-fall not far from the camp. In the Himalaya avalanches make one jumpy; one never seems very far from the reach of them, and their frequency is a sign that the mountains are still young, and have not yet reached the degree of stability of other ranges like the Alps. In the Alps, wherever there is danger, it is usually sufficiently obvious to the experienced eye, so that it can generally be avoided, but in the Himalaya experience is no guarantee of security, and often, when the camp-site seems quite safe, there is still a lurking sense of anxiety. The Himalayan scale, too, is so gigantic that it is difficult to gauge the limits of the avalanches.

At one o'clock in the morning of June the 21st we were off. There was a crystal-clear quality in the moonlight, and the snow was sparkling like diamonds in its rays. The Bhotias were bubbling with energy and high spirits; like us they were relieved that the long period of waiting was over. Marching up the upper part of the Kamet Glacier to its head, we pitched a light camp, consisting of one tent for Pierre and myself, and a second tent for seven Bhotias. Our altitude was probably 20,000 feet, and the camp was on a rock-ridge, so close underneath Kamet that the upper regions of the mountain were hidden from sight by the steepness of the precipice immediately above us. The Kamet Glacier that day was so easy to walk on that we had already established ourselves in camp by ten o'clock in the morning. I took some photographs of the magnificent sweep of the glacier, looking like a great frozen high-road, and winding away below us down the valley in symmetrical curves till it disappeared round a mountain-corner to join the Raikana Glacier and feed the head-waters of the Ganges.

On the way up during the morning I had found myself gasping for breath most uncomfortably. It is common in these mountains to suffer acutely from mountain-sickness at a relatively low elevation, and to feel discouraged in consequence, because one hastily assumes that the symptoms are bound to get worse as one goes higher. But this is not the case, for the attack wears off as often as not, and probably does not recur till a much greater height is reached. To-day we were unlucky, for the weather was unfavourable; it was just the sort of day that is most trying, hot and cloudy without any breeze, and although we both felt well when we arrived, we soon had splitting head-aches. This year's experience confirmed our conviction that much of mountain-sickness, in this district, at any rate, is caused by the sun shining with terrific force through still air that is not dense enough to give adequate protection. The Bhotias' habit of lying flat on their faces fast asleep in the sun probably accounts for a good deal of the discomfort from which several of them were now suffering. Our head-man, Alam Singh was in a state of collapse. The thought of a meal made me feel sick, and the light seemed murderous in its intensity. It was not merely the direct rays of the sun, for even the glare inside the tent was intolerable, and I could well believe that sunstroke can attack one through the eyes. The extremes of heat and cold were astonishing; at almost any moment of the day sunstroke and frostbite were equally likely contingencies. I was conscious, too, of the effect that altitude has on the mind. As we climbed higher into the unknown, and penetrated farther into the secret and untrodden regions of this great mountain, the commonplace reality of every-day life faded from the landscape, while the sense of romance and mystery deepened. It was as if a gradually thickening veil was dimming our memories of the ordinary world. In the strange new world that we seemed to be partially conscious of, the fierceness of the sun's rays, the blinding light reflected from the snow, the savage cold, the clearness of the deep blue sky, as well as the magical purity and emptiness of the air, all combined to produce an impression of the most fantastic unreality. Yet at times a different impression prevailed. It was as if our normal, sea-level consciousness were acting as a veil of illusion, so that only at great altitudes, in such places as this, did the veil of illusion become thin enough for the true reality to begin to shine through it, supernatural, incredible and incomprehensible.

At such a moment we seemed, as in the fairy-story, to have climbed the miraculous bean-stalk, so that we were beginning to explore the magical country beyond it, and just as it must have seemed to the hero of that romantic tale, the inspiring adventure was both nightmare and fairy-story combined. Perhaps this strange experience, painful though it was in many respects, had in it some of the quality of ecstasy, and perhaps it was this peculiarity that gave it its irresistible appeal. Indeed, whatever agonies and miseries the sufferer may endure on his pilgrimage to the heights, and however often he may swear never to return there, the longing to do so is certain to recur.

The ridge on which we were now camped ran into the base of a broad snow-covered precipice supporting a saddle-shaped glacier-plateau which formed the depression between Kamet and its nearest great neighbour, Eastern Ibi Gamin, the peak of 24,170 feet that had frustrated us when we were attacking from the west. The precipice so dominated the camp that it concealed the saddle from view. It was necessary to climb the precipice in order to camp on the plateau, if we were to have any chance of getting up the final portion of Kamet, where the upper slopes rose from the saddle in a continuous sweep of pure ice and snow for 2,000 feet at an angle of 45 degrees. As the recent bad weather had loaded all the rocks above the camp with fresh snow, we decided definitely that we must wait for daylight before starting, since with heavily-laden porters it would be too dangerous to climb by moonlight. We had noticed that the forehead of the precipice 1,000 feet above our heads, and just below the plateau, consisted of a steep slope of snow, or perhaps of ice. If it were ice, of course, it might require prolonged step-cutting, a formidable job when one is above 22,000 feet.*

On June the 23rd, at three in the morning we emerged reluctantly from the tent to inspect the weather. The long ice-valley of the Kamet Glacier below us was packed tight with dense white clouds, and a haze almost concealed the moon. These banks of fog were obviously the approaching monsoon, and all the way down the valley we could see the clouds waiting patiently in queues, ready for the monsoon wind to give them another push, and sweep them over the passes into Tibet. There among the bleak parched plateaux and immense round-headed hills they would be dissolved in the thin, dry air. But it was too cold to linger outside the tent, and we quickly came to a decision to wait till the afternoon, so that if the weather became at all possible, we would try the ascent of the rocks and the snow-slope so as to pitch a camp on the plateau. It was meanwhile a considerable relief to be able to get back into one's sleeping-bag.

Curiously enough, we were now free from the attacks of breathlessness that affected us so unpleasantly, and for no obvious cause, several thousand feet below this camp. However, we felt bad enough in other respects, and although my head-ache had vanished after a night's rest, perhaps owing to a dose of bromide, I did not feel at all fit. Later during the day I was able to eat a small slice of barhal venison, slightly

---

* The Kamet Glacier up which we had come is formed at its head by the junction of two great ice-streams pouring down in ice-falls from either side of Kamet, to unite at the foot of the peak. One of them flows from the depression between Kamet and Mana Peak, and the other comes down from the ice-fields of the saddle that we hoped to reach, between Kamet and Eastern Ibi Gamin. This latter glacier is split into ice-falls by the rock-cliffs which we had to climb on our way to the plateau.

flavoured with petrol from a leaky tin. Probably our state of acclimatization was not sufficiently advanced to justify us in making such long stages between camps, as we were now doing.

Next morning, the 23rd, we dozed uneasily till nine o'clock, and then began the struggle with a defective smoky primus stove, a miserable performance which seemed to occupy most of the day. In fact, primus stoves react to altitude badly, much as climbers do. It was a wretched day, and as I crawled panting into my sleeping-bag for the night I noticed it was snowing and consoled myself with the reflection that it was not very likely in view of the weather that we should have to turn out in the small hours in order to toil farther up the mountain.

Nevertheless, on the 24th of June Pierre woke me at one o'clock in the morning with the news that it was gloriously fine, a clear moonlight night, and that we must start immediately. I at once reminded him that we had agreed already that the thousand feet of rock above the camp were in too bad condition to be safe for a night march with our laden men. So we got back into bed and remained in a state of coma, hardly to be described as sleep, till we eventually succeeded in setting out at 5.30 a.m., after eating an insignificant meal.

We soon found the ascent of the precipice trying owing to the quantities of fresh snow lying all over the rocks. Bhotias are in their element wherever there are crags to be climbed, but snow-covered rock is not what they are accustomed to, and consequently we had some anxious moments when the men launched themselves on to this snow-bound face, heavily laden as they were. A slip would have been fatal, and yet, such is the lethargic state of mind induced by altitude, that we neglected the elementary precaution of roping the party on these very treacherous cliffs. However, all the men climbed admirably, and at last we found ourselves on the supreme promontory of the precipice, where it abutted on the snow- or ice-slope that formed a sort of forehead just underneath the spacious plateau leading to the saddle, as we had noticed from the camp.

It was disconcerting when we came to the 'forehead' to find that it was a slope of steep, tough ice. Pierre, however, rapidly hacked a staircase up it in a style that perhaps only the best professionals can achieve. When prolonged step-cutting is required at such heights as this, the leader must be able to cut quickly, and balance himself in mere scratches in the ice. Time and energy are lacking for carving out the elegant 'soup-plate' steps, such as a talented guide will prepare for his clients in the Alps, and when at last the leader was up he was glad to recuperate for a while. Later, he threw down a combination of all the available ropes as a hand-rail to help the rest of the party to follow in their turn.

At the top of the 'forehead' began the lofty glacier-plateau sloping at an easy angle up to the high saddle between Kamet and Eastern Ibi Gamin. We were now in a strange paradoxical world, where the ordinary laws of nature do not seem to work. Snow here is soft, not because it is melted in the sun, but because it is frozen into fine dust by the intense cold. Here it is the relatively warm monsoon wind that brings the snow, and it is not the sun's warmth, but the icy northerly winds that remove it again. If the cold in such places begins to overwhelm the climber, it is useless for him to hasten the pace. On the contrary, he had better slow down, in order to diminish the rate of his breathing, for it is not inactivity on his part, but the violent gasping for breath in the thin cold air, that may dangerously deplete the vital store of warmth on which his life depends.

The endless monotony of toiling up the bleak slopes of

this ghastly plateau through an increasing depth of powdery snow, and under a burning sun became a torment. When at last we camped it was only eleven o'clock in the morning, but I felt incapable of moving another yard.

We were now wearing extra-dark snow-spectacles, our faces were smothered in yellow grease, to keep off the blistering sunshine reflected from the dazzling fresh snow, and we had specially large boots to allow room for numerous socks and stockings as protection against the arctic cold. Yet when I sat in the entrance of the tent, half in sun and half in shade, I felt myself grilling and freezing simultaneously. Our camp here seemed to be at the foot of the final ice- and snow-slopes of the peak, and I estimated that we were three or four hundred feet below the high gap between Kamet and Eastern Ibi Gamin, so that our height must have been about 23,000 feet, two thousand feet or more below the top of the mountain. The altitude was certainly very noticeable. Crawling into our sleeping-bags caused violent palpitations and fits of gasping. Any mild exertion brought on breathlessness and dizziness, with a curious empty feeling at the pit of the stomach. Probably we were insufficiently acclimatized to undertake an ascent of 7,000 feet in only two stages.

On the 25th of June there was intense and increasing cold towards the small hours of the morning, with a wind causing a horrid flapping of the tent. Our hot-water bottles had lost what little warmth they had, and the cold was depressing to our lowered circulations. We seemed too feeble to resist these low temperatures. It was difficult to produce hot water, for water no longer boils at a reasonable temperature at this height, and tea has to be stewed to extract any flavour from it. We dared not start before dawn for fear of getting frozen. To add to our discomfort the Bhotias had jammed the screw of the primus cooking-stove, so that it was almost dawn when Pierre at length succeeded in boiling some water for a refill of the hot-water bottles. Unfortunately with the arrival of daylight there was nothing for it but to get up.

As I poked my head out of the tent into the revoltingly cold air of early dawn, I observed seas of cold grey cloud lying in the valleys, but the far peaks were all clear, especially the gigantic Gurla Mandata, 25,000 feet high, rising into the Tibetan sky in superb isolation, a hundred miles away. The divine Nanda Devi, the only superior to Kamet, now showed her true height, and completely dwarfed the usually magnificent peak of Dunagiri which now seemed to crouch at the goddess's feet. The glittering ice-crest of the principal Mana Peak looked as if it were on our level, and its minor summits were obviously beneath us.

We stumbled unwillingly out of the tent, after much shouting to rouse the poor mountain-sick Bhotias who had been vomiting during the night. Starting at once with three men who seemed to be less ill than the others, we put one of them in front to make the track by stamping his way through the deep fresh snow. He was to take it in turn with the others, and we hoped that when they became exhausted we should be able to continue without them. I soon noticed, however, that the snow was getting deeper, and I realized from the state of my exhaustion at starting that it was a hopeless job, for I kept stopping to rest every hundred yards, sinking down in the snow, or leaning gasping and bent double over my ice-ace used as a support. At last, before we reached the top of the plateau, Pierre at my suggestion, left me and went on with two Bhotias, while I turned back with Shyamu. Pierre and his men then got as far as the foot of the ridge that ascends from the saddle to the top of Kamet. Here they tried the ridge and found snow above their knees, and the gallant Bhotias, who were still doing the leading began to stagger in their tracks. Further progress was impossible. Higher up it might have been necessary to take to the face where the slopes appeared to be in a dangerous state from avalanches, and Pierre decided to follow me back to the 23,000-feet camp, where he joined me about an hour after my return. From the saddle he had had a magnificent view over Tibet towards the north, apparently much the same panorama that we had seen from our highest points on the other side of Kamet during the previous year; a limpid brown landscape bright in the sun, containing hundreds of miles of rolling mountains like gigantic downs, and on the horizon a chain of snows. This peaceful undulating Tibetan country formed a striking contrast with the stormy sea of savage peaks which we looked back upon whenever we turned our eyes towards the Indian valleys, where the threatening monsoon-clouds were beginning their advance once more.

On the return of Pierre's party, Shyamu prepared some tinned fruit for all of us. On the previous day we had only eaten a few water-biscuits and drunk some cocoa. The plan of ascending by forced marches had not been a success, and we determined to get down to our advanced base at 16,000 feet as quickly as possible.

As soon as we had swallowed the fruit we began the descent. Fearing that the steps cut that morning in the ice-slope of the 'forehead' might have melted in the sun, we were tempted to try the descent of a broad easy couloir on our left. We had shunned this route on the way up because of its dangerous appearance, and now one glance at the various potential missiles lying about the brink of it convinced us that we had been right. So we made back to the 'forehead', and descended its steeply sloping ice with all our ropes tied together to form a balustrade, fixed to an ice-axe planted upright in a snow-drift, Pierre remaining behind to extricate the axe, and descend by his own unaided exertions. Pierre, on these occasions, seems to master any really formidable obstacles by means of a skilfully planned series of bold and determined dashes, on the principle recommended for cavalry action according to the drill-book, that is to say progression in a series of bounds. In this manner, therefore, he had soon descended to our level. But he was still separated from us by a precipitous ice-gully, and, to enable him to reach us, Alam and Shyamu, after many unsuccessful attempts, managed to throw him the end of a rope. Then, crossing the forbidding-looking gully in two or three deft and strenuous jumps, he rejoined us at the base of the 'forehead'. Thereupon, hurriedly coiling the spare rope, we embarked on the descent of the snow-covered precipice beneath. On these treacherous rocks I dreaded a slip on the part of our exhausted porters, but nothing happened, and we all reached the 20,000-feet camp without mishap.

The following day we descended to the advance base-camp on our way back to the plains and Bombay, where, a month after our defeat on Kamet we took ship for England.

Thus this expedition ended on the eve of the European war which put a stop to any further efforts. Failure on the mountain was not only due to the unconsolidated snow, but to mistaken method. In those days, however, it was still uncertain whether climbers could exist at 25,000 feet, and perhaps the effect of altitude was psychological as well as physical. It was supposed, too, that mountains of this height could only be taken by storm. Acclimatization at such a height as 20,000 feet was believed to be impossible. It was thought that owing to the demoralizing effects produced by the first few nights spent at great heights, it would be better to sleep at the higher camps as seldom as possible, and long forced marches were considered advisable in order to avoid doing so.

When we come to consider the effect of these methods on our campaign, there can be no doubt that this attempt to rush the mountain took too much out of us. Stages of only 2,000 feet, instead of intervals between camps of nearly double that distance would have been much better, and might have made all the difference to the result.

EPILOGUE

It was another occasion—the middle of August—and we were leaving the hills for the last time, on the way home by Niti and Joshimath to Europe. For nearly three months we had never descended below 14,000 feet. There were already remarkable changes in evidence since the beginning of the season. There was much more water in the rivers, no snow-bridges remained to help us across the torrents, and green crops were growing round the village of Niti.

A runner brought a pencilled scrap of paper from Joshimath to say that a man I had counted on as my ambassador there had "run away into jungle for fear of cholera disease". Presumably he had taken our incoming and outgoing mail with him, but that remained to be seen. Meanwhile our Bhotias by unmistakable and unpleasant signs made it clear to us exactly how people were supposed to be dying farther down the Ganges valley.

As we came to Malari, it was pleasant to see trees again, the great deodars that slanted across the path. At dawn and sunset the air seemed to be saturated with the scent of pine and musk. Later on at Surai Tota I noticed how the roaring of the torrents, swollen by many months' rain, became more savage towards nightfall, as the snow-water increased in volume. We heard continually that grim sound, the rumble and thunder of the invisible boulders as they bumped along the bed of the river under water. Everywhere there was an extraordinary luxuriance of grass, and as we descended ever lower on our journey, the dampness of the heat became oppressive. There were hordes of grasshoppers, as well as magnificent dragon-flies, particoloured in green and grey. One night an immense insect with a phosphorescent head-light in his forehead, watched me balefully from the roof-line of my tent, while I cautiously undressed. During the day flies plagued us incessantly, and the mess-tent became a sort of recreation-hall for them, although the insect population perished every morning when the tent was folded. The grasshoppers I observed to be of such dimensions that they thought nothing of springing on to the roof in a single bound.

Finally we reached Joshimath and thankfully discovered that our ambassador had returned safely from the jungle, bringing back with him the letters and telegrams that he had taken on his flight. Nothing now remained but the sadness of saying good-bye to our Bhotias, and good-bye to Garhwal. At Joshimath indeed, more than anywhere else in this country there seemed to be some compelling quality in the hills that made it especially hard to leave them. I remembered all the pain of my previous farewells to this place. Yet in the past it had not been good-bye for ever; I had not then been certain that I should never return.

For the last time I walked up and down in front of the bungalow on the little terrace that seemed almost suspended over the abyss of the valley. Gallant old Soba, the last of our followers to depart, came to say good-bye. It was a dull, grey evening, but on the hill-side across the valley there was still light enough to see the numerous tiny streaks indicating cultivated terraces. Clouds were curling round the flanks of the mountains, no clear sky was visible, and darkness was coming on fast. I knew that before daylight had returned I should be gone. Deep down in the valley I saw for the last time the thin distant thread winding uphill towards Badrinath.

Epilogue

It was the homeward path that the happy Bhotias were to take next day. Soba's good-byes were ended, and he strolled away carrying over his shoulder one of Pierre's final presents to him, an old flannel shirt. Crickets were singing their ceaseless chorus, and a wind came up from the far-away depths of the gorge, bringing with it a smell of the earth. For a moment I heard the sullen murmur of the snow-water in the Ganges as the sound came up on the wind, and ceased as the wind died away. Alas, it was good-bye to the Himalaya.

INDEX